WHEN I CAME HOME

WHEN I CAME HOME

GEORGE BRINLEY EVANS

PARTHIAN

Parthian
The Old Surgery
Napier Street
Cardigan
SA43 1ED

www.parthianbooks.com

First published in 2012
© George Brinley Evans

ISBN 978-1-908069-955

Editor: Jessica Mordsley
Cover: 'In The Bath' by George Brinley Evans, used by permission of
Aberystwyth University
Typeset by Elaine Sharples
Printed and bound by Gwasg Gomer, Llandysul

Published with the financial support of the Welsh Books Council

British Library Cataloguing in Publication Data

A cataloguing record for this book is available from the British Library.

CONTENTS

To my family: especially to the newest member, my beautiful great-granddaughter, Amelia Jayne.

BOOK ONE

1

I was, as Dylan Thomas would put it, in my twenty-second year to Heaven. I had had my twenty-first birthday homeward-bound on board the troopship *Monarch of Bermuda* anchored off Aden in the first week of November 1946. Now it was the 4th of January 1947 and I had arrived in Southampton to take a ship back to join my regiment in the Far East.

The trooper that we would be sailing on was the *Corfu*, but industrial unrest was bubbling to the surface in the Merchant fleet. Reading about the conditions the ordinary crew men had been made to put up with during the Second World War, the unrest was not unexpected. For instance, when a merchant ship was torpedoed and sunk, the time was logged by the Royal Navy escort as the surviving crew members clambered into the lifeboats. When the survivors picked up their pay they found they were paid up until the time they clambered into the lifeboat. The time spent in the lifeboat was not paid for.

The *Corfu*'s crew went on strike. What their particular grievance was we were never told. Hanging around Southampton was a bit of a bugger knowing that three hours' train ride away was home. The transit camp there was not the best-run in the British Army. Bob Bagley and I called in the office and asked if there was any mail. The corporal in charge was one of the most officious twats I had ever come across. He was older than we two but had no campaign ribbons up. Bob reckoned: 'More than likely wangled his way out of every overseas posting. And now it's all over is conscious of his bare chest!' With the cruelty that is just under the surface of all young men, the next time we called at the office we made sure we were wearing our campaign ribbons.

There was talk that we would be shipped out to Japan to be part of the Commonwealth occupation force. I started thinking of ways of getting a home posting; didn't fancy going to a new unit. I had in my Service book a letter from a MO at the British General Hospital Rangoon from the time Captain Belton had taken me there when he found out I was suffering from a severe bout of jungle foot rot. The MO had given me a letter saying 'it would be advisable if possible that this soldier be given a home posting' and a chit that I be issued with two pairs of Indian Army chapplies, sturdy sandals much like the ones you see the Roman soldiers wearing in paintings.

The following morning I went on sick parade. Showed the MO the letter and I was wearing my chapplies and got a home post as easy as blinking and dashed off to tell Bob. He immediately joined the queue at the MO's. Half an hour

4

later Bob came into the hut beaming. South East Asia Command had seen the last of us two.

We were kitted out: big pack, small pack, respirator, rifle (no ammo), greatcoat, the lot. Following morning on board a train for London then Thetford, Norfolk. I had never been on an underground railway before; with all our gear it was a bit of a crush.

When we arrived at Thetford railway station it was snowing heavily and was getting dark. A three-ton truck slid to a stop. 'Get in!' shouted the driver. The truck stopped. It was the first time I had seen an army truck with its headlights full on. When I had been driving them the headlights were masked allowing only a slit of light, sidelights and a small light above the white painted differential gear box in the centre of the back axle. That small light enabled the wagon coming behind you in the convoy at night to follow you.

'This is it lads. Get out!' ordered the driver. There were three of us. The third lad in our group was from Liverpool, a Scouser out of the Seventeenth Twenty-first Lancers. The Nissen hut's door was plaster with snow driven against it by the wind. We pushed the door open.

'Where's the light switch?' Bob had to shout against the howling wind.

A single light bulb flickered on. There were four beds, a pile of straw-filled palliasses and a stove. We each threw a palliasse and our gear onto a bed. Part of the hut had been vandalized and some of the wood strewn about the floor. We set about breaking the wood into pieces that would fit into the stove by putting the edge of the piece of wood on the concrete hearth of the stove and jumping on it. Some straw from one of the spare palliasses and we had a fire going.

The stove was still smouldering in the morning. I bunged on more wood. It was comfortably warm in the hut. The snow had blocked all the cracks and crevices. We dressed.

'Wonder where the cookhouse is?' muttered the Scouser. The hut door wouldn't open. The three of us pulled and got an opening enough for us to squeeze out and snow tumbled in. The world was white; not a branch, twig or blade of grass without its covering of snow. This day would go down in history – January 21st, 1947: the day the whole island was held fast in the grip of winter; Food having to be parachuted down to the people of East Anglia, trains frozen to the tracks, thousands of cases of livestock buried alive. I was to find out later my uncle Jim had lost his entire flock at Llwynrhyn at the top end of the Swansea valley.

We were on a giant disused American Air Base in Norfolk. We saw a bloke struggling through the snow some fifty yards away. We all shouted. He stopped.

'Where's the cookhouse mate?' Scouser yelled.

The bloke pointed to a rise in the ground and indicated with his hand, over the hill. It was the biggest Nissen building I had ever seen and when we got inside it was even more amazing. When this great air base was fully manned over one thousand men messed in this very building. The counter, the hot plate must have been thirty yards long.

A Thetford girl told us that this place made the local newsagent a very rich man. The *Daily Express*, The *Daily Mail* and all the other newspapers were stacked shoulder

6

high. A local girl stood by each stack with a pail on the floor. The Yanks simply threw their money into the pail, never waiting for change. That morning there were no more than fifty of us sitting down to breakfast. A sergeant came over to our table.

'You three up from Southampton?'

'Yes Sarg,' Scouser answered.

'There's a group of huts. You can see them across the fields. A jeep will pick you up. Take the jeep, pick up your gear and move into one of those huts. There's some lads already in there. Ok!'

There were twenty blokes in the hut: a mixed bunch, all out of different regiments. Only one coldwater tap and one lavatory was working in the ablution block but it had an adequate amount of firewood.

Some of the lads were taken to help the local people out who were in a very bad way. Coal was in very short supply; people were queuing at half six in the morning for half a hundredweight of coal. Their houses were in a bad state of repair; many had suffered bomb damage with slate roofs blown off and just a canvas covering remained which kept out the rain but not the cold. In those days if you broke a pane of glass in a window there was no way of getting a new pane and a piece of cardboard would have to do.

Many of the farm workers' houses were very old. They were not the sturdy brick and stone houses we had back home. I went one day with a bunch of lads to help free a bus. The snow by then was turning to ice and I still only had my Indian army sandals to wear. Sitting by the stove that night I took off my sandals and socks.

'What the bloody hell happened to your feet, Taff?' Scouser gasped. Both my feet were black but there was no pain. There was a thump and the hut filled with smoke. The spectacle of my feet was instantly forgotten. Padgett out of Signals had put a house brick in the stove then into his bed as an improvised hot water bottle. The straw in his palliasse smouldered then had burst into flame.

The following morning I trudged across the fields to the MO to be greeted by one of the most forlorn sights I have ever seen. A huddle of men, about fifteen of them all wearing army greatcoats over civilian dress and all handcuffed; six Red Caps smoking and chatting, their backs turned towards their charges. The King had granted an amnesty to all deserters and these were but a few of them. Not all deserters had jumped ship because they were afraid to fight; many stayed because their families were in desperate straits and unlike the well-to-do, were unable to stay at home on compassionate grounds alone.

'Yes?' barked the MO.

'My feet, Sir!'

'Your feet! Your feet! Clear off! Clear off! For goodness sake clear off!' His heavy Ulster accent rang in my ears. Later, with hindsight, I thought that perhaps the sight and the disagreeable task in front of him of medically examining the hapless group of handcuffed deserters had the same demoralizing effect on him as it had had on me.

Back in the hut the lads were flabbergasted.

'You've got to go back, Taff. For fuck's sake!' Scouser was emphatic.

Before I went into the surgery the following morning I took my sandals and socks off. The MO looked at my feet then at me almost in despair. 'Get him in to sickbay!' My feet wrapped up in thermal dressings, I was out of the cold for ten days. The MO issued me with a chit on leaving sickbay. The orderly drove me into Thetford town to a shoe shop and got me two pairs of black shoes not boots.

I wouldn't have anything said against Ulstermen after that.

Riley had joined us by the time I got out and so had our old Company Sergeant Major: the guy who had a nervous breakdown just before the rest of us boarded ship to take part in the main sea assault to try and recapture the City of Rangoon. He had us on parade, inspected us but didn't show any sign of recognising Bob, Riley or me.

We were taken into Bury St Edmunds for a bath in the public bathhouse which was a great relief. We were now in a fit state to be posted. I was the first to go, posted to Plymouth to the *Royal Citadel* right on Plymouth Hoe. The ceiling of the barrack room was at least fifteen feet high, the stone walls painted white, the wood floor polished so that you could see your face in it. There was a green wardrobe-style locker between each single bed, greatcoats buttons polished, hung on hangers, sleeves folded behind into belts. On the white wall they had a striking effect. The cleaning was done by German prisoners of war. Two years after the end of the war the former prisoners of war had still not been repatriated.

There were white bed sheets and pillowcases. I was in Montgomery's army. For the first time in the history of the British Army, British soldiers were issued with bed sheets and pillowcases. Until then the issue had been two wool blankets, groundsheet, no pillow and one of the blankets would be your shroud and coffin if you fell in action.

Our style in shirts was changed at the end of 1944. Until then a British soldier had worn the same style shirt as a convict, just the colour was different, the convict's was grey and the British soldier's khaki. No collar just a white band as a neckpiece. A collar I expect could have got in the way of the noose.

I had to report to Frobisher Terrace Company HQ. In a week Riley and Bob had joined me and we were billeted to Western Kings, a coastal battery that looked out over the Sound. Just seven squaddies, a wooden hut with cork lino covered floor, better than some holiday homes. A mess we shared with half a dozen Royal Artillery lads and their cook.

We caught a bus to the Barbican each morning, to work on boats that were as different to our launches as different could be. Some with triple Perkins Diesel engines capable of a speed of twenty-one knots. Life was especially pleasant working on the Barbican as you were physically aware of the history around you such as Pilgrims Point from where Captain Jones set off with his ship the *Mayflower* for the New World. We had breakfast at one of the ancient eating-houses. The backdoor opened out onto the water where French and English fishing boats tied up. The fish we ate for breakfast had been swimming in the channel the night before. If there was a better breakfast to be had anywhere I never found it. I remembered thinking to myself at the time that the wartime army had been the most democratic organisation I had ever belonged to. If there were fourteen biscuits and there were fourteen of you, you got one and the CO got one.

One spring evening a soldier turned up at our billet asking to see the senior soldier.

'Why? What do you want?' inquired Bob.

'I called at the office. I want a bed for the night and CSM Matthews told me to come here.' There was an empty bed as Lang had gone home for the weekend. The lad looked clean and well scrubbed.

'What do you think?' Bob asked me.

'We'll change the sheets before Lang gets back.'

The soldier left on the Sunday night. We would get the clean bed sheets on Monday morning. When we awoke on Monday morning Lang was already in bed; he'd had a lift back. So we decided the best thing to do was not to mention the lodger.

The coming weekend Lang was off home again. Then, travelling to work on the bus in the middle of the following week, we noticed Lang scratching himself.

'Bloody hell I'm itching all over,' muttered Lang.

'Get yourself to the MO,' advised Riley.

The doctor asked had he been home and had he slept with his wife.

'Yes.'

'Then you'd better telephone her and tell to go and see her doctor. You have got a bad dose of what you lot call the crabs. You'll have go into hospital right away!' He telephoned his wife and he had infected her. We never ever did tell Lang about the lodger.

The spring turned to summer and with little money the only free recreation was swimming. Something Riley and I should not have done; within a week both of us were down with otitis media, an infection we had picked up in Burma – the propellers of our boats would become jammed by the often dense vegetation in the rivers, we would go over the side to cut it away, little realizing that we were being infected by a very virulent little bug.

We found ourselves in the Royal Naval Hospital Stonehouse, Plymouth. Riley tormented the ward Sister for a week. Both Riley's ear drums were perforated. He'd wait until he'd hear Sister's footsteps coming down the corridor, take a deep drag on his cigarette, putting his hand over his mouth, and hold his nostrils blowing out as she came through the door. The sight of smoke pouring out of both of Riley's ears brought a sharp and loud reprimand, 'Riley!!' that could be heard in the next ward. We were both sent before a medical board. There was a lot of muttering and head shaking.

'Stay out of the water!' warned the old doctor who had examined me.

The week I joined up I volunteered an allowance home to my mother of seven shillings a week out of my twenty-one shilling a week allowance. My father had opened a post office account and banked the money in my name which meant I had the cash for the train fare at the weekends when I was free to go home and take Peg out.

At Aldershot on October the 4th 1947 my service with the colours came to an end. I was put on reserve and I was awarded eight shillings a week war pension compensation for the infection in my ears. I never saw Riley again to ask him if he had got the same.

2

I had twenty-eight days' leave and I was going to spend each and every day with Peg.

In Banwen, the weather was absolutely gorgeous. I gave my father a hand on the fruit round some days which gave me a chance to meet people I hadn't seen for the best part of four years.

The family's fish and chip shop still qualified us for free passes from three cinemas. Peg used her father's car if we went to Glyn Neath or Seven Sisters, the bus if we went to Neath. If you travelled by Western Welsh bus you could use the same ticket to come home by train. The bonus came in the privacy of getting a compartment to yourselves in a non-corridor train plus the compartments were still fitted with wartime low-wattage light bulbs. Most of the valley's young lovers travelled that way especially on the last train on Saturday night. It was their only hope of having time on their own.

Not one house had been built for more than six years. It was quite common for three families to be living in one three-bedroom house. I remember being told that at one time six hundred people lived in Roman Road and the few houses on top of the colliery.

Five thousand men worked in the small valley. Twenty-four hours a day, seven days a week, the sound of the winding engines filled the air with noise; trucks were shunted, buffers clanked, hobnailed boots rang on the pavements. The valley was part of the old Glamorgan that, even with coal exports falling dramatically away, still earned more money than the rest of Wales put together.

A new doctor's surgery was opened in the village. The miners had decided, although the NHS was coming into being, they were going to have their own clinic close to home so that people when they were unwell would not have to travel all the way to Swansea or Neath. The new clinic would be funded by the miners paying fourpence in the pound of their earnings. When the NHS came into being that contribution would be halved. Manned by two doctors, Dr Thomas and Dr Littlewood, and a full time physiotherapist, Mrs Tyler, the Clinic would provide heat, radio, wax treatment plus X-ray. The Clinic was open from nine in the morning sometimes until nine at night.

It didn't go down well with everyone. We already had a surgery with Dr Thomson. He lived in the village and worked with Dr Armstrong who lived on a large prosperous farm in Crynant and had twice been the Lord Lieutenant of Breconshire. Their surgery was held twice a day, seven days a week except on Sunday; Sunday morning surgery only – surgery seven days a week because there were no antibiotics, so dressings on wounds had to be changed every day. With five thousand miners working the valley, some days the doctors must have thought they were working in a field dressing station on the Western Front. If a post mortem was required Dr Thomson carried out the surgical work in the garden shed if there was one; on the kitchen table if there was not. As far as Dr Armstrong was concerned people did not really care; he was gentry. But Dr Thomson lived in the village in a company house and both his children attended the village school. People were concerned about his feelings.

Dr Thomson had looked after my family for years. I remember the care he took of my brother David when he had a very badly infected knee after falling into a blackberry bush and a thorn had lodged itself deep under his kneecap. Doctor Thomson removed the thorn, carrying out the surgery in the back kitchen with Dr Armstrong assisting. David was ill for a long time, missing his eleven-plus exams. For a time they suspected he had developed tuberculosis; Doctor Thomson called to check on him at least once a week for months on end.

Another time was on a beautiful Sunday morning just before dinner. The table was laid for dinner and Drs Thomas and Armstrong called, Armstrong as usual dressed in his deerstalker's hat and riding britches. They had called to see my grandmother, my mother's mother, who had been living with us since my grandfather died. We two were on the best of terms. I used to run up to Mrs Williams the Tuck shop for her to buy her favourite 'losins' as she called them and she gave me a half penny to buy one fag. I smoked it sitting on the fender so that the smoke went straight up the chimney.

'Elisabeth!' Dr Armstrong greeted my grandmother. 'Come into the backyard would you please. There's better light out there.' It was the first time I'd ever heard anyone using her name. We only called her Granny. She was seventy-five, almost as tall as my father, with jet black hair plaited and worn in two side buns and would not have looked out of place sitting by a gypsy camp fire.

I read years later that people like her, from mid Wales, were called the dark Welsh. Her sister Caro was as dark and as tall as she, so were Caro's two daughters Lillian and Miriam. Before my grandmother was married she was a Prytherch from Llandovery, fluent in both Welsh and English and able to translate the Latin mottos on the army badges I had collected.

Dr Armstrong put his head around the door. 'Could you pass me a dessert spoon please, Gwladys,' he asked my mother. My grandmother came back into the kitchen and sat in her high-backed chair. She smiled and winked at me. A week later they took her in to Swansea General Hospital and she was given radium treatment but she died within weeks.

Working back underground in the January of 1948 I realized there were definite advantages. Down the mine the weather always stayed the same. But there was a hiccup. When France fell in 1940, the orders for Welsh anthracite coal were lost not just for France but Holland, Italy and Belgium as well. Three hundred men lost their jobs at Banwen, those of military age and physically fit went straight into the armed forces; a dozen went over one weekend, plus all the men that belonged to the Saint John's Ambulance Brigade of military age. The younger ones like my brother David were sent away to train for war work in munitions or aircraft factories. Darrel Baker was one of these. Three months later the factory he worked in was destroyed in a bombing raid. Darrel was immediately called up. He served in North Africa, Sicily, Italy and France. Demobbed, Darrel returned to Banwen Colliery only to find that his entitlement to a collier's number had been taken away from him.

Because I was only fifteen years of age I was sent to the Rhas, a new drift mine that was still in the hands of the contractor, Phil the Pant. It was there I had served my time as a collier-boy. The Rhas colliery was owned by Evans-Bevan Ltd., who had owned all six collieries at the top end of the valley. Nevertheless, once under the new ownership of the National Coal Board, a self-appointed clique had made up their minds. According to them, the likes of me had been away serving in Churchill's army, unlike the Russian army, who according to them 'had been fighting for the freedom of the ordinary men and women of Europe'.

These were the very same blokes who had been frantically calling and holding meetings and rallies demanding a Second Front to help the Russians in 1942 when there were not enough guns to go around to set out on a decent rabbit shoot.

I remembered my uncle Fred Jones, the sawyer at the colliery, making wooden rifles out of Norway four-and-a halfs to supply the valley's Home Guard platoons to practise arms drill. Some of the men who had been in the army just twenty-one years before in the First World War and others who had served as peacetime soldiers enjoyed showing that they had not forgotten how to slope arms, present arms or port arms with their wooden guns that couldn't shoot.

Until then I had been attending the Young Communist League meetings. 'From each according to his ability, to each according to his need.' There was something fundamentally humane and I thought Christian in that sentiment; it made me accept the Russian invasion of little Finland, believing what I had heard that the Finns had been secretly siding with the Germans, as indeed the English Black Shirts and some Irish and Welsh nationalists were. I was also attending communion classes at St David's Church at the same time. My father thought it was wrong and not fair to the curate of St David's. I could understand the deep concern that the comrades, as they called themselves, had for the lives of the Russian soldiers who were being slaughtered by the thousands, witnessed every week on the cinema newsreels. What I couldn't understand was their complete lack of concern for the lives of British solders and taking into account the Russians had started out the war fighting on the side of the Nazi Adolf Hitler.

Now four years later the same clique had decided to make plain to the returning ex-servicemen the error of their ways by taking away the qualification earned by the serving of an apprenticeship and seniority entitlement by denying them a collier's number, automatically demoting them to labourers. The good money was made by the colliers on dayshift, the coaling shift. Everywhere else in Britain returning ex-servicemen and women were reinstated with their seniority restored.

One of the privileges the self-appointed commissars bestowed upon themselves was, after raising their lamps, which had to be done before 7am or 'stop lamp', returning to the canteen to discuss the running of the colliery, staying there for two hours or more, despite the fact that one of the most competent mining engineers in Wales, John Williams, was in charge of the colliery.

It seemed to me at the time the committee was dominated by one man: Arthur Jones from Cadoxton. Thin, gaunt, intense, with his raincoat always almost touching the ground, he reminded me of the KGB men I had seen in the films, with a burning zeal to hand out to the returning ex-servicemen a lesson he felt sure they thoroughly deserved.

The ex-servicemen, the very men who had suffered being the lowest paid group of all for the five years of the war; one pound one shilling a week for a private soldier on active service in Burma when at the same time a girl in a munitions factory in Resolven could be taking home four pounds a week and still be able to sleep in her own clean, dry bed at night. Nevertheless I still found the home-grown commissar a bit comical, as did quite a few others. Fraught, edgy, always looking as if he was mounting the gallows steps, but he had his principles and was sticking by them. Later I felt guilty and a bit ashamed I had thought him comical on finding out he had been through the mill, gassed on Flanders Field.

I was working nights in the Grey's district with my father and Alf Ashley, a tall rangy West Country man in his fifties; still getting used to being home, odd things like sharing a towel and a bed with my brother David after four years of having my own towel and bed, even if sometimes my bed had been on the ground or at best on the bilge boards of our boat. Both Alf and my father had come into mining by way of being farm labourers and soldiers in WW1.

Their attitude to work took a bit of getting used to. They

worked as if the colliery belonged to them. One night they had bored five coalholes across the face of No. 6 Gate End. The seam of coal was about a yard thick, the intention being to fire the holes then fire the six holes bored in the ten-foot-thick rock bed overburden, and making sufficient room to take a twelve-foot steel arch.

The shots-man arrived, hitched up all six coalholes, walked back to a safe distance unwinding his cable my father had gone into the face to stop anyone coming down. Alf and I went back with the shots-man, got into the side with him and he hitched his cable to the battery.

'Fire!' he yelled at the top of his voice and turned the handle.

There was a huge bang. We walked back to the face, the thick white smoke cleared quickly. All the coalholes had fired bar one. The detonator wires were still hanging from the hole. Alf went back and brought the electric drilling machine and the five-foot long drill. My father came out of the face and knelt down next to Alf. Carefully they guided the drill into the unexploded drill hole, my father with one hand holding the detonator wires to one side. The drill twisted easily into the clay ramming, the clay changed colour; they were into the gelignite. There were four sticks of gelignite in the coalhole, the last with the detonator inside it. Their lives depended on their judgement.

They withdrew the drill and uncoupled it from the drilling machine. 'Here George, take this back and wash it.' What they had been doing was against the law, the shots-man conveniently disappearing. Suddenly he was back, my father and Alf recharging the hole.

I had been away for four years and had forgotten one cardinal rule of coalmining: after handling gelignite never rub your hands in your face, especially your forehead. After washing the muck off the drill and unfastening the bit I did not then wash my hand properly in the water in the sump. Within thirty minutes I had a splitting headache so bad that I had to go out and go home.

Working nights with Alf Ashley and my father was, I felt, keeping me out of the swing of social life in the colliery. On the Friday when I came to the colliery to collect my pay I met Mr Williams the manager on the colliery path.

'Hello George! How's things going?'

I stopped. 'Not too bad thanks, Mr Williams. Mr Williams, there's no chance of me going days is there?'

'Ashley and your father take a bit of keeping up with, George?' asked the manager, smiling.

'Well yes, and working nights is a bit of a bind.'

'Listen, they want help on the timber on E conveyor down the four. Come in Monday morning! See John Stevens, George! All right?'

The following Monday I reported to John Stevens, a quiet; tall man in his sixties, a devout Jehovah's Witness. He had known me all my life and had lived only a few doors away from my grandfather and grandmother in Roman Road.

'I'm going on to E supply road now. I'll take you there, George.' I followed the old fireman or deputy as they had began calling them. Firemen were the people directly in touch with the men, below the firemen came the shots-men who were responsible for firing off the shot holes. Above the fireman was the over-man; he would be in charge of a district and would have perhaps four firemen under him plus two or three shots-men. A large colliery such as Banwen would have two under-managers and a senior mining engineer as manager.

The supply road was the out-by for the air from the face. E face had no coal cutter. The coal was drilled and blasted with gelignite. The smell in the supply road was a mixture of fresh-cut timber and gelignite smoke. In the middle of the road stood a sawing horse and hanging on the horse a bow saw with a gleaming sharp blade.

Matt Owen, a lad about seventeen years of age, was the timber boy. I knew Matt's family well, his father Will Owen had been a boxing sparring partner to the world famous Tommy Farr. I was a bit of a novelty, having served in the Far East, with an air of the odd man out, maybe because there had been so few British soldiers in Burma compared to other theatres of war. There were seven Indian soldiers for every one British soldier serving in Burma. The 2nd Division was the only British division. There was one British battalion to each India division, no British battalion in the two African divisions.

Later in the week, John Stevens came onto the supply road with three young trainees. I knew all three by sight, what family they were out of, but not by name. When I left Banwen all three were still at school.

'George, I'll leave these lads with you. Get them to tidy up the place,' John Stevens ordered. There were four and a halfs and flats that had been unloaded all over the place. 'You heard what the fireman said,' George directed nodding at the piles of timber. They got on with the work right away. I got on with sawing timber to the lengths to meet the orders being shouted up from the face. By snap time the supply road looked a lot tidier.

'How long were you in Burma, George?' asked one of the lads.

'Month short of two years.'

'What was it like?'

'Hot and sticky!'

Neath or Porthcawl was as far as these lads had travelled, and as far as I had travelled until I joined the army. The war had put a stop to what little travelling the likes of me did anyway, what with food rationing and one thing and another.

'What about these brothels in Bombay then George? Foster reckons the girls stood in the doorways begging you to come in? Is that right? And Foster reckoned they were real stunners? Was Foster having us on, George?' asked the biggest of the three, grinning and by the look of him earnestly wanting the right reply.

'Yes there was this street in Bombay; well more an alley really, where the girls stood in the doorways. And yes, they were really gorgeous. They had to be. The lads wouldn't give their money to some toothless old bag, would they?'

The big lad laughed and looked threateningly at his two mates. 'And there's us had to make do with an old mongrel bitch on heat on our last summer holiday, before we left school,' he smirked and pushed the smaller of the lads. 'Didn't we?'

His two friends were engulfed by embarrassment. They dragged him to the ground, punching him as they did.

'Don't listen to him, George! He's lying! He's a fucking liar!' the youngest and smallest shouted, trying to put his hand over the big lad's mouth.

'I'm not a liar, George!' The hand went over his mouth again; this time he bit it and turned his head away. 'What I'm saying is true, George! Honest to God! On the third day Jack Best came down the shed and caught us and yelled at us at the top of his voice, "Clear off from here you dirty little bastards!!"'

They let him get up off the floor. 'Don't listen to him, George,' growled the one who had not said anything to date, completely humiliated by the obscene outburst, and punched Mr Bigmouth in the ribs.

But their tormentor wasn't finished with them yet. 'We were on pins for the next couple o' weeks wondering would Jack tell PC Jenkins, weren't we?' He rounded on them.

'He's a fucking big liar. George don't listen to him!' The smallest looked as if he was going to take a swing at their aggravator.

'Hang on now! Hang on! Calm down now. Calm down,' I coaxed. I was worried John Stevens would come back. Fighting underground and you were instantly dismissed. I didn't want it to look as if I couldn't manage three sixteen-year-olds.

The tormentor was a bit of a scamp. Was he telling the truth? I had no idea; he came from a family that said outrageous things, often infuriating people but very often making people laugh. They said things for the hell of it, plus the family had the advantage of having a resonance in their voices that captivated the listener.

I told Tom Martin about the lads scrapping on E supply road. Tom worked on the Gate End, the tunnel that ran parallel with the supply road, and he had heard the gossip.

'There's no telling what blokes get up to George. We had a fat little cook when we were stationed in Bermuda and half the battalion was sticking it up him.' He laughed. 'Know what they say. A standing prick has no conscience!'

The following Sunday evening Peg and I did what we did on many a Sunday evening if it was fine – we would walk along the railway line to the Price's Arms to see her brother Dai and his wife Nana. Pubs did not open on Sundays in those days. Nana would have been to church where she often played the organ. I told them about the lads fighting – scuffling would be more accurate – and why they had fallen out.

'It goes on all over the place,' Dai laughed. 'In Port Suez they put on shows with a woman and a donkey.'

'Not all over the place! It's against the law in this country,' Nana said sharply.

'Aye, but not everywhere! In Scandinavia it's not,' Dai insisted.

'Well, look at things like the ancient Greeks and their mythology – I mean! According to the Greeks the Goddess Europa had three sons. What were they called? Minos, Sarpedon and I can't remember the other one, all sired by a white bull.' Nana was better-read than any of us, and a better scholar; she had gained her cap and gown. We were happy to listen to her.

'Go away, Nana! They made fairy stories like that up to cover up for a bloody horny old woman,' sneered Dai to provoke Nana. 'There was one Greek queen who had a wooden cow made so that she could get inside to be serviced by a bull.' He turned to me. 'And George boy that was a few hundred years BC. A few thousand years before your horny little buggers in Banwen! And where the hell did the Centaurs come from I ask you? Fairy stories to cover up what the dirty old buggers were up to!' Dai rounded off his argument.

'Can we talk about something else please,' begged Peg. It was how Sunday evenings were spent at the Price's. Talk about anything and everything, but never politics or religion.

3

I got home from work one day to be greeted by Peg.

'There's a letter for you from the War Office!'

I picked up the buff colour envelope and threw it on the fire.

'Shouldn't you have opened it?' Peg asked, concerned.

'No it's just some old bull I expect,' and I really thought it was.

A few days later a registered letter arrived from the War Office telling me to report to a Motor Boat unit at Newport, Isle of Wight by 23.59 hrs that coming Sunday or consider myself to be absent without leave. If I didn't they would then telephone the local policeman and he no doubt would have picked me up. I got into the car and drove to the colliery post-haste to see the manager. He wasn't there. Drove down to his house, Maesmarchog House, a large detached house at the end of the village. John Williams came to the door. He smiled as he read the letter.

'George is this you? Waterman Evans? A kind of Gunga Din?' he laughed.

'I served in Waterborne Mr Williams on motor boats. They call soldiers who ride horses Troopers and us lot Watermen, that's the army for you.'

'Don't worry about it, George. I'll tell them the colliery will come to a stop without you!' He grinned broadly and shook my hand.

Another he helped was Gavin Scott. Gavin had been taken prisoner at Singapore and had spent three and a half years of hell in a jungle camp but was still recalled. John Williams had him transferred from surface work to underground. Tom Martin, a good mate of mine, was recalled. He had served through the war with the Gloucesters. I told him that I had been to see John Williams and he had sorted it out for me.

Tom was anti-authority in every shape or form. When the Queen gave the Military Police the honour of the added title Royal he was spitting teeth. He had spent some time in army prisons. They were brutal places and were called Glass Houses. There was a scandal concerning one army Glass House about a young soldier being beaten to death. I had witnessed a little of that brutality too escorting a prisoner into Rangoon's notorious Insein Prison. Tom ignored the War Office letter and was duly picked up.

A week or so later I was finishing off a smoke before going down on nightshift. A light was coming up the hill towards me from the lamp-room and the rocking to and fro of the light had about it the gait of Tom Martin.

'How did you get out?'

'I sat on the bed and cried every day for a fucking week!' laughed Tom and slapped me hard on the back. Tom had had

28

a bad injury to his knee about two years earlier and the army doctor had slung him out. He had been a boy solider and had come to Banwen on leave during the war with his mate Cawsey and had met the very pretty Meg Evans. Tom used to think there was no one in the world like her and still did.

'First real home I ever had see, George!'

Tom was a large man weighing between seventeen and eighteen stone and worked like a dog, every shift clearing twenty ton and more of shale and boring five shot holes five foot in length ready for the next shift. He needed the money. He liked spending it on his home, keeping Dawn his daughter in private school and downing a dozen pints on Saturday and Sunday at the Belt.

Meg spoiled him. We always worked Sunday nightshift. Tom usually brought in two snap boxes on Sunday night. One snap box had in it bread and butter sandwiches, the other four or five lamb chops. Shinc Brynceiliogau, one of Tom's closest mates, got to know about it.

One morning at about half one Shinc turned off his lamp, crept forward, took the snap box, ate the succulent tasty lamb chops, then put the bones back in the box and crept away, very well pleased with himself. At two o'clock in the morning, snap time on E gate end, all hell broke loose.

'Which one of you lousy stinking bastards 'as eaten my grub?' Tom threw the bones at the lads sat on the side.

'It wasn't one of us!' grinned Paddy.

Shinc strolled up. 'Hi up! And what the bloody hell's all this uproar about?' Deliberately picking his teeth he gave a broad smile.

'Shinc! You greedy cunt!' spat Tom and threw the last of the bones at him.

'My compliments to the lovely cook, Tom!' laughed Shinc. They all laughed and Tom sat down, scowling, to eat his bread and butter sandwiches.

I was recalled for the Korean War because I was on reserve, so were the rest of them. I was kept on reserve until 1959 without pay. All together, with the colours and in reserve, fifteen years.

The main reason I did come back home was because I didn't want to take Peg away from her father's business. He depended on her. After working underground from the age of thirteen his health was failing; chronic bronchitis, no doubt brought on by years of riding the trams from the warmth of the nine-foot seam, six hundred feet down, along a mile-long drift to the surface into bitterly cold, early winter mornings. Peg staying gave Sam, her father, the feeling that things would stay as they were and it pleased Peg no end.

My father had always regarded me as the steady one who'd turn up for work no matter what. These assumptions tied Peg and myself to what should have been obvious: a dead end in a community that had reached its peak in the prosperity stakes. Within ten years all the collieries in the valley would be closed, five thousand jobs lost, and property prices would be at rock bottom.

As well as the fish and chip shop, we also had a fruit, vegetable and fresh fish round. My father started that round during the war when he was appointed to distribute white fish for the district. Fish was never put on rations but it did have a controlled price, hake at one shilling and eleven pence a pound, heads off. The round was carried out on a Monday, Wednesday, Friday and Saturday. The fish arrived at Onllwyn Railway Station on the 8am train, five stone to a box, headless and it would arrive still packed in ice, loaded on to our flat cart pulled by Danny Boy, a very good-looking bay pony with two white socks on his back legs. Danny Boy also ran in the local races his jockey was young John Wilton.

Danny Boy was our second pony. The first pony I owned my father bought me when I was fifteen – a beautiful palomino mare: he paid eight pounds for her, expensive for that time, local ponies could in those days be bought for three or four pounds. Mr Tom Bowler travelled to Dowlais by bus to make the purchase then walked her all the way home to Banwen. The war was on and transport was out of the question. It was summer time and she was kept in Tafarn-y-Banwen's small field, next to Mr Fry's bungalow alongside the inter-valley road. Someone opened the gate and she wandered out onto the road in the blackout. The bus driver didn't see her and her back was broken. I was in Port Eynon with the Naval Cadets when it happened.

I never ever understood my father's attitude to politics. He got on well with everybody, the local Bobby too, but always asked for the money when he served him with fish and chips. He would have been mortified if someone had offered him anything and not expected him to pay for it and very likely thought PC Jenkins would feel the same. He hardly ever joined anything. He joined the ex-servicemen's club because they asked him; they wanted as many ex-servicemen to join as possible as it would look better when they applied for a licence. He belonged to the Foresters Lodge in Crynant that he and his brother Jim had joined on leaving the army: never went to meetings but always paid his dues – paid Lloyd George's stamp from the same time when many didn't pay it until they had to in 1947.

My father bought a new up-to-the-minute frying range for the fish and chip shop, black and white crystal glass with chromium surrounds and a counter to match. The range had the very latest steam extractor that fed the steam on to the fire that heated the fryer, not allowing the steam to escape into the shop. It cost as much as a new Rolls Royce would have cost at the beginning of the war: twelve hundred pounds.

The sight of that elegant range I believed made some people jealous, which caused, I think, one or two on the committee of the Ex-service and Working men's Club, on whose land the fish and chip shop stood and had stood since the mid-1920s, to demand the shop and outbuildings be pulled down. They covered their real intentions by saying they wanted to make a bigger concert hall. There was enough room to build two concert halls with no need to pull the shop down.

The threat to the fish and chip shop resulted in my father making the biggest business mistake of his life. Years later I realized I had contributed to him making that mistake by coming back to Banwen to work. My father bought the billiard hall to acquire the land that went with it to rebuild the fish and chip shop. The property consisted of a billiard hall with four Burroughes and Watts full size tables, over three large cellars and a boiler room for the big Robin central heating boiler and a well-laid-out confectionery and tobacconist shop, ice-cream making facility, living quarters (one bedroom, one living room, outside toilet with no window), a stable, a very large garden and a bungalow that was rented out to Mr Dai Jones and his family.

The main living quarters that went with the billiard hall and confectionery shop were not at all what my mother wanted. She would not go to live there. Gavin Scott and Dai Thomas, both carpenters, worked for the best part of twelve months putting in new floors, walls and an inside toilet. Mr Lewis, Lew-Lew, an old friend of my father's, worked on the drainage. The first important job was to connect the men's urinal to the mains sewer pipe. Until then it had been just soaking away into the ground. My father asked me to help Mr Lewis, using china drainage pipes, the joints sealed with hessian cord rolled in wet clay. It was December and very cold, my fingers were frozen but Mr Lewis, who was in his seventies, seemed not to feel the cold. It amazed me. What was it about that generation: had the brutal working conditions they had endured as boys made them oblivious to pain?

I also had the job of painting the very large and very high billiard hall ceiling, fourteen yards by ten yards, that had turned dark brown in colour from the clouds of tobacco smoke that had floated up against it for more than forty years – two hours every morning after coming off nightshift. At the beginning of the two hours my neck measurement was fifteen and at the end of the two hours it was sixteen.

As much as I liked working in the colliery I wanted something more. The potato crisp idea came to me in bed early on a Sunday morning. My brother David had married, so had my sister Ceinwen, but they both still helped in the business. There was not a soul about when I started work in the fish and chip shop early on that Sunday morning. I lit one fire, cleaned some potatoes, then with a hand peeler I sliced them into the thickness of crisps, tested the fat with one long, thin sliver of potato. The fat bubbled. So I dropped a handful of the thinly sliced potatoes into the fat that immediately frothed up. I shook the crisps with the wire scoop; the crisps were stuck together in a ball. I turned the fire down.

The thinly sliced potatoes left in the bowl were wet and stuck together, that, I guessed, must be the problem. I spread a clean tea towel on the counter and tipped the wet crisps onto it, then dabbed and fluffed the crisps until they were dry, turned up the fan on the fire, waited a minute or two, then scattered the dry crisps into the warm oil, and stirred the crisps with the wire scoop. Success. The crisps floated, frying to perfection. I drained off the crisps, put them in a greaseproof bag, cleaned out the fire and presented the crisps to the rest of the family just before tea that Sunday.

We bought a crisp hand-cutting machine from Preston and Thomas in Cardiff, and took it down to Matt Price garage, James Street, Neath, to have an electric motor fitted. That didn't work; it was cutting too fast. There were three blades on the cutting drum. Dave Dawson, a friend of mine and a colliery electrician, came to look at it and suggested we turn two of the blades upside down. It worked.

The next problem: drying the crisps before frying, Dry White, alum, was the answer. That made me smile remembering the remark the MO had made in Calcutta to one of the lads who had picked up a knap hand of a girl he was told was a virgin.

Next was a fat extractor to dry the crisps before packing and, that was the most expensive bit of gear. Palm Kernel Oil was the oil we had always used for frying fish and chips but was just a bit too heavy for frying crisps so we bought a forty-gallon drum of the very expensive Tea Seed Oil and that turned out to be an outstanding success. Waxed cardboard boxes with a cardboard foil-covered lining were used to hold 24 packets of crisps. These were heat-sealing packets with blue squares to hold the twists of salt, and a name: 'Enterprise Crisps, D.R. Evans and Sons, approximately one ounce'. Within weeks we were selling as many boxes of crisps as we could make.

But we had to pull down the fish and chip shop, which put paid to Enterprise Crisps, D.R. Evans and Sons.

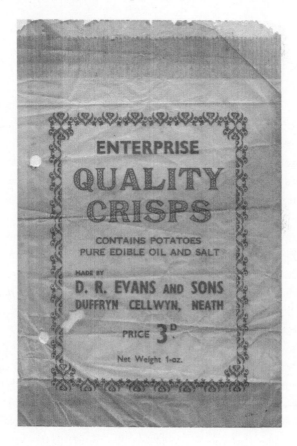

4

The uncertainty, the haggling, the worry went on for about two years. In the meantime I too had got married at Coelbren Church on Boxing Day 1949. Christmas Day fell on a Sunday which meant Peggy got three days off on a trot, and my mother and father too had been married on a Boxing Day.

Rationing was as bad in 1949 as it had been in the war. My mother bought clothing coupons on the black market – 52 coupons at half a crown a coupon: £7-00 – so that I could have two tailor-made suits to go on my honeymoon. She bought the coupons off Jack Bach the Butchers wife, bottom house.

The cornerstone of the black market as far as food was concerned was the local grocer shop. A grocer would have, say, one hundred families' ration books registered with him, a holding of about four hundred ration books. At least ten to twelve per cent of the families would be low waged.

Amongst the lowest-paid families were the families of servicemen. When the quarterly gas or electricity bill arrived, they had a choice: pay the bill or buy your ration and have your supply cut off. The grocer was in possession of the ration books at all times however. He'd take them along to the warehouse and buy the entitlements of the books. Rations that were not then bought by the person whose name was on the book went under the counter, where they then could be sold at double their market price or given as a sweetener to a councillor, policeman or even a magistrate sometimes in order that the grocer could make his way up through the ranks, perhaps to becoming town mayor.

I had never been measured for a suit before. My mother had always taken my brother David and me to Hodges on the same street as the Star Supply Stores in Neath where she bought her groceries, and Hodges always gave a new pair of braces with the new suit or blazer and grey shorts, usually the week before Easter. The new suits would be for Sunday best, the previous Sunday clothes would be for school, and the school clothes for out of school running around on Saturday or to wear working in the fish and chip shop, picking whinberries, going to Saturday matinee, Band of Hope and Mark Podger's boxing club.

Mr Podger was a former Imperial Services welterweight champion. At first we practised and trained in his back yard which had a glass canopy, like all the houses in School Road, which meant we could carry on training even if it was raining. We paid thruppence a week to belong to the club, supplying our own shorts, vest and daps and turned up spotlessly clean to be inspected by Mark who was an ex-army PT sergeant. In the last tournament the club put on, Vernon Edwards won Boxer of the Tournament Award. Vernon was killed in Normandy.

Our wedding breakfast was at the Price's Arms. Dilwyn, Peg's brother-in-law, who was a master baker, made the wedding cake with four tiers that everyone thought was a masterpiece and that some clown dismantled before a photo was taken. David my brother was to be my best man but didn't turn up until after the ceremony. Dai, Peg's brother, stood in. David said when he did turn up that his van had broken down.

It poured with rain, so much so we had to go into the village hall to have our wedding photographs taken, on the stage which had been dressed for the Christmas Pantomime. The wedding breakfast was just one course, mainly ham from a pig reared in somebody's back garden, pickles, beetroot, boiled potatoes and the cake.

Both families trooped down to Neath General Railway Station to see us off. Five pounds' return from Neath to Paddington. Peg's nine-year-old nephew John got on the train with us. Peg had taken him everywhere since he was able to walk because he lived in the same house as her from the day he was born. Dilwyn his father had been away in the army for six years and his mother Marie, Peg's sister, was the mainstay in running the Williams family bakery, so John lived with his grandparents. When I started taking Peg out after I got home from duty we always took John with us to the seaside, the cinema or wherever. So it was little wonder he thought he was coming to London on honeymoon with us. There were a lot of tears and quite a bit of struggling to get him off the train.

London in 1949 was still threadbare and shabby with great gaps like a mouth with missing teeth, where buildings had been blown away and the rubble removed. The only time I'd been there before was three years earlier travelling from Southampton to Thetford, Norfolk, but that was just to cross London by tube train. Staying in a hotel was new to us as a couple. Usually we'd go to stay with an aunty for a day or two; that would be our holiday. I had stayed in a hotel only once before, with my mother and sister when I was about seven. It was in a boarding house on the seafront at Swansea. There was a balcony that we used to stand on to watch the ships come in. Swansea was a very busy port in those days, exporting anthracite coal and tinplate and handling all the tankers for the giant oil refinery at Llandarcy, but the ship we enjoyed seeing the most was the white Fyffes Banana Boat which the landlady had told us about. For the last two days of our stay an air circus roared its way around Swansea's beautiful bay. Everyone was talking about a famous air ace from the Great War. We had a first-class view from our balcony.

Peg was 21; I was 24. Our room in London was large with a very high ornate ceiling, and cold. We cured that by getting into bed as quickly as we possibly could. The following morning, a pleasant if a bit embarrassing surprise. A young maid about Peg's age, in a black dress, white pinafore and a small white headdress, wheeled in our breakfast. Peg laughed and pulled the bedclothes up to her chin.

'Hello!' She spoke to the girl the way she spoke to everyone, as if she'd known them all their life. 'We're not dressed yet.'

The maid smiled in reply. 'There's tea and coffee!' and

left the room. Breakfast was cornflakes, fried Spam, scrambled eggs and toast.

We got a taxi to the Tower of London and enjoyed listening to the Beefeater's interesting and grisly tales. I felt there was something a bit tacky and evil about the crown jewels. Karl Marx had found a small corner in my conscience and I was happy about that. Afterwards we sat on a low wall drinking a mug of hot Bovril we had bought off a mobile stall. A street photographer was setting up his tripod a yard or two away; he put his black camera hood over his head, he then emerged from under the hood with a beaming smile on his face. 'Lovely!'

He walked towards us with a photograph, still wet, held by a wooden clothes peg. 'How's that then?'

It was a very nice sepia photograph, postcard size, of Peg and me.

'Seven shillings and sixpence for six! And I guarantee you won't get a better bargain anywhere in London!'

Lots of people had given us presents. There were very few things you could buy that were off rations, to say thank you. Peg went to open her handbag.

'No, no! The gentleman will give me the shillings and you lovely lady shall cross my palm with a lucky silver sixpence.' He definitely had the gift of the gab; he was well turned out and good-looking. I thought, if you're not careful, this bloke could talk the shirt off your back.

'Now don't open the envelope for two hours, let the image settle on the card.' He put the envelope into Peg's still-open handbag.

At dinnertime we took a taxi to Lyon's Corner House, Piccadilly. The times my mother had told David, Ceinwen and me about this place. That was thirty-five years before, in 1914, when she worked as a nurserymaid for a well-to-do Welsh family. When they could afford it, she and Edie Beer her friend would treat themselves to tea and cakes at this very place. We had lentil soup, cod and chips and rice pudding, then off to the shops.

Selfridges was a must; Peg's sister Marie never tired of talking about it from the time she and her friend Mary Whitney had come back from holidays in London. So too had my mother and it was everything they said it was. You could put all the shops in Neath and Swansea into this one, massive emporium. We rode up on the escalators, the moving stairs my mother had called them. Everything was polished and sparkled in the torrent of light pouring from what seemed like hundreds of chandeliers.

I had booked seats to see the highly controversial nude show that had been brought from Paris to the London Hippodrome, the *Folies Bergere*. I had booked at Tricks the Neath auctioneer. Just being sat in the London Hippodrome was a thrill for us both. The *Folies Bergere* was spectacular and the audience gave standing ovations to the stage sets – London audience that had seen it all but at the end of the week the Lord Chancellor closed it down.

After the show the taxi driver took us back to our hotel by way of a famous railway station, St Pancras, for us to hear the starlings. The massive building was completely smothered in chattering birds. According to the taxi driver it was something most visitors to London wanted to hear. It was a spectacle. I wondered who'd be cleaning up the mess, but we were glad he took us as it would be something to talk about when we got home.

41

Bob and Pat Bagley came up from Slough on New Year's Eve.

'God it's cold in here! Put the fire on!' Pat asked shivering.

'Don't know how,' said Peg.

'Who's got a shilling?' asked Pat.

'I'll do it,' said Bob. In a blink of an eye the room was filled with a warm red glow from the large gas fire.

'There's an envelope on the dressing table, Pat. Open it, there's some photos in it,' muttered Peg, putting the finishing touches to her lipstick.

'There's no photos in here. Just some plain cards,' said Pat.

I must have stuck out like a sore thumb, caught first day by a spiv. From then on Peg took charge of the money.

We went to see Sid Fields in *Harvey* that night at the Prince of Wales and afterwards joined in with the crowd at Trafalgar Square waiting for the bloody 1940s to be behind us and welcome in 1950, the beginning of the new half century. Shook hands and kissed everyone within reach and wished them a happy New Year. Kisses and hugs to wish Bob and Pat goodbye with heartfelt promises to keep in touch, on Paddington Station.

On the train back to Wales Peg still would not believe that the name of the hotel manager was Allcock. When you've lived your life surrounded by people with names like Jones, Lewis, Davies, Williams, Evans, and very occasionally a Smith, Allcock takes a bit of getting used to.

5

We went to live with Peg's mother and father, Sam and Sophia, at 9 Gordon Terrace, Onllwyn, a semi-detached corrugated iron bungalow. There were two such terraces, each of ten bungalows, the other being named Khartoum. Named to remember the great anti-slaver General Chinese Gordon. The London firm that manufactured these bungalows exported them to every corner of the British Empire, to mining communities especially, the first flat-pack houses. Three-inch by four-inch hardwood timber frames, corrugated iron sheeting, the inner walls and ceiling, pine tongue and groove planed planks, the cavity filled with horsehair for first-class insulation. Three bedrooms, a large living room with a big fire place, a box room and pantry. A lean-to, divided between a small kitchen and a bathroom. The most comfortable house I have ever lived in.

In the kitchen, a Dover Stove that burnt anthracite and on windy nights the hobs of the stove would glow red-hot.

9 Gordon Terrace was a company house, as were ninety-nine per cent of the houses at the top end of the Dulais Valley, owned by the mine owner Evans Bevan Ltd.

Sam was entitled to thirteen tons of concessionary coal a year as the householder; as well as being a newsagent he was still a pumps-man by night at Onllwyn No. 1, and I got six tons a year being in apartments as they called it. The fires were kept going twenty-four hours a day and we had coal to spare.

The Price's Arms' overheads were heavy: a very large, very cold old building. Dai and Nana were lovely people but not the best at business, plus Dai socialized more than he should have with the customers. A couple of bob to Jack Tongue the coal haulier and Dai would get one of his father's tons or one of mine. Nana (her maiden name was Hanna Roberts) came from a Cardiganshire family who had lived some time in Cheltenham; her father, a master carpenter, had worked on many of the churches in the town and had returned to South Wales to work on Abercraf church and St Margaret's in Crynant. When her father died Nana was still very young; she and her mother went to live at the Onllwyn Inn with her uncle Jim Jones, landlord and mining contractor.

The Onllwyn Inn was one of the three splendid pubs built by the Evans Bevan family at the top end of the Dulais valley. The interior was fitted out in a first-class Edwardian style and was, architecturally, amongst the finest commercial buildings in Wales.

Jim Jones looked like Wallace Beery, the large tough American film star, and he acted the part. Nana would say there were times when he would lock himself in the beer cellar and drink himself into oblivion. One time he emerged to stand on the upstairs landing proclaiming at the top of his voice that Jesus had told him, 'Jim Jones you're a good man'.

He was a fanatical fan of the great Welsh boxer Tommy Farr. In 1937 when Tommy Farr fought Joe Louis for the heavyweight championship of the world, he had an artist paint a ten-foot high, three-foot wide portrait of Tommy Farr in a fighting stance. He hung it in front of the Onllwyn Inn surrounded by coloured lights. Nana worked behind the bar as a teenager with her mother and generally helped out with the housework and cleaning the pub. Onllwyn No. 1 colliery had about eight hundred men working there on three shifts. The lamproom was just five hundred yards away from the pub, and when the dayshift knocked off at 2.30pm the bar was packed out. Then it would become busy again after the men had got home, and had bathed and changed. They would spend the evening supping beer, playing dominos, tip-it, cards, darts, or just chatting.

Dai, who was eighteen years older than Peg, started courting Nana. He only lived ten doors away in 9 Gordon Terrace. They were married at the beginning of the war with a Home Guard honour guard. Afterwards they went to live in apartments with Bopa Mary Anne and uncle DL in a house on Main Road, Dyffryn Cellwen.

The tenancy of the Price's Arms was on offer: a Simons-owned pub, the only non-Evans Bevan pub at the top end of the Dulais. With Nana's years of experience they thought they would apply. They got it. Peter their son was born. Within months Dai was called up. He no longer worked in the mines so was no longer in a reserved occupation. He served with the Royal Engineers in Egypt.

I had started driving underground winding engines when a driver was missing and I got a shift a week allowance for that. The extra money came in handy when Owen was born in March 1951 and I asked to go on nightshift in the summer so that I could work our ice-cream round by day.

Peg was always a touch unpredictable. Doctor Boladz called that morning. He was a large, striking figure, Polish. He strode out of the bedroom.

'Zeorge your baby will be born today! I'll arrange for an ambulance!' He was out of the house and into his Land Rover and gone. In those days all first babies had to be born in hospital.

Enid, who was married to Peg's cousin Dai John Jones, had come down to the house when she saw the doctor's Land Rover. She was known as Enid Loud Speaker because she was the daughter of George Williams Loud Speaker, one time CSM in the Welsh Guards and now an officer in the Saint John's Ambulance Brigade and Ambulance man at Onllwyn No. 1 Colliery. He used to cut my hair in his garden shed; glass of cider to start and a clean pinafore around my neck. My hair in those days grew as vigorously as wild gorse.

'The only thing missing on your head Evans is the fence!'

One time he came to see me. 'You know Mr and Mrs Biggar are on holidays and I've been left in charge of their chickens!'

'Bloody hell, the dog!' I said. 'He hasn't killed any as he?'

'No! But he's undressed most of them, George!'

Enid his daughter was just as colourful.

'I'll go with Peg, Aunty Sophia,' she offered.

'Thank you, Enid.' Sophia looked worried. After all, Peg was her baby: eighteen years younger than her brother Dai and thirteen years younger than her sister Marie. As usual she spoke to Peg in Welsh: '*Dod cariad fach i fy* (Come my little darling),' she said quietly, gently pulling the collar of Peg's coat snugly about her neck.

The ambulance pulled up outside.

'One of my earrings is missing,' said Peg, turning to go back into the bedroom.

'Nobody will notice, Peg,' Enid protested.

She came back out of the bedroom fastening the retrieved earring to her ear. She looked at me. 'You're coming aren't you?'

It was touch and go but we got to Neath General Hospital in time. John was still confused about how he was related to Peg and me. I was looking after the shop that afternoon and John came pedalling up at full speed on his bike. Didn't bother to stop, jumped off his bike and landed on his knees in the shop.

'We got a brother, George!' he gasped.

What a difference the arrival of a seven-and-a-half-pound baby boy made to the rhythm of life in 9 Gordon Terrace. My working week was full, not a minute to spare. Got home from work by 6am, bath, cup of tea then straight to bed. Peg was already at work sorting the papers and there were an awful lot of them. In those days on a Thursday with *Radio Times*, *Woman* and the *Women's Own*, the parcels would weigh a hundredweight or more. Every house had one newspaper delivered, sometimes two plus magazines and comics. Peg had an extraordinary memory, able to remember what newspaper, magazine and comic each house took, from the Seven Sisters end of Pantyffordd to the houses on top of Banwen Colliery two and a half miles away, and remember them at speed.

I would be out of bed by midday. Peg's mother would have my breakfast ready on the table. I'd reach the billiard hall by 1.30 to load the cold boxes onto the ice-cream van. The long triangular tubes had to be removed carefully from the brine in the main freezer and placed one in each corner of the cold boxes so that they would fit around the stainless steel cylinders containing the freshly made ice cream; portable thermos cylinder, nail brush and towel for hand washing, stainless steel serving tools, boxes of wafers, cone biscuits, a bottle of raspberry flavour sauce and a box with five pounds in assorted coins.

We used Griff Morgan's recipe to make the ice cream; it was well tried and very popular. Griff had been using it before the war, so there was no trouble selling it, and we always went home sold out. I'd start the round when the children came home from school at 4.30 and finish at about 7.30 then unload the van, drive down to Ton-y-castell farm where the cows had been milked, the milk cooled and put into a five-gallon churn ready for me to take back to the billiard hall. The milk was poured into a stainless steel boiler fitted with a large agitator; as the heat built up, sugar and the ice cream powder mix was emptied into the swirling milk. When the milk came to the boil the heat was turned off and a tap that let ice-cold water into the jacket that surrounded the boiler opened. This drastic change in temperature was supposed to kill off any remaining bacteria. Once cool, by way of a tap the mix was run into a two-gallon white enamel jug and emptied into a refrigerated mixer and within minutes the finished ice cream was ready to be scooped out into the stainless steel serving tubs.

The van was a blue Bedford, tastefully painted with D.R. EVANS, in gold, with a very handsome young boy painted at one end and a very beautiful young girl at the other end, both holding ice cream cones. It was painted by one of the most talented artists that had ever lived in the valley, Ken Lewis. He worked driving a winding engine underground at Banwen colliery and attempted to be as bohemian in appearance as possible, even turning up for work underground wearing sandals until, coming on shift one day, he bumped into Mr John Williams the manager, who explained to him very politely that the prescribed footwear would be more suitable. His eccentric behaviour did nothing to lessen his outstanding ability. He could paint as well with his left hand as with his right and his eye for colour and proportion could not be bettered. Alas his domestic life was not as complete as his artistic talent and a gifted painter was lost to the community.

After the round, tea and a piece of home-made cake, teisen-lap, with my mother, then wash and put on a spotlessly white apron and coat. The Victoria Laundry at Cadoxton picked up eighteen white aprons and coats every week from the billiard hall and the fish and chip shop that was now up and running and being looked after by my sister and her husband Des Jackson. Des was not really a fish and chip shop man. He worked as a collier by day and a first-class one at that. In his younger days he had played football for Merthyr Town in the Southern League and had been capped for Wales as an amateur. He found working as a collier and playing football as an amateur was his best option; colliers were better paid than footballers in those days. It was hard work but he was as fit as a fiddle. One time he came off nightshift, bathed in the pit-head baths at Seven Sisters as there were no baths at the Rhas then, travelled on Gables colliers' bus to Merthyr and travelled with the team to Gillingham, played the full ninety minutes, travelled back in the team bus to Merthyr then caught the colliers' bus on Sunday morning to Banwen. Des was a clubman; every day, no matter how busy he was, he'd find time to go to the club. His burning ambition was to be on the committee and a leading light on the committee, an ambition he achieved. This was an ambition somehow alien to me, and to my father too I thought: to our cost I am sure.

Des and I had been good friends since school days. At sixteen he could notch timber better than most colliers and he had an obsession with keeping his shoes shiny. If Swansea was playing home on a Saturday I'd ask William Harries the under manager if Des and I could finish in time to catch the eleven o'clock South Wales Bus so that we'd get to the Vetch for kick-off. He never once said no.

I remember one Saturday, it was a week or two after the terrible bombing raids of February 1941. Thirty thousand incendiary bombs and eight hundred high-explosive bombs were rained down on the important seaport town killing two hundred and seventy of the town's inhabitants and injuring over four hundred others. The roadways had been cleared but the skeleton-remains of all those buildings had about them an air of eeriness. When we got off the bus at St Mary's church the church was gone and the smell of burning still in the air.

I didn't mind cleaning the billiard hall, brushing and ironing the tables but watching blokes come in at 9.30 in the morning and play almost continually until midnight was something I didn't enjoy or understand. Especially one bloke: he played all day on a Saturday then at half ten at night reached for his two walking sticks and limped home; he was on a permanent sick note I think. Watching the Burroughes and Watts man recover a table was a joy to see. Each of his fingertips was splayed out like a duck's bill. He would spread the beautiful dark green cloth evenly over the two-inch thick slate bed, tacked the one end, filled his mouth with tacks, and walked to the other end of the table. With his left hand he pulled the cloth straight and taut, drew it tight down over the edge of the slate bed with an iron grip and tacked it to the wood frame, then all around the twelve foot by six foot table, hence the reason for the large hands and duck-billed finger tips.

6

When Owen was two, we were allocated a brand-new council house in Seven Sisters, but sadly we were never able to move in. Peg's mother Sophia collapsed with a heart attack. So it was back to square one. Owen didn't mind; he loved living with his grandmother and grandfather – they did whatever he wanted them to do and all in Welsh.

Eighteen months later when I got in off nightshift Sophia was up and waiting for me. It was quarter to six in the morning.

'Owen's not well George, you'd better fetch Dr Thomas!'

The doctor arrived, took one look at Owen who was by then unconscious.

'I'm going back to the surgery. There'll be an ambulance here right away. We'll take him to Hill House!'

Hill House was the isolation hospital. Peg's young cousin Avril had died of poliomyelitis just a few years before. The very name Hill House sent a shudder through the family. Thankfully it was not poliomyelitis but peritonitis.

Owen was transferred to Swansea General Hospital. We had a telephone call to come down to the hospital to sign consent forms so that they could operate. We had an Austin A40 by then and Gwyn, who was a bus driver for United Welsh and the late Avril's father, drove us down. Thankfully there was very little traffic on the roads. We were well over the speed limit for most of the way. We signed and Owen was on his way to the operating theatre but we were not allowed to see him, as were the rules in those days. The next time we saw Owen was three weeks later, when we went to bring him home. Owen sat in the back cuddled up to his grandmother Sophia.

They were bridging the last gap in the new bridge over the river Neath, the biggest built in Wales for a hundred years. We took Owen to see it. It looked magnificent towering above the river as it flowed out into the sea; what Owen made of it at four years of age goodness only knows.

Peg worked from six in the morning, sorting the hundreds of newspapers and magazines into bundles for the rounds; her hands and face would be as black as a collier from the inferior print still being used even after the war. A wash and change of clothes, then in the shop until seven in the evening from Monday to Thursday, on Friday until nine or ten in the evening, Saturday half day.

Christmas was her busy time; every shelf in the shop would be full of annuals. Peg ran a Christmas annual savings club. Each saver was issued with a club card with their name and the book or books they were saving for. All of the annuals like the *Dandy*, *Comic Cuts*, *Wizard*, *Adventure Play Box* and *Girl's Own* were half a crown each. Thirty pennies so if a boy or girl got their card at the beginning of November they'd have, not counting Sundays because the shop was not open on Sundays, forty-six days to save for their Christmas annual. Peg would keep the shop open until eleven at night on Christmas Eve to make sure every child got their book and if no one called to pick up their book Peg would deliver it.

Sophia ran the house. She saw to the food and ironing, cut my box for work and Peg's father Sam's box; he still worked nights on the pumps at Onllwyn No. 1. Saw to it that everything was ready for my bath at the end of the shift and Sam's bath first thing in the morning as there were no pithead baths. Or if I was going to one of the many boxing matches held in South Wales, usually at St Helens, Swansea or Coney Beach, Porthcawl, my clothes, shoes and clean socks would be ready, even down to a clean handkerchief in my pocket. The boxing trips were organized by Herbie Regan and he'd drive Len Potter's colliers' bus. They did not always run without a hitch. One time it was a blazing hot day, four o'clock in the afternoon on our way to Porthcawl. There was a traffic queue from Baglan to the policeman on point duty on the square in the middle of Port Talbot.

Len Potter's bus was old and very warm, moving a few yards at a time it took us three quarters of an hour to reach the policeman. The policeman held up his white-gloved hand to the stop position and called the traffic coming down from the valley across our front on their way to Aberavon. Everyone dressed in a navy blue serge suit, white shirt and coloured tie, the going out uniform of the anthracite coalminer and everyone sweating profusely. The policeman turned smartly and his white-gloved hand beckoned us on.

Herbie put the bus in gear and the engine stalled. The engine was inside the bus next to the driver's seat. Herbie put his hand down and pressed the starter. There was a loud bang and the bus filled with blue smoke. Herbie looked suicidal. Gasping and coughing we all tumbled off the bus. The bus had to be moved; it was holding up a mile-long queue of traffic. There were thirty-two of us, pushing to the cheers and applause of the afternoon shoppers. We pushed the bus down a side street and then went into the nearest tavern.

Things were ticking over very busily, but evenly. Then like a bolt out of the blue Sophia developed dementia. It was unbelievable, this highly capable and very handsome woman that we all depended on, still only sixty-one, suddenly could not even tell what day it was.

Peg and Marie paid Sal Williams, one-time cook at Llandovery College, to stay with Sophia and Sam and do the cooking. Sam was by then suffering badly with bronchitis and had stopped work. Marie, Peg's sister, was still the mainstay of the Bakery. Three bakers worked by night to meet demand. Two delivery vans on the road six days a week, Marie with an assistant, usually Betty Parry, on one and her husband Dilwyn with an assistant on the other. Dilwyn also worked as the third baker. He was a Master Baker having won more than a thousand trophies but it was Marie who was the bookkeeper. There were the takings to be counted and checked then banked, wages and tax and national insurance to be deducted, bills to be paid, government subsidies to be claimed... without Marie there would have been no bakery.

Marie was a first-rate scholar and gambler. When she was fifteen she was caught taking bets on the horses, she had a clock under the counter in her father's shop. That was illegal in those days and she was taken to court and fined but her love of gambling stayed with her to the end. She was also very good-looking and that got her out of a few scrapes. During the war she was an auxiliary ambulance driver. Jenkins the wholesale confectioners of Skewen, large delivery vans were temporarily converted into ambulances and Marie drove one of them in the blitz on Swansea.

Sophia was admitted to hospital. She had only been there a week when Peg went to visit her and found her soaking wet in bed. Peg immediately drove back home and went to see her auntie Lizzie, who at one time had been a senior nursing sister. Peg called at the house, collected clean clothes for her mother and drove back to the hospital. Aunty Lizzie told the matron, 'We're taking my sister home!' As time went by Peg slept virtually with one foot on the floor because Sophia had taken to wandering about at night, once preparing to light the fire with paraffin: a fire that was already lit.

I asked Gomer Jenkins the overman could I go onto the afternoon shift so that I could help Peg by taking care of Owen in the mornings and he said yes. They wanted a winder driver in the Tabor's district. I found to my surprise that driving this small Picrose winder could be quite a dangerous job. They had driven a Hard Heading from the four-foot seam down to the eighteen-foot seam off Tabor's level. The winder was tight against the rail track facing in by the Hard Heading. Down to the eighteen was off to the left and Tabor's level went thirty yards up a gradient, on to a dead end that had a large sheave fitted, which the rope was threaded around. The winder would pull the full trams up the Hard Heading to the sheave. The rider would change the points, so that the full trams would run past the winder to the main drift. The rider signalled double two, which meant slack out at full speed. The six full trams would career past at full speed, not even a guardrail for protection. If the trams jumped the track it would be curtains for the driver and his engine for sure.

7

Dai Jones and his family who lived in the billiard hall bungalow were allocated a NCB house in the Moorlands. My father decided to renovate the bungalow for Peg and me. Ned Pedricks, my brother David's brother-in-law who lived in Resolven, took the job on.

It was a wooden bungalow, three bedrooms, a large living room with the normal open fire place with oven and hob and an outside lavatory. The timber used to build the clinger-built bungalow was top grade, bought at Wards the ship breakers at Giant's Grave, Briton Ferry, in the twenties, a kind of tropical hardwood so hard it was impossible to hammer a nail into it without the nail bending. You needed to start the nail hole with a gimlet. A new coal-burning Rayburn cooker was fitted that heated the hot water. All the inside walls and ceilings were lined with hardwood and plasterboard sheets, relaid floor, new doors and a brick garden wall to give the bungalow some privacy.

One day Sophia appeared to be her old self again. Asking me how my mother and father were and delighted with the way Owen and John (who was now a teenager) were coming on, and her two grandchildren in Coelbren, Peter, and Janet, who were the same age as Owen and living with their mother Nana and father Dai at the Price's Arms. Dai was constantly in and out of the TB sanatorium first at Cimla, Neath then at Talgarth. He stayed in sanatoriums for months at a time, Peg driving the family on visiting day one week and Marie the following week. Nana was not able to drive. As ill as Dai was, no one ever suggested he stop smoking; Peg took him a pack of two hundred Players cigarettes on each visit.

I was helping Ned Pedricks renovate the bungalow and my mother called me from the open kitchen window of the billiard hall.

'What d'you want?'

'Peg's Mam has died!'

The day before Sophia had been her old self. I decided not to rush home to Gordon Terrace right away; Sophia's sisters Lizzie and half sister Vi along with Marie, Nana and cousin Enid would be there with Peg and Sam. They were in times of grief a quiet family; like most mining families they didn't go in for the howling and wailing performances.

Months later Peg's cousin Enid told me how she'd come out of the bedroom and told Peg that her mother was dead. Peg fainted and how that had shocked everyone in the room, to see this strong healthy young woman who had attended to her sick mother and father over the last two years, who was first up every morning and last to bed every night, out in all weathers running her newspaper round, collapsing into a dead faint.

By the time I got home aunty Lizzie, aunty Vi and cousin Enid were there; the living room as usual was sparkling, polished brass reflecting the bright glow of the fire. Peg came into the room dressed in a white plain blouse and black skirt, no sign of tears, her black wavy hair smoothed down into her favourite pageboy style. She was twenty-eight-years-old and as far as I was concerned the loveliest, prettiest girl in the world.

She hated her wavy hair, especially when it rained – then it became curly. Her mother had made her a velvet glove to smooth her hair down and make it shine. The shop didn't open on Sundays, so Peg had a lay in on a Sunday morning. I would wake first and would often look at her, her dark hair on a white pillow, her spotlessly clear complexion and wonder: How did an ugly bugger like me land up in the same bed as her?

Nor did the billiard hall open on Sunday. I'd pop up in the morning after breakfast to clean up after Saturday night, brush and iron the tables and tip the cues that had lost their tips over the last week. Then home for Sunday dinner. Sunday evening listening to the wireless as there was no television then. I'd listen to the wireless and draw, Peg would read and listen to the wireless, Sam would lay back in his chair and doze, Sophia would crochet, the same comfortable routine every Sunday evening. I'd begin to sketch Peg and she'd look across and catch me.

'Mammy he's staring at me again.'

Sophia would gently scold Peg in Welsh and laugh. Peg's family were fluent in Welsh. Sam and Sophia only ever spoke Welsh to each other and very likely did their courting in Welsh and it had nothing to do with being nationalistic. It was the language they had been spoken to as babies but Peg would not speak Welsh. They would be together as a family the five of them, her mother, father, sister and brother all speaking Welsh. They would speak to Peg in Welsh and she'd answer in English.

I used to think it was to do with the way we got our entertainment, at least twice a week to the cinema. There were Saturdays when we'd go twice in one day, first to the Windsor and then in the evening to the Gnoll or Empire. I thought that Peg wanted to be a proper modern Millie, wanting to sound like the film stars Deanna Durbin or Judy Garland. Peg's easygoing attitude to what seemed everything and every occasion often sent people barking up the wrong tree, me included.

Later I found out, or half-guessed, there was a deeper, more personal reason. Peg's mother's father, David Thomas, a deputy at Maesmarchog colliery, Banwen, had died after helping in the rescue at the explosion at Seven Sisters pit in 1907. On his death certificate it had 'cause of death pneumonia', very likely it would have been from smoke inhalation but in those days that was not taken into consideration.

Her widowed grandmother, with four children, then remarried old William Bowen. Mr Bowen had lost his post as choirmaster at the chapel, which he had held for twenty-five years, because he had married her grandmother. She was clean-living and hardworking but she was also the landlady of the Half Way Inn and marrying a publican was more than the chapel deacons could put up with.

Peg's resentment of the chapel was shared by many of her friends, not against the people who spoke Welsh like her mother and father and my father, but to the people she felt peddled Welsh, the self-righteous bigots who had publicly humiliated her stepgrandfather whom she adored, and a young unmarried woman too, in front of the whole chapel's congregation, because she had fallen pregnant. A young woman who like women the length and breadth of the country, at that time, were risking their lives for eight hours a day every day. Twenty-seven young women were killed in the Bridgend ammunition works in one blast. Workers there also had the appalling indignity of having their skin turn yellow, a yellow that would not scrub off, caused by handling deadly nitro-glycerine.

On Coronation Day Peggy put out the Hammer and Sickle flag along with the Union Jacks. Years later Dr Aubrey Thomas teased her, 'You're a compulsive rebel Peggy!' This just about summed her up. If someone spoke against the Queen she would automatically stick up for the Queen.

The bestselling newspapers on her round were the *Daily Mirror* and *Daily Herald*, the *Communist Daily Worker* then the *Daily Express*, *News Chronicle* and *Daily Mail*. On Friday two extra parcels of 'Daily Workers' arrived, one parcel for the lamp-room of Onllwyn No. 1 the other for the lamp-room of Onllwyn No. 3, and every copy that was not sold was paid for by Dai Turk Davies on Saturday. Dai was a communist who didn't need a boss – he worked from gong to gong every single shift.

Peg had quite a few characters among her customers. One who used to call to pick up the magazine the *Writer*, Bert Lewis Coombes, who lived at Nantyfedwen Farm and worked nights in the colliery and was quite a famous author. His book *These Poor Hands*, won 'Book of the Month' by the 'left' book club. I got to know him by sometimes driving him home on Saturdays if it was raining. He was interested in my paintings and drawings. He would fascinate me with tales of meeting and talking to people like George Orwell.

A chance to go on piece work turned up, cogging on E conveyor face. The work was hard; it involved knocking out or cutting out the roof supports to allow the roof to collapse into the waste, the area from where the coal had been removed, the gob. The face was one hundred and fifty yards long and on average three-foot-ten inches high.

The conveyor was the jigger type, a steel trough that was noisily rocked to and fro by a large heavy drive arm attached to the master pan in the middle on the conveyor, controlled by the button boy who sat on the electric drive motor. There were fifteen colliers each with a ten yard stint that he was expected to take forward a yard a shift, ten tons cut and shovelled on to the rocking trough in seven and a half hours, about one hundred and fifty tons a shift. The noise was deafening.

Each collier would timber his stint using posts and flats: eight posts, four flats to a stint. At the end of shift there would be a timber-lined corridor one hundred and fifty yards long and about three-foot-ten inches high, rising from the Gate End on a gentle incline to the supply road. Every post had to be dead in line with the next as the face captain would check and so would the deputy and over-man.

Keeping the point the surveyors gave for any roadway in a coalmine was of paramount importance. The conveyor turners worked middle shift unbolting the trough into sections called pans, turning each heavy pan on its side and sliding it forward between the posts, lifting the rocker wheels that were resting on an 'S'-shaped cradle, two to a pan, and throwing them forward into the new track. The heavy electric motor was moved forward by using a Sylvester, a strong comb-like bar, the handle of which gave the purchase. It had a short bar at the end that fitted between the comb's teeth and when pulled, levered the load forward with a chain at one end and a hook at the other to work as an anchor.

Once the heavy steel trough was resting on the idlers and the idlers resting on the 'S'-shaped guides, the pans bolted, and the drive arm bolted to the master pan, the jigger was ready to go but not until the coggers had dismantled the forty cogs and rebuilt them tight up to the jigger, from the Gate End to the Supply road; cut or knocked out all the posts and flats left in the old track and made an eight cubic yard long pack, tight to the roof, of rock supported by a dry stone wall.

Coggers got a penny point four for every post knocked or cut out, fourpence a foot for the building and taking down of a cog, one shilling and eight pence a cubic yard of packing and there was about one ton of rock to a cubic yard. Before the steel automatic cog releasers were brought in, we used half a house brick at each corner in the middle of the cog. To release the cogs that were jammed tight between the roof and the bottom you smashed the bricks with a long-handled four-pound sledgehammer.

If there had been a squeeze overnight, downward pressure from the top, the bricks would have been crushed to just about an inch thick or less and would have had to be dug out with a mandrill: a light pickaxe with very sharp pointed blades taken out to the blacksmith to be sharpened and tempered every few weeks.

A cog was built of sawn oak blocks six inches square and two-foot-six inches long. The first two blocks were laid parallel with the coalface north to south about twelve inches apart, the next two on top east to west, until it reached the top putting releasers at each corner halfway up. You had to be ultra alert watching the roof above the cog as you smashed the brick; sometimes with little or no warning the roof would come crashing down and you would have to scurry away as fast as you could on your hands and knees. It was a work that did not allow for daydreaming. I remember Tommy Jenkins Cwmaman once saying, 'If we were doing this in a circus George we'd be getting a hundred quid a night'. The idea was to bring tens of hundreds of tons crashing down into the waste or cob. This greatly assisted the ventilation by forcing the air along a restricted corridor.

There was a time on number six face in the Grey's seam when the face turned five times and they failed to bring the top down. A great black space over one hundred and fifty yards long, the centre of the waste, the roof sagging hazardously and looking menacing, the pressure making the timber in the face sound off like the timber of a ship in a storm. One day there was one almighty crack and the whole one hundred and fifty yards came down with such a power it drove the air back up the in-by with such force it opened the air doors on the main drift. People talked about in awe for years afterwards.

I was to join Dai Penclawdd and Tommy Jenkins on E conveyor. To cut or knock out sixty posts, dismantle and rebuild forty cogs and pack an eight cubic yard pack in a shift, the three of us had to go flat out from gong to gong. Then Will John Jones the over-man told us that unless a post was cut out with a hatchet we would not be paid for it. Cutting out posts was against the law; they had to be pulled out using a silvester, but that took too long. Will John knew that but it didn't matter to him. We were earning good money and he was going to put a stop to it. So when we did knock an easy post out we took a few slices out of it with the hatchet.

Dai was a tall rangy man in his forties who had worked in the very dangerous pitch veins in the Gower and chewed one whole plug of twist a shift. He chewed the hard black tobacco as if it was chocolate. When Dai began working at Banwen colliery, he travelled every day by bus from Penclawdd, a round journey of about forty miles and four and a half hours at least in the bus. He would arrive in Banwen outside the Pantyddraenen Hotel at a quarter to eleven at night, then a ten-minute walk to the lamp-room where he would rise his lamp by eleven o'clock. Tommy Jenkins travelled by Cables colliers' bus from Cwmaman, Aberdare. Tommy was as tall as Dai but heavier built, a bit of a ginger, a rabbit catcher, rat catcher and first tenor in Cwmaman male voice choir.

When the pithead baths opened in Banwen it meant Dai did not have to take his pit clothes into someone else's house and he came to lodge in Banwen, first with Mr and Mrs Smith 'council houses', then with Bowden Green. One or two would not use the pithead baths even though they had the reputation of being the finest colliery baths in the country, the clean locker bays separated by the bath area from the dirty locker bays; and a first aid room with an attendant nursing sister, so well equipped that if necessary emergency surgery could be carried out there. Strict discipline, no wandering into the clean area before bathing, failing to take home dirty clothes to be laundered, one warning then banned from the baths, by order of the union.

It had its funny side too. There was one bloke they called Jack the bantam who had served with a Bantam regiment in the First World War. Men who failed to meet the required height of five three but who were perfectly fit were formed into Bantam battalions. The Cheshires, Lancashires, Yorkshires, Royal Scots and the Highland Light Infantry, so many that they created the 35th British Light Infantry Division.

Jack was in his fifties then, originally from Lancashire and always in good humour, just as well. In the baths he found himself in the next cubicle to Telec Evans who, like his brother Wat the Glo Evans, had a voice that could be heard a mile away.

'Look at this! Hells bells! Look at this!' Telec was yelling standing under the shower. 'It's like a baby's arm! Like a blinking tom cat with its ears back!'

Telec Evans reckoned it was like a baby elephant coming at you and it must have had a very demoralizing effect on some of the bigger men that Jack outmeasured by a mile.

For all that, the pit-head baths were a godsend. Years later, nominated by the pop star Bonnie Tyler, the pit-head baths would be acclaimed by BBC's Wales' *National Treasures* television programme, profiling the most iconic treasures from the National Museum of Wales as Wales's national treasure.

On Fridays we would not take a snap break, so that we could finish early and get down to the Pant for a drink before we went home. The Pantyddraenen Hotel was built by the Evans Bevan family for the needs of the twelve hundred colliers then working in their colliery. Architecturally it was a very fine building, I thought the best in the valley or the town of Neath for that matter. Built of top grade Bristol red brick, it was a brick baked so hard it had the smooth surface of a tile with one of the longest bars in Wales which was beautifully furnished with mirrored shelves and mahogany counter. It had a parlour with cushion bench seats against the walls, round mahogany tables with a cast-iron open lace designed leg and mahogany chairs; a billiard room that had one full-sized billiard table and bagatelle table and small bar, singing room with a piano, wall bench seats and tables with back-less benches. Upstairs a very large function room was furnished accordingly.

Some said the Evans Bevan had built the pub in order to get their hands on the workmen's pay. True! If they had not someone would have come along and built a pub perhaps like the Price's Arms: when you went to the toilet and it was raining, you stood there getting soaking wet. Not so in the Pant or the other Evans Bevan pubs.

The singing room would be pretty full by the time we got there. Before there was a pithead baths we would still be steaming with sweat when we arrived especially if it was a cold night. Dai would go straight to the piano, Tommy and I would fetch the drinks. Other than John Owen Williams, the renowned choir master of the time, Dai was the best piano player I had ever heard and there was dead silence when he played. The music would stop when Tommy and I went in with the drinks.

'Tommy! Tom! What about a song Tom!' the shouts would go up every week the same. Tommy Jenkins was a shy man.

'Come on Tom! Tommy mun come on!' Tommy would step up, put his pint on the piano, take off his cap and the steam would rise up from his still-wet hair. He turned to face the wall as Dai started to play the introduction. You could hear a pin drop.

Tommy's clear tenor voice was as clear as a bell. 'I think that I shall never see. A poem lovely as a tree' but to me it was the line 'A tree that looks at God all day'. That was the line that seemed to please the colliers most in the warm crowded sing-room, rivulets of sweat making white scars on their coal-black faces.

I watched Tommy Jenkins perform, putting every fibre of his being into his singing as he did into his work. Afraid of nothing, he'd put his hand in a hole and pull out a live rat and kill it with one blow; then almost dying of a broken heart when his young daughter died of polio.

8

E conveyor face turned every day for a year. One of the main reasons for that good progress was that we were working a face slip. That meant the coal leaned out towards you. The slips of coal were the layers of coal, between twelve inches and eighteen inches thick, that made up the seam coal of about three-foot-ten inches to four-foot high. Working a face slip the collier could timber tight up to where the coal supported the roof. A back slip sloped away from you like the roof of a house so that the collier could not timber tight to where the coal supported the roof.

F conveyor face worked a back slip. It travelled in the opposite direction to E face, and they were lucky if they turned three times a week. The result: great pressure was brought on the face and gate end. Twelve-foot steel arches were squeezed down to half their height because they could not get the roof over the gob to collapse.

We had a surprise visitor at the end of one shift, the under-manager.

'I've come to ask a favour lads.' He explained that he'd like us to go over to F conveyor face and bore uppers into the roof over the gob and fire them. It was dangerous and against the law. Gas being lighter than air could rise into the boreholes and cause an explosion when the holes were fired. But he was a good man and worried sick by the way things were going on F face.

Dai held the heavy drilling machine fitted with a short drill, Tom and I put a four-foot long railway sleeper under the machine. Dai held the drilling machine and squeezed the trigger, Tom and I lifted the sleeper pressing upwards and the drill cut into the soft shale. F was a wet face so there was no trouble with dust. They fired the holes after we three had left, the fewer witnesses the better. On Thursday we got the master docket. The amount was split three ways. No bickering over tax or a shift off.

Since Nationalisation nothing now was decided at the colliery. Came into work one day and was told the four feet was to stop, that it was now to be worked from Pentreclwydau in the Neath Valley. I was sent down the eighteen feet, the 'dwy-naw' or the two nines as the old-timers called it. It was the deepest seam worked in Banwen, about eight hundred feet down and at the far end two miles in.

I worked with Dai Hopkins who had a very good smallholding on March Hywell mountain. Legend has it that it was so named to mark the boundary of the land of the ancient ruler of these parts, Hywel Dda, Howell the Good, and that he even had a law made that protected cats.

There were no conveyors down the eighteen feet. It was stall and pillar. The colliers worked the top nine feet of coal leaving nine feet or so of coal underfoot. The downward pressure from the top forced the timer uprights down into the soft coal bottom that caused the bottom to rise, they called this pokkings. Eventually the roadway that had been nine-foot high at the start would be reduced so that a horse was unable to travel in and out with a tram.

Then they'd go back to the entrance of the stall, heading or level and start again by cutting and filling the bottom coal. It was an economic way of working, reusing the same timber. Usually the timber was not broken by being pressed down into the bottom coal; often twisted out of line but easily put right with timber clamps, large hooks with a short chain attached. The collier would drive the hook into the upright that was out of line, push a bar through the big link at the end of the short chain and lever the upright back into place.

Dai Hopkins and I had the job of changing any timber that was broken. The collars, the cross timbers, would break and form a 'V' sticking downwards. The sharp ends would skin a horse's back as he travelled at speed, so the problem was a serious one.

Two of the colliers in one heading were in their seventies but filling as much coal as anyone else. They were dead keen to make sure that one did not have more tram than the other; they got paid by the ton on piece work. Hundreds of colliers worked on the coalface well after turning seventy during the war. People retired when they wanted to or if their health gave out. On Thursday we got our pay dockets and on Friday our pay packets. One Thursday afternoon the old timers had a letter attached to their dockets. The letter, typed on the cheapest paper possible, told them they were on fourteen days' notice as from Monday of the following week. No 'thank you'; no redundancy pay. One I knew had started work at thirteen. They would be going from ten or eleven pounds a week, which in the mid-1950s was a fair wage, to an old-age pension of about two pound ten shillings a week.

My seventy-seven year old uncle Alf was one. He worked on his own by night on the Far End, about a mile away from anyone else, his only companion his old horse Hector, as old as Alf was in horse years. There were sixteen colliers working on the Far End by day and afternoons, each one in his own stall or heading. Alf would drive out every full tram to the double parting, an underground marshalling yard, and take in an empty tram loaded with whatever supplies that particular collier needed, timber, rails, and sleepers.

Uncle Alf was a Londoner, a Cockney, married my aunty Mary, my mother's sister, during the First World War and came to live and work in Banwen. My aunty Mary had died and he was on his own. My mother had him to come down to the billiard hall and asked him would he like to keep an eye on the billiard hall during the day; that way he could earn a few bob and have his meals with my mother and father.

It was then, I think, that people began to think of the NCB as the N C Bloody B. Ninety-nine per cent of the houses in the valley had been owned and built by the Evans Bevan family. They had kept a permanent maintenance crew at Dyffryn Cellwen and Seven Sisters. The houses were painted every four years. If a slate blew off it was put back that day. They built three-bedroomed houses which had hot and cold water, bathrooms, front and back gardens, a brick boundary wall the length of the gardens in School Road and a front garden with a low wall topped by wrought iron railings and a wrought iron gate; Highland Crescent – semi-detached, back yard facing the road. The walls facing the road were high; red brick topped by dressed limestone, giving complete privacy. The wall was also the back wall of the coal house and had in it a small wooden door to receive the deliveries of coal. The back yard was covered by a glass canopy itself protected by a wire mesh screen. The front garden walls of Moorlands Street were capped with curved terracotta tiles.

Since the NCB took over, if a slate came off the rain would have damaged the ceiling before the NCB came around to repair the roof. Number 63 Roman Road actually fell down because of lack of maintenance. Once, Peg and I went away for the day and when we got home we found that the NCB crew had painted our house without opening either the doors or windows; We were unable to open the doors or windows, everything was stuck fast. That on top of the old-timers being sacked made me resolve to do something about it.

My mind was made up by an article in the *Llais Llafur* (the Labour voice), the local weekly newspaper, written by a prominent NUM official, on the housing programme in Communist Hungary. The paper shop was closed on Sundays; I collected up my drawing gear, drove up to the shop knowing I would have peace and quiet there. I copied the famous carthorse used by a very well-known cartoonist to represent the TUC, the workers of Britain. My cartoon showed the carthorse walking out of his safe stable into danger and no one lifting a finger to stop him, implying that those that should were concerning themselves with international politics and not the plight of men who had paid their wages and put clothes on their backs. *The Llais* published it.

A day or two later I was walking past the manager's office and I heard my name being called. At first I could not make out where the voice was coming from. Then I noticed that a small window was open so I walked over. John Williams was taking a shower.

'Well done, George boy! Well done!'

John Williams was the manager of Banwen colliery, one of the most competent mining engineers in the country and easily the best man-manager. He got a message out to all the old-timers to report to the canteen and stay there for the day with free tea and sandwiches. He signed them all on, that qualified them to one pound a week pension and house coal.

He then became a victim of what was jokingly called long-range management. A plan was thought up somewhere a long way from Banwen colliery to change the rope on the main winder. They wanted to increase the diameter by a half inch. John Williams tried to explain to the two of them that the journey (train made up of trams) was just about heavy enough to pull the existing rope to the mouth of the level that led onto the Far End. The system had worked for sixty years.

I was privy to the conversation because on that day I was standing in for the absent engine driver. John Williams came into the engine house looking worn out. 'George ring for the spake, please.' The heavier rope was fitted. Every fitter, fitter's labourers, blacksmiths with their strikers, rope-smiths and two winder-men all in work one weekend to fit the huge new rope to the massive drum of the Big Drift winder. First the excising rope had to been wound off on to a nine-foot diameter wooden drum and it had to be coiled properly. Then the new rope had to be fastened to the winders drum and that had to be coiled to perfection on to the winding drum. Otherwise all kinds of damage could be done when the winder was travelling at top speed and it travelled at top speed all day except when lowering or rising the spake, the train that carried the men.

The new rope was coiled on to the drum. The rope-smiths had capped it and it was hitched to a journey of seventeen empty trams. The rider knocked three on the signal wires and the engine man eased the journey up. The rider swung the oak safety block clear of the track then knocked double two on the signal wires. The journey freewheeled at speed towards the mouth of the drift running nicely, smiles all round. At the quarter of a mile mark the rope they were watching, which was making a pleasant ringing sound as it spun the shining, spinning idlers suddenly went slack then stopped. The journey had reached the old nine feet where the drift levelled off and the extra weight of the new rope was more than the weight the journey could manage. To their dismay the journey had come to a stop.

The rider knocked three on the signal wires and the journey was hauled back to the surface. The head mechanic got on the telephone in the old lamp-room.

'Will John! When you get the double two! Let her go flat out! Give her the gun! Right!' The rider gave the signal and jumped on the last tram as it sped past. Four times they tried it and four times it failed. Put another three trams on the journey.

'There's no room for twenty trams in the mouth of the Far End.'

'Let's get it down over the Hard Heading: we'll sort the bloody room out after!' the head mechanic shouted. With the extra weight the journey made it over and down the Hard Heading.

The Hard Heading was six hundred yards long; called the Hard Heading because it was driven down through solid rock. The coal seams had been thrown down by a major geological fault when the earth's surface was ripped apart three hundred million years before, the rock beds standing vertical allowing water to pour down everywhere. The work must have been brutally hard, no smooth bottom to shovel on and the tram they were throwing into higher than their shoulders. They must have been men of steel.

It was a prime example of first-class mining. Each time you walked down – walked the wrong word, stepped, it was that steep, would be a more appropriate description – you marvelled on how the old-timers had managed such a feat.

John Williams had warned them there was no room for twenty trams at the mouth of the Far End but by then the two know-alls were long gone and no doubt would have picked up a bonus for their efforts at Banwen colliery.

Reversing the decision was out of the question. What would you do with a second-hand, mile and a quarter long wire rope when the solution was going to be expensive anyway. John Williams decided to make the incline of the main deep more acute and make a double parting (marshalling yard) large enough to take twenty full trams and twenty empty trams.

It was then I worked with Jack Llewellyn for the first time. Jack like the rest of his family was a smallholder and a miner. He stood out a bit being six-feet-four inches tall. His mate was Alby Thomas and barely five-feet tall. Alby would go down with the flu but would still come to work. Down a mine what one bloke breathes out the other breathes in. Alby would lay Jack up every winter.

'Alby if you come in here sneezing and coughing again, I'll buy the biggest goldfish bowl I can find and jam it over your bloody head!!' Jack threatened.

Jack and his wife Mary had no children and they took a shine to Owen. One night I was dressed ready to go to work, the Cables colliers, bus stopped outside the house and there was a knock on the door. It was Jack Llewellyn. He was carrying a hessian sack and something in the sack was moving. Jack opened the sack and out shot a very robust six-month old Collie pup, straight behind the easychair at the side of the fireplace. What I saw of it, it was a dark slate grey with a white collar and a white tip to its tail. Not the best-looking dog I'd ever seen.

'For Owen!' announced Jack with a large smile. 'Do you think he'll like him?'

'Yes!' Peg was delighted. She had had a red Springer Spaniel from the time she was six until she was eighteen; she liked dogs. Little did I know the trouble I was letting myself in for by accepting Jack Llewellyn's gift. They named the dog Cymro (Welshman), the same name as Peg's Springer Spaniel.

Work would start at the mouth of the main deep, taking second rippings that would make the main deep wider and higher. Over the years its height and width had been greatly reduced by all round pressure from the roof, sides and floor. The great thirteen-foot collars (cross beams), eighteen inches in diameter, were as smooth and as hard as marble, seasoned by the constant flow of air being sucked over them by the giant fan a mile away on the surface. The bark had long gone over sixty years.

Dai Jones (Cardo) and his son John were given the job. Work would be carried out on nightshift when there was no coal to be hauled out. Jessie Jones was put in place of my uncle Alf driving on the Far End by night. 'Jess' was known as a bit of a lad. Once he'd got the horse out on the main drift he'd get up on its back and ride out. It was against the law but it made no difference to Jess. If I was walking out and Jess came by he'd shout 'Get on the collar, Sahib!'. The name Sahib referred to my time in India.

One day as the horse was bounding up the steep Hard Heading, Cyril Boyce (a collier and uncle to Max Boyce) caught hold of the horse collar on the other side.

Jess looked down at him. 'Get off the collar,' Jess snapped.

'Piss off,' growled Cyril as we raced along over the steep, rough wet ground.

'Get off the collar you long streak of piss or I'll get off this horse and snap you in half and I'll fight the fucking two of you!'

I collapsed laughing on the side of the road and so did Cyril who was big and strong enough to have knocked Jess's head off.

Peg's father Sam became ill and had to be taken to Llandough Hospital, Mabon's Ward, named after the famous miners' leader of the nineteenth century. The South Wales Miners' Federation funded all the research into lung disease that went on at the hospital and the hospital became a world leader in the treatment of miners suffering from pneumoconiosis, or 'black lung' as the Americans call the condition.

He was on oxygen a great deal of the time and had difficulty walking just a few steps. It was a fine hospital but Sam was homesick. So Peg asked could she take him home. Cymro, who had lain outside the door of Sam's empty bedroom the whole time Sam was away, went berserk at the sound of the old man's voice. The dog spent his days with Sam whilst Peg and I were at work.

Cymro had developed one very irritating habit. Every day Peg sorted the papers and magazines into parcels: Roman Road, Main Road, School Road, Moorlands. The half past eight United Welsh bus would pick the parcels up and drop them in the doorway of the shop a mile away in Dyffryn Cellwen for the paperboys and girls to collect.

Cymro would slip out of the backdoor and be at the paper shop to meet the bus, then stop the paperboys and girls picking up their parcels. He'd stand snarling, hair standing up on his back. The kids were terrified of him. The bus on its way back to Neath would stop, the driver would shout to Peg and tell her what was happening; she would go to collect him. He'd jump into the car wagging his tail. He obviously thought he had done a first-class job of guarding the papers.

I told Jack about it, he said, 'He's like his mother. One day Mary and me were walking down to catch the bus at the Angel. The mail van was going up to the farm and the postman waved to us. When we got home that evening the mail van was still in the yard. The postman was up in the loft of the barn and Cymro's mother sitting at the bottom of the ladder, wagging her tail. It's in the breeding George boy!' Jack laughed.

Sam did seem to gain some ground. He had a cylinder of oxygen next to his bed that he was able to help himself to. We were on piped television by now and that helped. Peg had Sal Williams in to help. Sam still had his rough days. Then, he'd want Peg close by.

On Saturday evenings when Peg, Owen and I went to the cinema, which was now just next door at the new Miners Welfare Hall, our neighbour Mrs Pegley would kindly sit with Sam and they'd watch television. On sunny days Cymro would lay basking on Mrs Pegley's front doorstep. On Fridays the packman would be on his rounds. He got his title from a case he carried that had in it ladies' headscarves, also handkerchiefs, ties etc. He did his rounds on a Friday because Friday was payday. This Friday he made the mistake of turning the handle of the door, slightly opening the door and stepping over the dog into Mrs Pegley's house. Another peculiarity: Cymro never barked, just took a bite. Cymro lifted his head up and snapped. Peg reckoned the packman gave one yelp and was off down the road like an express train.

It was 1956. There was talk of converting Tir John power station from burning anthracite duff to oil burning. Tir John had been the salvation of the Welsh anthracite coalfield. It had saved the region from the depression suffered by the other coalfields of Britain. Plus it had supplied an unlimited amount of electrical power to keep the biggest munitions works in the country going, helping Britain to survive the Second World War.

From Glyn Neath to Pembroke the anthracite villages were unique and stood out as the best places for a British working-class family to live. Better houses, playing fields, parks, silver bands, welfare halls and cinemas, better health care, all provided by the Fed because of the prosperity Power Stations like Tir John had brought. Until these wonderful generators were developed, the duff, the very fine anthracite, could not be burnt. Ten per cent and more of the coal cut by an anthracite miner was cobbed, thrown away, so they were not paid for it.

I turned again to my drawing pen to protest against the sheer stupidity of the idea of converting it, and drew a cartoon showing a ship named *Coal*, figures representing the Neath Valley and the Swansea Valley clinging to a life raft, and a hand, palm open, marked Dulais Valley sinking into an ocean of oil. The *Llais Llafur* published it. The cartoon was prophetic; Nasser seized the Suez Canal and oil prices shot up.

Because of the work that had to be done, making the room for a marshalling area that would hold the extra trams needed to pull the new heavier rope, I found myself driving the big winder at the bottom of the Hard Heading on night-shift. The winder was housed in a large engine house cut into solid rock. It had the look of a very large Heath Robinson creation, made from spare parts bought from all over South Wales more than fifty or sixty years before. A huge electrical resistor standing about five feet high and a yard square gave off pulses of heat that got hotter as the driver moved the control handle around the brass buttons that indicated the speed. Just one gear, haul in; to slack out put the winder into neutral and control the speed with the brake. The brake pedal, a steel chequered plate, measured six inches by four on top of a ratcheted vertical lever that you pushed down through a hole in the steel floor. From the raised engine house floor the driver looked out over the two large winding drums into a tunnel that curved off to the left; the second drum was for the tail rope that serviced the far end. The wire rope sloped down to the coiling sheave on the cusp of the curve and twenty yards away the rope was hitched to a journey, around the corner out of sight.

Shinc came out of the mouth of the Far End level, leading Major, a new horse who, like all horses on their first few shifts underground, was nervous, acting up and prancing around, not wanting to be led. As quick as a flash his two hind legs skipped over the taut wire rope. 'Wow lad, easy boy, easy now,' Shinc coaxed, but there was no quietening Major. The rope chafing against the inside of his rear legs seemed to excite and frighten him all the more. Within minutes he was ten yards along the rope standing on his front feet and suspended like a side of beef, the rope by now against his stifle or sheath.

Shinc, usually a calm customer, had a touch of panic in his voice. 'Easy, boy! Easy, Major lad!' Then shouted to me: 'Make sure that bloody brake is on fast, George! The smallest move will cut his prick off and he'll bleed to death! I'll go and scotch up the trams! Not a bloody inch now, George!'

Shinc ran off and disappeared around the curve of the

drift. He would have to scotch each wheel on seventeen trams, sixty-eight wheels, and scotch them tight to be sure that the journey would not move a fraction when I slacked off the rope. I stayed standing on the brake watching the horse. He had become perfectly still as animals do when they're in deadly danger. After what felt like an age Shinc came back, out of breath, panting and sweating.

'Try it. Just a small bit, George. For Christ sake careful now.' Shinc stood away from the horse. 'Careful now, George boy! Careful now! Just a bit at a time!'

I pulled myself slowly forward by holding onto the guardrail with both hands and slowly let the brake lift a fraction. The rope sagged. I let the brake lever up slowly, the drum turned and the rope fell to the floor. Major's rear hooves were on the floor; his whole body shuddered. Shinc, relieved, led Major away from the ropeway and loosened Major's feed bag from under his head. The horse pushed his muzzle into the bag of chaff and oil cake.

Shinc's proper name was Jenkin Williams Brynceiliogau after the smallholding he was born and brought up on. He was one of those extremely strong men who, after a couple of pints, would lift one of the round mahogany tables with cast-iron legs off the floor with his teeth for a laugh in the Pant. His grandmother Marie had her picture in the *Western Mail* shearing sheep when she was one hundred years old.

That spring Sam's condition became worse. Dr Thomas decided it would be better if he went in to Adelina Patti castle. The great singer's home had become a TB hospital for children in the 1920s. Now in the 1950s with TB eliminated the hospital had been turned over to the care of elderly coalminers. Sam was on oxygen for most of the time. At visiting time you'd just sit while he lay there eyes closed, sometimes opening them and giving a thumbs up then closing them again. If Peg was not there when he opened his eyes, he'd ask where she was.

I got home from work one morning. Peg was busy sorting out the papers.

'George! Daddy is worse. Marie is with him. I'll go over after I've finished here to let her come home.' She kept working as she spoke.

Sal was preparing dinner ready for Owen, when Peg came into the bedroom to wake me to tell me she was leaving to take over from Marie. Owen wanted to know where his mother was when he came home from school.

'They're short of nurses because of all this old flu that's about and they want Mammy to stay to help out,' Sal explained as she set his plate before him.

'How long will Mammy be?' Owen asked, looking a bit puzzled.

'Only until Aunty Marie takes over,' I reassured him.

'Is Dad very bad?'

'Yes, Ow.' Owen got on well with his grandfather; he had lived with him all his life. They, sat out in the garden together in the summer time ever since he was a very small boy. His grandfather spoke quietly to him, telling him stories and always in Welsh. Sam bought him odd presents. One day Peg came in and got the fright of her life. Sam had bought two baby rabbits for Owen and had hung them from the ceiling of the lean-to in a string bag.

His grandchildren meant a great deal to Sam, perhaps because of his own childhood. His mother Mary died soon after he was born; his father Owen had two other children, David John and Mary Ann. Sam was fostered out to a couple, a Mr and Mrs Howell; they had no children and they gave Sam a good home. They lived in the same street as Sam's father Owen, who was known locally as Owen Saint because his father had been a pit sinker and had in the 1870s gone to Utah in the USA with the people of the Church of Jesus Christ of Latter-Day Saints, who referred to themselves as Saints. He came back to Wales and helped in the sinking of the Dulais Higher Pit known as Cwm Mawr and, as normal for Wales, the name Saint stuck.

Sam was minus half his thumb, half his forefinger and half his middle finger on his left hand. When he was a young boy he had picked up one of the new brass detonators that had been left on the Onllwyn Colliery tip. The colliery was part of the village; it was not fenced off. He had seen other boys open the top of the detonator, tip out the cordite, then burn out what was left inside with a match to make a whistle. When Sam did it the detonator exploded.

The doctor came to Onllwyn on horseback in those days. Sam's foster mother wrapped his hand in a towel and placed him down on the kitchen settle. When the doctor arrived his foster mother sat on the settle, putting Sam face down in her lap. The doctor put Sam's shattered hand on the seat of a kitchen chair that was covered with a clean cloth and carried out the amputation. The doctor gathered up what he had cut away into the blood-soaked cloth and put it onto the blazing fire in the grate.

The doctor lifted up Sam's face. 'You're a brave lad, Sam! But you stay away from the colliery, or your Dad could be getting the sack! Alright!' That was the way Sam told it, never with bitterness, never angry or with malice. He would make the boys laugh by pretending to have pushed his fingers up his nose and told me that more than likely it had saved him facing the horrors of the trenches in the Great War.

Because he had no proper grip with his left hand he could not be a collier. He had a way with horses and by his middle twenties became a master haulier. When a new horse was bought, always geldings, usually from Ireland, Sam had the job of breaking him in and was paid extra for it. The method he used was he'd have a small piece of pencil, because they were made from soft wood that did not splinter; he would carve a groove in the pencil, tie a soft shoelace tightly around it. On the other end of the shoelace he would make a loop, put the loop over the horse's ear and drop the small piece of pencil into the ear. The horse would be worrying about the small object moving about in his ear instead of working out ways of kicking or biting Sam. Then he became a rider, a dangerous job, riding the journeys from underground to the surface. Being a rider gave a man a bit more status.

He married Sophia Thomas daughter of the Half Way Inn, who according to Arthur Jones Finley was the prettiest girl in the valley, and it was in the Half Way by the strangest of coincidences he became a newsagent. It was in the twenties. The rep of the *News Chronicle* was in the bar looking for someone to sell his newspaper in the valley. The papers would leave London by train at 12.30am, be in Neath Central by 5.30am, be transferred to Neath Low Level and be in Onllwyn by 7am.

The rep had a *News Chronicle* with him and turned to the racing page. 'Listen if I give you a winner will you take me on?'

'Right-o,' agreed Sam.

The horse came in first. The following morning a quire of *News Chronicles* arrived on the 7am train at Onllwyn.

John Williams built a bakery at Dyffryn Cellwen and two smart double-fronted shops. Sam rented one of them when it became vacant after the Hopkinses moved to their new grocery shop. Sam sold stationery, tobacco and newspapers. As a direct news agency, Sam got 33% profit and not the 10 or 12% they would get off a wholesaler.

With Marie's help Sam built up a very successful business but still worked nights as a rider. In 1938 he bought a royal blue Morris Eight off Baker's of Merthyr Tydfil, £112.00 brand new, taxed, on the road. Peg was ten years old at the time; she grew up with a car and according to Marie became the first car thief in the valley. When Peg was fifteen the car was parked on the road outside the house. Because of his business Sam was allowed a small ration of petrol. Peg got into the car, started the engine and drove the three and three-quarter miles to Glyn Neath. Trouble was she did not know how to turn around. So she drove the ten miles down to Aberdulais, then the ten miles back up to Onllwyn, popularly known as the 'round the valleys run', using up her father's petrol ration for the week. Most men would have been pretty angry to say the least, not Sam. In Sam's eyes she was the valley's answer to Amy Johnson; the times he told the story of Peg's solo drive around the two valleys in the bar of the Half Way Inn and told it with pride.

Marie drove me over to the Hospital to relieve Peg. The night sister met us and walked with us into the small ward where Sam and two other old miners were being nursed. She called Peg to the door.

'Could one of you stay the night with your father? We're short-staffed because there's so much flu about. If one of you can operate the oxygen?' she asked.

I volunteered. It was late spring. I spent most of my time on the bedroom's balcony looking at the Rock of the Night, 'Craig-y-Nos', silhouetted against a star-filled sky and thinking maybe, just fifty years before, one of Edward Prince of Wales's lackeys perhaps, given this room at the back of the castle, would have stood here – whilst his master was in Wales, sponging off the great Patti's generosity.

The three old-timers were no trouble. They slept through the night. Marie brought Dai over to relieve me. Peg woke me at midday.

'Daddy's died, George.'

I caught around her. We lay back on the bed, her head on my chest. She had lost someone who had worshipped the ground she walked on from the minute she was born. Peg was not crying. I had the feeling she was in some way paralysed, overwhelmed by her great loss. Something had happened she never believed would ever happen.

On the day of the funeral, the large table was opened out with plates from the best tea sets filled with all kinds of different sandwiches. Dai was first back from the cemetery and sat down at the table.

'How much money is there, Peg?'

'None!'

'Bloody hell! Bloody hell!' Dai was angry. It was out of desperation; he wasn't a violent man, just the years of never facing up to everyday things like looking after his health. He was a bright intelligent man. First job colliery electrician, in the 1930s as good a job as a working-class lad could hope for. He was a bit of a daydreamer like Nana, and like him she too was brighter than the average bear – gained her cap and gown in music. Their lifestyle plus illness had robbed them of the chance to earn real money.

Then in 1944 Dai, now not in a reserved occupation, was called up to the army and was posted to Egypt. On his return he had contracted tuberculosis. Some of his friends when he came out of the sanatorium would persuade him to keep the bar open until one or two in the morning and he'd be back in the sanatorium within the year, but only his two sisters along with Nana would be his regular visitors through the long months of recuperation. He did have great help from Dr Aubrey Thomas who got him an army pension. Peg gave him Sam's Half Hunter gold watch.

9

Other things were changing in the valley too. The Yellow Houses known as 'Y Tai' were to be pulled down, so were Khartoum and Gordon Terraces; sixty families to be moved to Neath. Built in 1845 by John Williams the Iron Master to house the workers at his Onllwyn Iron Works, there were forty-four houses with one small single-storey house that was used as a school. The children paid two pence a week to attend. John Williams had been transferred to another colliery and people were knocking off work hours before time. The eighteen-feet district at Banwen was stopped. The big drift after one hundred years would be no more. Banwen colliery was big: stables for one hundred horses, two very large winding houses and a smaller winding house for the Cornish drift. Electrical engineers, workshop fitters, workshop, blacksmith shop and saddlers shop, first aid room. There was a very large screening plant and crusher, weighbridges for trams and rail wagons, pithead baths, large new state-of-the-art lamp-room but the most iconic feature of the complex was the beautiful red-brick arched entrance to the big drift. That's where photos were taken in the thirties to mark it as the first thousand-ton-a-day anthracite mine in the world or when the baskets of food were ready to be taken down to the stay down strikers accompanied by the local Bobby PC Woodhouse.

I was sent to the Cornish drift to work; it was where they had worked the white four and the eighteen feet, but now only the eighteen feet, on the topside of the fault and geologically the most disturbed seams in the area. In some places the eighteen-feet seam was more than forty-feet thick. In Ron Day's heading they filled coal on one pair of rails for a month. It was worked by pillar and stall method. The white four had been worked by conveyor method and was the wettest coal seam anywhere. There was a main and tail winding engine that I would drive if the driver was missing, but in general my work would be what it had been down the eighteen feet, with one important difference: the water. The Cornish was wet; the old eighteen feet was bone dry, so dry that the rat population thrived there. In the quiet of the nightshift the baby rats cooed like pigeons as they were fed by their mother. There were a lot fewer once the NCB appointed a rat-catcher or rodent officer as he was known.

If things were quiet on nightshift, some of the lads would purloin a brass detonator or two and borrow the shot's man's firing battery, cover the detonators that were placed in the middle of the road with chaff, wait until there were a good few rats at the party and fire the detonators. There were always real ructions afterwards. An already unpleasant place was made worse by having bits of bloody rat stuck to everything.

I remember characters better than I remember places. One was Will Merthyr, small, wiry, worked in an airway off Will Fry's heading that had an air door shutting off its entrance. The door had painted on it in large white letters: 'The Vulcan piano downstairs.' The Vulcan was the pub where Will spent his pleasurable hours in the company of his closest and dearest friend Jake Fredricks. Jake was a huge man standing well over six feet; he had a head on him the size of a boulder and looked ferocious. He wore his hair in a skull crop with a fringe about two inches wide like a paintbrush. He had served seven years with the colours in India and had a tattoo of the Taj Mahal across his chest and belly, a belly that was swollen by being filled with large volumes of bitter beer at weekends, which made the Taj Mahal look as if it was suffering from structural subsidence. At a Merthyr Fete & Gala in the 1930s the story was that Jake carried a donkey across his shoulders, with its feet tied, from the road up to the castle some five hundred yards away. He told us how his brand new wife sewed a button back on to his working shirt. Like most miners he wore a dark blue flannel shirt to work. It was the top button and, not able to find a button but anxious to please her new husband, she knocked two holes in the tin top of a Guinness bottle. He told her as gently as he could, because she had only been a wife for a week, that the buttonhole was 'too small' for her very large improvised button. He got his shirt back to go to work that night and she had made the hole big enough to take the Guinness bottle top.

Jake never tired of telling stories about his good friend Will Merthyr like the time he went to call him to come for a drink down the Vulcan. The radio was on; it sounded like Henry Hall.

'You clear off from here Jake Fredricks!' Will's wife screeched.

'Shut your mouth woman!' Will boomed in his unusually loud voice for such a small man.

'No I won't! You get away from my door Jake Fredricks!' she yelled loud enough for next door to hear.

'Keep that gob of yours shut or I'll put that bloody wireless over your head,' boomed Will.

'Go on then, you bloody try it.'

'Duw, there's embarrassed, I was standing there and her with all valves and wires in her hair,' said Jake.

The story I enjoyed the most was the one about the lead water pipes. The street Will lived in had been built to house the workers of Merthyr's great iron works and the street was to be demolished. On this Saturday Will's house was the only one left standing; it was to be demolished on the coming Monday. The local scrappy was paying good money for old lead. Will turned off the stopcock at the end of the street and dug a trench all the way to his house, cut the pipe, rolled it up, put it in a wheelbarrow and off to the scrappy. Sweating! Back to the house to wash and change then up the Vulcan. He turned on the tap. No water.

One sixth of Peg's income would be gone with so many families being moved to Neath, and Peg had become pregnant. Owen had turned nine years of age and we had given everything away: pram, pushchair, cot, the lot.

'Stay away from me you awkward bugger!' laughed Peg when I went to kiss her.

94

It was a bitterly cold day on December the 27th, 1960. Peg had finished sorting the papers and the parcels had gone out to the delivery boys and girls.

'You'd better go and fetch Nurse Miller, George,' Peg said and went into the bedroom.

I followed her. 'Now?'

'Yes, now!'

The road was like glass. Thankfully there was no other traffic. Nurse Miller lived halfway down Pant-y-ffordd's big hill. She was ready and looked every inch the dependable District Nurse: good-looking, immaculate in her dark blue uniform with white piping, the uniform that at times of worry and sometimes panic gave families a feeling of confidence and security from Land's End to John O'Groats.

'Is Peggy all right, George?'

'Yes! She's gone to bed, Nurse.'

Owen had gone next door to stay with Aunty Annie, old Mrs Williams. She wasn't his Aunty but had lived next door for donkey's years and in a Welsh coalmining village that qualified her to the title.

I had banked up both fires – the Dover stove in the back kitchen and the open fire in the front room – so the house was lovely and warm. Within what seemed no time at all Nurse Miller came out. 'You got another boy, George!' she smiled. Another boy, and born in the same room that his mother had been born in thirty-two years before.

The front door opened; it was Aunty Vi the Half Way, Peg's mother, half-sister.

'Is the baby here?'

'Yes! It's a boy!'

'I got a name for the little bugger!' she laughed and marched straight into the bedroom. I could hear the nurse, Vi and Peg laughing. Vi was a Blue Riband singer. Singing was her life, competing in eisteddfods locally and nationally. That was how Geraint got his name; Vi was Sir Geraint Evans's biggest fan. Peg and I decided that his other name would be Samuel in memory of the father she had adored.

That evening the living room was packed, my mother, my sister, Aunty Roseina from Glyn Neath and her daughters, Peg's sister Marie and of course John and Owen. Geraint was asleep in his brand new pram and he was not a bit like the description people make about newborn babies; he was very beautiful with lovely pink cheeks like his mother. I went to fetch Nurse Miller at about eight in the evening; it was still bitterly cold and care had to be taken driving and walking. We came out of the freezing cold night into the very warm living room.

'George! What are all these people doing in the same room as this newborn baby?' Nurse Miller scolded. She knew everyone in the room and was on friendly terms with all of them but tonight she was the District Nurse and they were just people.

At the billiard hall in the spring there was an important difference of opinion going on. Danny Boy had not done any work for a very long time. He was stabled in a roomy loose box and spent most of his day watching the world go by with his head out through the half door of the stable, or grazing and rolling around in the warm grass in the field my father had rented off Evans Blaen Nantcellwen farm.

My father went to Neath every Wednesday, market day, and always had a stroll around the livestock. He was still the countryman at heart and hoping for a chance meeting with some of his nephews still in farming, John Ty-Mawr perhaps. Danny Boy was quite well-known in the local horse world. He was fourteen years old but still when you put a halter on him he arched his neck, and lifted his tail when you led him.

Some bloke inquired about Danny Boy. My father told him if he was interested to come up and see him. The bloke arranged to come up on the following Saturday. My father told my mother wished he hadn't before the day was out. She could not believe how heartless, how money-grabbing, her husband had become.

'Danny Boy has earned as much money for this family as any of us!' That was her opening line. 'For shame on you, Davy!'

The bloke came up, but went away without Danny Boy.

Maybe it would have been better if he had been sold. Danny Boy was a gelding but he never thought he was. In those days mountain ponies still roamed about the place. The mares came into season that spring; Danny Boy thought he was in with a chance, jumped out through the half door, taking half the door with him, over the garden fence and away on to the mountain. We hunted everywhere for him. A week later Stewart Jackson, Des's younger brother, called to see my father. He had found Danny Boy dead by Pont-yr-Offeririad (The Parson's Bridge), a bridge the railway company had to build across the Neath and Brecon line in the 1860s by the church so that the Parson could travel from one church to another in his horse and trap. Danny

Boy had been killed by one kick to his chest in a fight with a young stallion. My mother wanted to know what would happen to Danny Boy. My father told her they had buried him using a JCB. He had not. He had got in touch with Orion Morgan head horstler at Banwen who got in touch with Court Herbert, and Danny Boy was fed to the Court Herbert hounds, as were all colliery horses that were killed.

Working in the Cornish I was expected to cover if a pumps-man was missing. The Cornish was a very wet drift with pumps and siphons everywhere. They had had a very dangerous break-in of water some years before. No one was killed; Stan Lopez the under-manager was very seriously injured, and but for the fact he was wearing a boiler suit he would have drowned. The air trapped in the suit caused him to float. Some of the lads saw him sailing by and grabbed him. Almost every bone in his body was broken. Now he was back, working like a dynamo. The only physical mark – one of his legs was a bit bent. He wasn't big, but he was one of the toughest men I had ever met. He belonged to the strong Spanish community that lived at the top end of the valley. His brother fought against the Fascists in the Spanish Civil War along with young James Strangward, killed in the battle of Ebro River, young Francis Zamoro, killed on the Teruel Front, and Glyn Price, now back working in Banwen, seriously wounded at the age of 24. The headmaster of our school Mr William Edwards had been the chairman of the Spanish Aid Committee that included all the Chapels, Trade Unions, Miners Welfare, the Communist Party, even the Ladies Knitting class.

When I was a boy I had worked with two of the original immigrants Mr Esteban and Mr Rodriguez. They were in their seventies and as tough as old boots. One of them told me he had served in the Spanish Foreign Legion and that the sergeants carried whips that they would lash you with if they lost their temper. Not everyone was enamoured with the Dulais Valley's pro-Republican stance. Kate Roberts, regarded as one of Wales's best women writers, said, while a schoolteacher in Aberdare, that she would kill herself rather than live in the Dulais Valley. Many thought that was down to the fact that Saunders Lewis, who was a strong supporter of Franco, was her lover.

Bill and I were waiting to have our lamps tested and the customary search on the surface when Stan walked hurriedly over to us.

'Bill, George! I want you to go down right away. There's a horse locked in the first level off to the right after the double parting. Right away now!' he ordered.

Water was the controlling element in the Cornish Drift. The chimney of the fall disappeared up into the darkness; water dripped everywhere. Separating each of the bands of rock above the seams of coal was a very thin coating of mud; if it was dry you'd mistake it for part of the band of shale. If however it became wet it became a lubricant able to move mountains. The main slab of rock on the left hand side of the fall must have weighed ten ton and more, and our light beams reflected off its mirror-smooth surface. I scrambled up the front of the shale pyramid of the fall. There was a small gap at the top. I shouted down to Bill and Will Morgans.

'There's a bit of an opening!'

Bill scrambled up and lay beside me. 'Bit of a job getting through there, George.'

If anyone could get through there it would have to be me, I was the slightest. I took my lamp battery off my belt; I didn't want it catching in anything as I squeezed through the narrow gap. I lowered the battery into the darkness and holding the lamp in my hand I slid through the gap headfirst. I could hear the horse snorting, making known he was glad of the company. He pushed his muzzle against me. Horses, even horses that work under the most brutal conditions, are very social creatures. I patted his neck and stroked his muzzle. I stayed with him for a while; it was obvious he didn't want to be left alone. I climbed back up the shale pyramid and out through the narrow gap.

'Is he alright?' asked Bill.

'Aye but I expect he's missing his grub.'

The lads on afternoon shift had come down. Bill and I made a collection of sandwiches and I crawled back in with banana, cheese and tomato and jam sandwiches and pieces of cake the lads had taken out of their snap boxes.

Will-Puss Morgan, Bill and me got on with clearing the fall. A feedbag of chaff and oil cake was sent down from the stables. I took it in over the fall before we went off shift. When we got in the following afternoon the horse had been got out. The opening he had been brought out through was no more than four feet high and four feet wide. It was unbelievable that a horse at least fourteen hands high and weighing about fifteen hundred weight could have got through an opening that size. What had happened was Tom Ellis Jefferies, a collier and a smallholder, had gone through to the horse, got behind him and coaxed the horse to walk in front of him. The horse must have bent its legs, literally crawling out on its knees. Anywhere else Tom Ellis would have had a medal. Medals and commendations for bravery were very, very rarely handed out in the mining industry.

Joe (Tex) Williams was our fireman, lovely bloke, but he must have been the most nervous fireman in the South Wales coalfield. He couldn't even take the time to put his food into a snap box; instead he simply wrapped his sandwiches up in newspaper and stuffed them under his pullover. The other thing Joe would not do was carry water. One afternoon three of us were working in a spout hole: an airway, just big enough to crawl through – Billy Brec, Will Knot and me. We were squatting down having our snap break when a light showed at the entrance to the spout hole.

'If it's Joe and he asks for water leave it to me, Ok?' laughed Will Knot.

I wondered what the ex-paratrooper was going to do. Joe scrambled into us.

'Lads! How you doing?' Joe inquired.

'Ok, Joe,' we all answered. Everybody liked Joe. He was never quite sure what he wanted you to do or indeed what he wanted to do himself. He was a worrier of the first order. Some of that, I expect, was down to the fact that John Williams the manager was his cousin and he didn't want to let him down. He was married but they had no children which made you wonder why he kept chickens and had an egg round, when he earned good wages as a deputy. He called at our house every week with eggs.

'Can I say you'll be finished here today?' Joe asked.

'Yes!' said Bill Brec.

'Good! One of you got a swig of water to spare?' Joe asked.

'Me Joe!' Will Knot said and took a drink from his bottle. As he drank Will let a mouthful of crumbs into the bottle that could clearly be seen floating up through the clear water by the lights of our lamps. Joe could not refuse when Will handed him the bottle. There was an age-old important practice to be adhered to if you worked down a coalmine: carry your own water.

The one time Joe's nervous disposition had quite an effect on Peg and me was the time after days of torrential rainwater broke into the main Drift. Joe came rushing onto Will-Puss Morgan's level.

'George will you go back to the big Turbine!' Joe was out of breath. 'It's not holding its own. Go back straight away, George! Have you got a watch?'

'Yes!'

I set off back to the main sump. The Turbine was a spectacular looking machine. Standing on a heavy steel frame ten feet long and five feet high, pumping six hundred gallons of water a minute along an eight-inch diameter pipe a mile long. Water was rushing into the sump. I measured twelve inches back from the water and marked the rail with chalk. I looked at my watch. It was five minutes past five. Joe came running back. 'How is it, George?'

'I've marked the rail. I'll walk out to see how things are. Right! Won't be long!'

I set off up the drift, the water swirling with some force. It was halfway up my shins. Not to have my feet swept from under me I had to hang on to the armoured cable draped along the side. At the seventh manhole from the mouth there was what I was looking for. Water was spouting out of the manhole full-bore. My guess was that the bottom of one of the large lagoons on the opencast site above us had given way, and was letting water pour into us. The clay bottom of the lagoon must have been breached somehow. I was so near the surface I carried on to the shed where we left our fags.

It had stopped raining. I lit a cigarette and looked out over the lights of the colliery and the massive floodlights of Maesgwyn coal site. In 1947 Irish workers ran away from this site because of the Jack-o'-lanterns – methane gas igniting on a warm summer night and its blue ghostly flame flitting across the huge peat bog. The Irish knew too that the area was known as the fairy-haunted land of the Banwen Pyrddin. The incident was reported as far away as Australia. I finished my cigarette and walked back down to the Turbine.

'It's stopped raining.'

'Stay by here, until I find someone to change you.' Joe gave me my snap bag and hurried away from the din of the turbine and the sound of the rushing water.

I looked for a dry place to sit down. Slowly, very slowly, the force and the speed of the water slackened and the Turbine began to gain on the flood. I looked at my watch; it was a quarter to midnight and no sign of a relief. At half past one the nightshift fireman turned up.

'Sorry, George! I didn't know you were still here!'

I got out to the lamp-room and Peg was there. I was flabbergasted.

'Didn't Joe call to tell you?'

'No. I haven't seen anybody.'

Joe actually got off the bus in front of our house then walked down the brickworks road home at the end of every shift. The following morning Joe was in our house first thing and could not apologize enough and even brought Peg a dozen eggs to say sorry.

Sam's will was sorted. Peg was granted probate; the newspaper franchise was safe. Geraint was to be christened at the Methodist church that Peg had always attended and where Owen was christened nine years before. The Rev Davies would conduct the ceremony. It was a beautiful afternoon, the first Sunday in April. His brother Owen was there, his cousins Peter, Janet, Kingsley and Julie, John his Godfather and John's sweetheart Carol who was to be his Godmother. There too was his aunt Marie, his aunt Ceinwen, and uncle Dilwyn and uncle Des. The Rev Davies gave a short sermon at the end of the ceremony. Being a very traditional Welsh preacher he got himself into a *hwyl*! That means raising the rafters. After the service we called to see my mother and father. My mother asked seven-year-old Julie how she liked the service?

'Until Mr Davies lost his temper I did.'

We all trooped over to the Price's Arms. Nana had laid the table for tea in the Bar. Peg had arranged for Ken Lewis to take photographs. He was as competent at taking photographs as he was at painting. My favourite was Geraint in his christening gown lying on a table looking at the camera with Owen standing behind him. I didn't go to work that Sunday night, the 9th of April 1961. Carrying and fetching all day had worn me out.

10

Friday April the 14th 1961. I'll remember this bloody date for the rest of my life.

Bill and I had been told to change a pair of timbers on Will Fry's Heading at the mouth of Ron Day and Edgar Pugh's level. One of the arms (uprights) had been squeezed out by pressure from the sides and was protruding out into the roadway and hitting the trams as the horse pulled them past, causing the trams to jump the rails. We hung our snap bags high enough and far enough from the side so that the rats could not be tempted to feed on them, inspected the job we were to carry out and decided what tools we would need. We walked back to the bottom level where we kept our tool bar, Bill unlocked the padlock and threaded the saw, our two shovels, hatchet, sledgehammer and bar off the tool bar.

A close inspection of the offending upright followed: it was about twelve inches in diameter, a hefty piece of timber. An armoured electrical cable was fastened to it by a loop of signal knocking wire. Large chunks had been knocked out of the upright by the passing trams and each time the tram had hit the upright it was moved, so that the collar was barely on the upright but was resting mainly on the side. Nevertheless we decided that we would put a post in the middle of the road to support the collar before removing the offending upright arm.

First we had to remove the wire loop holding the heavy armoured electrical cable. We both put our hands on the upright meaning just to ease it away a little from the side. One end of the wire loop shot out from behind the arm and the chisel-sharp end went straight into my right eye. I put my hand to my cheek and felt a blob of what felt like jelly. Bill was looking at me. He seemed to be struck dumb.

'Stay there, George! I'll fetch Joe!' gasped Bill. He sounded breathless and was gone. I stood there on my own, feeling odd, thinking I did four years in the army, two years in Burma and now this back at home. Bloody hell!

Bill was back in no time with Joe.

'George bach! George bach!' Joe was shocked and was trying to comfort me, at the same time opening his first aid box.

'Take your cap off George,' Joe instructed, pulling a pad of cotton wool with a bandage attached out of its sterile package and gently put it over my eye.

'I've told the engine driver to phone the first aid room so they'll be waiting for us when we get out,' said Joe as he pinned the bandage at the back of my head. 'There, you can put your cap and lamp back on now, George!'

'You alright, George?' asked Bill very concerned.

'Ok, Bill.'

We set off in single file, as there are very few places down a mine where you can walk abreast. We had about three quarters of a mile to go to the mouth of the drift, then about a quarter of a mile to the pithead baths and the first aid room.

'You sure you are all right George boy?' asked Joe, his hand on my shoulder. Joe and Bill kept inquiring from time to time and I kept answering, 'Yes!'

Will James was the first aid man on duty. Everyone called him Will Shanny but not to his face. He was in his sixties, a tall lean man and had about him a presence that at times stopped people in their tracks. People didn't mess about with Will James. He had known me all my life. '*Eistedda* (Sit),' he said to me in Welsh.

He was smoking his pipe as he bent over me and changed the dressing. I had picked my fags up from the shed on the way down, took one out of the packet and put in my mouth. 'Anybody got a light?' Four or five lads had gathered round by now and it seemed all of them struck a match. One of them burnt my finger. I took a few drags and handed the fag to one of the lads.

I left my lamp in the first aid room, walked over to the dirty lockers, undressed, put my dirty clothes in the locker, took out my soap and towel and turned on the shower, keeping my head to one side not to wet the dressing. I was not very dirty. We hadn't been underground that long. Dressed in my clean clothes, we went out to the car and bus park. Not many people brought a car to work then. Bill looked at the gear lever on the steering wheel of the big Vauxhall Velox.

'Never driven one of them. Get someone else to drive, George!' said Bill anxiously.

'Jump in! I'll drive,' I said. Standing out on the road outside the Clinic was Dr Aubrey Thomas. When he saw me getting out of the driving seat his face was like thunder.

'What the hell do you think you are doing you stupid bugger! Come down the surgery!' I followed him into the surgery.

'There's an ambulance on the way to fetch you!' he growled, looking like an angry rugby prop forward with a stethoscope around his neck.

'I'm not going anywhere till I see Peggy!'

He took the dressing off my eye. 'Did you have a blue eye and a red eye when you went to work?'

'No!'

'Then you got to go to bloody hospital!' He walked out through the door of the surgery and called 'John! John! John can you drive?'

Young John Gibbons came to the door. 'Yes Doctor I can drive.'

'Then drive this silly bugger home! Please John.'

Peg was ironing when I got in, Geraint was sleeping in his pram and Janet his cousin, Dai and Nana's daughter, was there. She was ten, the same age as Owen and like all little girls liked helping to look after small babies.

'What has happened to you?' Peg asked, a bit shocked at the sight of the bandage around my head.

'Nothing much! Bit of a wood chip gone into my eye and they can't get it out. Ambulance will be here in a minute!'

'Ambulance! Go into the bedroom and I'll get you clean underclothes! Quick now!' I did as I was told. Bill who was sat on the chair by the door smiled at me. He, like me and every other bloke living in the coalmining valleys, knew that you did whatever you liked outside but in the house you were definitely second in command.

The ambulance arrived and took us to the General Hospital in the centre of Swansea. It looked more like a castle than a hospital. A porter took us into the Eye Hospital. A nurse brought hospital pyjamas.

'Here, put these on and get into bed,' she told me gently. It wasn't a big ward, ten beds, all occupied by old men bar the one they put me in and the bed next to mine. Cataracts were the main reason for the old-timers being in hospital. It was quite a long job, a week completely blinded.

Two porters came into the ward with a trolley. They wheeled me into an operating theatre. There were two nurses wearing white facemasks and a surgeon in a white gown and white facemask. The porters lifted me onto the operating table under some very powerful lights.

The surgeon looked down at me.

'What have you been up to George?' I could see he was smiling under his mask. The nurse who had helped me dress in the ward was holding my left hand. The hands of the nurse standing behind my head came in to sight holding a syringe. Her wrist rested on my forehead and she pressed droplets of a cool liquid out of the syringe into each of my eyes. The nurse standing on my right-hand side opposite the surgeon was holding the lids of my injured eye apart. The surgeon was bent right over me looking through a magnifying glass attached to his head. I could see the needle slowly coming towards my eye with the thread hanging from it then going up and back again then up and back again. He was sewing together what was left of my torn eye. The nurse holding my hand kept squeezing it. The thread was cut, then the lids of both my eyes were sewn together.

'Right! George, I'll be in to see you in the morning. And my name is Billy Rees by the way. Ok!'

The nurses wound the trolley up so that they could bandage me up, a felt pad over each eye fastened with tape then the bandage. I thought I must look like an Egyptian mummy. They wheeled me back into the ward and put me to bed.

'Are you hungry?' a nurse asked.

'No. But I could do with something to drink.'

'Here we are,' the nurse said gently. During that next few minutes I found out what a devastating disability blindness can be. I felt the beaker against my lips and went to take hold of it.

'No, let me hold it,' said the nurse. The newly blind are not able to find their own mouths without tipping over whatever it is they are trying to feed themselves with. You suddenly find yourself completely helpless, more so than a newborn babe who is unaware of its helplessness.

The ward was quiet.

'My name is Bill Morris; I'm from Bryncoch,' a voice said to my right.

'George Evans; Banwen.' Conversation seemed out of place at that particular time. I had a million things to think about. Peg on her own with two young boys, Geraint just six weeks old and the business to run.

I was suddenly conscious that my right hand was hurting. One of the lads so anxious to give me a light for my cigarette in the pithead baths had burnt my hand. I felt along the cold steel bedframe for a place to put my hand to ease the pain that was causing me more discomfort than my eye. I didn't remember going to sleep. I did not know it then but the nurse had put something in the drink she gave me.

When I woke up the following morning there was quite a racket going on in the hallway. A nurse whispered in my ear: 'Harry Secombe is coming to see you George.' I immediately thought they were playing a trick on me because I could not see but the laughter and racket got louder and it was right by my bed.

'This is George, Mr Secombe. They brought him in last night from Banwen.'

He was standing at the foot of my bed, one hand on each side of my feet.

'Banwen! I used to make the pays up for Cefn Coed colliery before the war when I worked for Amalgamated Anthracite, George!'

I didn't tell anyone as they may have thought me potty, but even with my eyes sewn up covered in felt pads then bandaged over, I felt I could still see Harry Secombe. He was such an exuberant, jolly man. The place was in an uproar. He had come to visit his mother in the women's ward upstairs. It was a day Swansea Hospital would remember for a long time and a day I would remember too.

We had our breakfast; I had to be fed. I asked the young auxiliary how long this would go on for. She said, 'Only until they take the bandage off your uninjured eye.' I was dying for a smoke but afraid I'd set the bed on fire.

The senior consultant Roy Thomas came to see me.

'Hope you are comfortable, young man?' he asked me in one of those cultivated Welsh voices that are bred in places like Cardiganshire.

The hospital Matron did her rounds of the wards. You could have heard a pin drop. I was unable to see her but it felt a bit like the Regimental Sergeant Major inspection.

'Where's George, Dai?' It was Peg's voice and she was standing right by my bed with her brother, because of the disguise of the bandages and the hospital pyjamas they had failed to recognise me.

'Peg!'

'George!' She squeezed both my hands. 'No wonder I didn't know you. Look at these awful pyjamas. Get them off!'

'How you feeling wus?' asked Dai.

'Well OK like! Thanks for coming down with Peg.'

Peg asked a nurse for a screen so that I could change into the pyjamas she had brought down for me.

'What have they done to you? All these bandages and things!' Peg asked as she took my pyjama jacket off.

'They've repaired my damaged eye and they've bandaged the two up to stop me moving my eyes. Where's Owen and Geraint?'

'Owen is outside in the car; he's not allowed in and Geraint is with Bopa and DL. Take your trousers off.' I did as I was told. 'I've put a carton of cigarettes in your locker, toothpaste, toothbrush, clean towel, soap, and do you want any money?'

Dai was chatting to Will Morris and Mr Abbott, my neighbours.

'Peg will you light me a cigarette?'

112

'They don't mind you smoking, do they?'

'Well somebody's smoking, I can smell it.'

'Put this ashtray on your lap then and be careful.' Peg put the ashtray off the locker on my lap while Dai chatted with everyone by the sound of it – he was used to hospitals, having spent a great deal of time in sanatoriums because of TB. Peg just sat there holding my hand until it was time to go.

'So long then, George!' Dai tapped me on the foot as he passed the bed.

Peg kissed me softly. 'I'll be down tomorrow. And don't smoke unless there's somebody with you.' I lay back and for a long time enjoyed the scent and taste of her in my pitch-black world.

The following morning Bill Rees the surgeon came to see me. A nurse lifted me into a sitting position, removed the bandages and the felt pad over my right eye.

'How are you feeling George?' Mr Rees asked.

'Bit hot.'

The nurse replaced the bandages, fluffed my pillows up and lowered me back me down.

'George I am going to give you an injection and I am going to inject Bill Morris in the next bed to you. This injection will bring on rigors, shivering fits, and you will become very hot. Now don't get alarmed. Nurse Blunsdun will stay here sitting between your two beds. OK!'

The sleeve on my left arm was rolled up and the skin just below my bicep was rubbed vigorously. I hardly felt the needle go in.

'Right George!' Mr Rees sounded satisfied.

'Want to listen to the radio George?' Nurse Blunsdun asked.

'Yes please. The home service please!'

Nurse Blunsdun fitted the earphones to my head.

'Loud enough?'

'Great!'

There was the end of a talk on about the losses being incurred by the NCB especially in the South Wales Area. Then, thankfully, of much more interest, a talk on the intelligence and industry of the Welsh Black honeybee. I very rarely listened to music programmes on the radio, preferring the sound of the human voice.

Later on there was a commotion going on around Bill Morris's bed. By the sound of it the shivering fits had started for him. They put a screen up around his bed. Me – nothing and I felt a bit guilty. People were to and fro around Bill Morris's bed and from time to time asking me how I was. They brought me dinner and fed me. Waiting until the spoon touched my lips before opening my mouth was one of the weirdest experiences I had ever been through in my thirty-six years of being alive.

Peg arrived with her sister Marie. I told them why there were so many people around Bill Morris's bed and that I had been injected too.

'Why?' Peg asked.

'We both got an infection in our eye socket and this is the best way of treating it,' I said. It was an answer I'd made up but it satisfied Peg. That was one of the main reasons I loved her and married her; she never made mountains out of molehills.

Peg sat there holding my hand. 'David's coming tonight; wonder will Joan come with him?'

A kiss each, off Marie and Peg.

'Is there anything you want?' asked Peg and I got an extra kiss.

'No. Give the boys a kiss from me!'

After tea David arrived.

'Joan's made you some trifle. I'll put it in on the bottom shelf of your locker. I'll ask the nurse to put it in the fridge before I go.' He patted me on the shoulder and sat down.

There were only eighteen months between us. He was heavier built than me, very good looking, and a lot cleverer than me. It was he who took me to Neath, on our own for the first time, to the new Windsor Cinema to see my first continuous film, Errol Flynn in *Robin Hood*, and to Porthcawl on our own for the first time in the summer of 1936. My mother had given me half a crown to spend on the fair: at a penny a ride, thirty rides. We went into the Arcade to the slot machines. In my excitement I put my half a crown into the first machine I got to, instead of a penny. Sir Leslie Joseph owned Coney Beach in those days. David marched me up to the office.

'My brother has put a half crown into that machine.' David pointed. The attendant was a middle-aged man.

'What is your brother's name and address?'

'George Brinley Evans, 10 Beacons View, Dyffryn Cellwen, Neath.' On the following Tuesday a letter arrived in our house addressed to me with a two shillings and six pence postal order inside. I remember forgiving David then for telling the man my middle name, Brinley.

Now he was looking after a small mine part-owned by my father and was almost living in work.

115

'I'll cut some firewood tomorrow and take it up for Peg.'

'Thanks. How is everybody with you?'

'OK George! I'll call with Mam and Dad as well.'

'Aye, tell them not to worry.'

Brothers, even when they are the best of friends, have very little to say to each other. David patted my shoulder.

'Take care.'

The nightshift came on duty. The staff nurse stood by my bed. 'Sit up George. I'll make the dressing more comfortable for you,' she ordered me. With the help of a nurse she started to unwind the turban-like dressing.

'God almighty! What happened here?' The staff nurse sounded shocked. 'Go and telephone the senior house man!' she ordered the nurse.

'But look what time it is Staff!' the nurse protested.

'I don't care what time it is! Go and phone him. Now!' I put my hand to my head. My skull was covered in hard lumps the size of hazelnuts. Literally plastered!

I felt something against my lips.

'Drink this!' instructed the staff nurse.

'What is it?'

'It's what we give women when they're going to have a baby.' I downed it in one and that was the last I remembered.

The next few days were a bit of a blur. Dr Aubrey Thomas told me years later that they had very likely upset the chemical output of my brain by the introduction of a pyrogen into my blood to bring on the rigor: the uncontrollable shivering fits and the rise in body temperature. My body became ultra sensitive. I was daubed from head to toe in calamine lotion. Mr Bill Rees came to check on me a couple of times a day. On the fifth day, with Mr Rees in attendance, they removed the bandages.

'Let's have a look how things are shaping, George!' Mr Rees removed the pad over my good eye.

'Lay back now George and I'll remove the stitches.' The staff nurse brushed my left eyelid with something cool. I heard a snip then felt the thread being drawn out of my eyelid. I looked up. In the picture was the staff nurse's face. After the total blackness of the last few days it was like looking at the most beautiful thing in creation.

'All right, George?' she asked.

'Yes.' Because I could see her face and her lips moving, her voice sounded more part of my world, less alien. I was back in the human race. Behind and above her lovely face, brunette hair well brushed and crowned by a starched white headdress, was the old ward's ceiling that was badly in need of painting, stained by years of tobacco smoke.

Mr Rees took the pad off my right eye. The staff nurse snipped the stitches that held the eyelids together. Mr Rees switched on the small light he held in his hand. Slowly and carefully he scanned my eye examining minutely every miniscule part.

'You're allergic to penicillin, George?'

'Yes doctor.'

'We'll put you on a sulphur-based antibiotic.' He reached for a small brown bottle off the trolley and read the label and handed the bottle to the staff nurse.

Staff put drops in both my eyes and the pad back on my right eye.

117

'There! Your visitors will be here shortly.' She fluffed my pillow before she left.

Peg and Marie arrived with the other visitors. Peg was delighted.

'That's better. Must have sixth sense, I put your specs in my bag.' She took my spectacles case out of her bag and put them on my locker. I needed them for reading. I tried them on; because of the felt pad on my right eye they wouldn't fit. I was having my first real good look at the ward and my fellow patients.

'I've brought something for the nurses too,' Peg grinned. She put a small cardboard box on the bed. Inside, there were six paperback copies of *Lady Chatterley's Lover*, banned since 1928, now newly printed by Penguin. She had called in at George Williams Wholesale Stationers and Bookseller. They were the people she bought all her magazines, comics and annuals from. Peg was a believer in what could be called lightheartedly white bribery.

Marie was chatting to old Mr Abbott, one-time dock worker, who was proving to be a bit of a character. She noticed he had most of his fingers missing on one hand.

'How did you lose your fingers, Mr Abbott?'

'One at a time my lovely.'

That evening a nurse came into the ward.

'Mr Abbott, will you come to your bed please.'

'Why?'

'I have a suppository for you.'

'Put it on my locker. I'll take it with my Guinness.'

The nurse pulled the screen around the bed.

'Come on Mr Abbott.'

He walked over to his bed and in a loud voice said to the nurse, 'You put plenty of chalk on the cue now.'

I was walking wounded by the middle of the week and was sat at the side of old Mr Gibbons' bed. He was retired and lived in Sketty; he had had his operation some days before and now was blinded by bandages and would undergo intense nursing for the next two weeks.

'George! I can see the most amazing thing! I can see a blue, the bluest blue I've ever seen!' The expression on the old gentleman's face described how he was relishing the experience. When I told Dr Thomas about the old man's obvious delight, he said he was very likely remembering all the blues he had ever seen in all his life.

BOOK TWO

11

By the end of the following week the infection had cooled down and Mr Rees said I could go home. It was the middle of May and the weather lovely. I washed and dressed and went out into the garden. They had told me not to overdo bending my head, so gardening was out for a bit. I thought I'd ask Peg to ask Johnny Bach Compo. He used to do the garden for Sam and Sophia. For years I had worked a twelve to fourteen-hour day, what with the fish and chip shop, ice cream round and the colliery. All the farmers or smallholders had to do the same. There were only two farms at the top end of the valley that were self-sufficient.

Now my life was completely disjointed because of the accident. I felt out of place and awkward doing nothing. Get up, wash, have breakfast, the district nurse would call, watch television if I felt alright. Other days if the pain was bad I'd go to bed and stay there until it had gone. The routine was only punctuated by trips to the hospital, the infection flaring up then cooling down. It was the first time I had ever had time to watch television. My moaning about the quality of the programmes got Peggy down.

'Shut up, George! You're spoiling it for everyone! Shut up and if you think you can do better, you write something! But shut up anyway! For goodness' sake!'

She came home from the bank the following week with a new portable typewriter. I couldn't type but I took the hint and started to write a script for television in longhand. I had no idea how the script should be laid out.

It was called *The Fourth Device*. The story was about three men locked in down a coalmine by a roof fall and a surge of water. And how the three men being wet, cold, hungry and afraid over the days that followed become disoriented, individually and collectively. One of the men finds a length of cap wire, wire that was once attached to an electric detonator, and uses it to tie together splinters of wood in the making of four crucifixes. The crucifix symbolizes one of the cruellest methods of executing a human being, yet for millions across the world it is a beacon of hope.

Peg asked John's sweetheart Carol, who was working at her first job as a receptionist at the newly open, very prestigious Dragon Hotel, Swansea, if she would type the script for me. It was a bit of a bonus for me; I got to spend my weekends in the company of a gorgeous, seventeen-year-old redhead. She was not only pretty but clever as well.

Arthur Jones Finley came to see me and told me to put in a claim for damages against the NCB.

'You see George, cables are not supposed to be fastened to the side with wire. There are webbing straps provided!'

Arthur was, many thought, the best President or Secretary the South Wales Miners' Federation never had. He belonged to the old school. In his day he had been the best lodge secretary ever at Maesmarchog lodge but turned his talents and his outstanding ability to the breeding of dogs, Irish Red Setters in particular. One line of Irish Red Setters bears the prefix Roman called after Roman Road, Banwen, where Arthur lived at the time and that line of Irish Red Setters can still be found from Cardiff to Chicago. He became a top judge at dog shows all over the country including Crufts. I told Dai Richards our compo secretary what Arthur had advised and he agreed to put a claim in. Had a short but curt reply from the National Union of Mineworkers office St. James Crescent, Swansea, expressing the opinion that the NUM could not possibly sustain a claim for damage in this case. I told my father.

'Don't worry George, early days.'

Peg went to the bank on Wednesdays and did her shopping. I stayed home with Geraint. One Wednesday she came home with watercolour paints, brushes and art paper bought in Whittington's. Peg took as much pleasure out of my cartoons being used in the local paper as I did, but could sometimes be more than a bit critical about my work. I remember once, before the accident, an Archbishop had said he backed the bomb. The one thing I thought I was good at was drawing hands. I drew a left hand, nails beautifully manicured, a bishop's ring on the fourth finger and the symbolic mushroom plume of smoke rising from the palm. The right hand I drew with calluses across the palm, fingernails broken and a jagged hole torn through the centre of the palm made by an iron spike. It really upset Peg and she asked me to destroy it. I had put hours of work into it, but I could see Peg was genuinely disturbed and upset, so I threw the drawing on the fire.

The next time she went to Neath, Geraint and I went with her. I went to Whittington's and bought three large sheets of specially-treated rag paper. I had in mind using all the small pencil drawings I had made of Peg while we watched television into a portrait of her. I didn't tell her.

Then as I had done before and would do many times again I lulled myself into a false sense of confidence, persuaded by five weeks of peace and quiet. Back to hospital, this time to the new outpatients department at Singleton. The main hospital was still under construction. After carefully examining my left eye, Doctor Rees went to the door and called Peg in.

'Peg I want George to come back into hospital, so that I can examine him more closely. The trouble is, Peg, eyes become, as we call it, sympathetic.' He looked at his watch. 'It's just one o'clock now. So if you'll drop George off at the eye hospital, Peg. Or I can call a ambulance.'

'No, it's no bother doctor! Be glad to be rid of him for a bit!' Peg laughed. She drove me back to the old hospital and walked with me into the ward.

'I'll come back down visiting time with your pyjamas and things.'

'No Peg! I can manage until visiting time tomorrow. Indeed now,' I protested.

I was feeling as guilty as hell. 'Please Peg!'

'Well, I'll telephone David.'

'OK! If you want to.' David turned up with a new toothbrush and soap and my own pyjamas.

126

'Nothing puts women off more than a smelly stale man,' he laughed.

And if anyone should know what women like and don't like, he should, I thought.

'Bit of bother at work,' he said glumly. He went on. 'You know the old man lets them take a bag of coal at the end of each shift, their house-coal. Well I got a tip-off. I went back last night, left the car and walked up. They were loading a lorry under the shoot. I told them to unload the lorry or I'd call the police. I was bloody dumbstruck.'

'What's happening now?'

'Well it's not just our old man, there's the other two partners. Anyway, what's up that you're back in here?'

'They want to do some more tests.'

The following morning the staff nurse came to my bed carrying a large jug of water and a tumbler.

'Want you to drink this as fast as you can George!' She filled the tumbler with water and handed it to me. I drank it up; she filled the tumbler again and I drank it up. She kept it up until the jug was empty. The staff nurse removed my pillows and I was laid out flat. The staff put some cooling drops in my left eye. The nurse held my eyelids open: my vision was blurred. The staff nurse was lowering an instrument down on to my eye. There was no pain. In a very short time she lifted the instrument off my eye.

'There we are George, that's us finished for this morning.'

The tests went on for a few days. David took me home on the Saturday.

The time flew by. Geraint's first Christmas was coming up, Owen had turned ten and if all the talk was true this would be our last Christmas in 9 Gordon Terrace, Onllwyn. I wondered what Peg thought of it. She had spent her entire life in this warm cosy wood-lined bungalow, one of thousands manufactured by a London firm and shipped to every corner of the Empire. I would miss it. Except for the accident, it had been the happiest, most contented twelve years of my life. Christmas came and Geraint's first birthday; he had what seemed like a house full of presents.

After the holidays I felt terrible; what was left of my right eye felt as if it was going to burst in my head. I looked in the mirror. The white of my right eye was blood-red. The pupil and iris looked a mess, badly scarred where Mr Bill Rees had sewn the eye together. The right eye looked like a broken stained-glass window, much smaller than my left eye and it was sightless and ugly. Peg called Dr Aubrey Thomas. He came into the bedroom and I sat up so that he could examine my eye. He took an ornate pill holder out of his waistcoat pocket, took out two very small pills and gave them to me with the glass of water off the bedside table.

'Peg will have to take you to hospital right away. I'll telephone them so they will be ready for you. Take the pills! They'll stop the pain!'

Mr Roy Thomas the consultant, Mr Bill Rees and a young Indian doctor examined my right eye. I heard the word 'enucleated'. Mr Roy Thomas put his hand on my shoulder.

'I'm afraid we will have to remove your right eye, George!' The ward sister brought a consent form for me to sign. They had put a screen around the bed and the nurses dressed me for the theatre. The ward sister injected me. I think they called it 'pre-med'; I felt completely relaxed. I remember them lifting me off the trolley on to the operating table. The next thing I remembered was Peg sitting at the side of my bed holding my hand.

I was home in three days. Every morning Nurse Betty Lewis called to wash my eye socket out with saline. She was a fresh-faced pretty woman, the wife of Llew Lewis. They lived in Coelbren. She brought with her the tool of her trade, what looked like a small teapot with a long spout made of glass, also a kidney dish and a large bottle of saline. She filled the small glass teapot with saline and stood it in a dish of hot water, waited until it was the right temperature and put a towel around my neck, giving me the kidney dish to hold against my cheek.

'Hold your head back, George!'

The gentle flow of water pouring into my empty eye socket soothed the bruising that had happened when my eye was removed. She put drops in my left eye and put a clean pad over the socket.

'See you tomorrow morning, then.'

It was a ritual that went on for weeks. Betty and Llew had no children and Betty started to take a shine to Geraint, and Geraint to her too. By the time spring arrived Geraint, almost eighteen months old, was demanding Betty's full attention, so much so she asked Peg if she could take him with her on her rounds. A long time afterwards she told Peg that baby Geraint's company had made her broody and along had come her daughter Helen.

I had an appointment at Neath hospital to see the artificial eye fitter. We didn't get off to a very good start. I was sat one side of the table, she on the other. She took a transparent plastic bag out of her case, full of blue plastic eyes, and poured them on the table. I laughed. She scowled at me. I stopped grinning. She spread the pile of blue eyes out across the table with the palm of her hand. I would have never guessed in a million years that there were that many different hues of blue. She stared intently at my left eye and just as intently at the spread of eyes on the table. She chose one and held it up, comparing it with my left eye. She took it over to the bosh and washed it thoroughly.

'Hold your head back please!' She opened my eyelids wide and the artificial eye fitted comfortably into the empty socket.

'There!' She held a mirror in front of my face. It was incredible; the match was perfect.

'Thank you!' I could have kissed her. She was smiling and gave me a round wooden box and what looked like a small white plastic tyre lever.

'Use this to remove the eye at night. Wash the eye then putting in this box until morning.'

The plastic eye being fitted was real progress I thought, but after an hour or so my eyelid began to swell up and I had the sensation that a tuft of hair above my right eye was being tugged. Peg went to Boots the chemist and bought me a black eye patch that she laughingly said made me look sexy. Dr Aubrey Thomas thought that the ultra sensitivity was because my body was reacting to the plastic eye. It could be the result of trying to bring on the rigors at the hospital. Nevertheless I persisted in trying to wear the plastic eye but to no avail.

I was given an appointment to see the consultant Mr Roy Thomas at his home in St James Gardens, Swansea. Peg and I were walking up the hill past the grand houses of St James

Gardens. I rubbed my eye and my plastic eye flew out and up in the air. I grabbed it on the way down. Peg was sat on a low garden wall laughing uncontrollably. She got up, caught around me kissing me.

'Sorry, George! Sorry! Sorry!'

We were both still laughing as she held her compact open so that I could see to put the eye back in but the eye was dry. I held the eye in the palm of my hand.

'Spit on it!' I told her. She did and the plastic eye slipped in to the socket. The receptionist must have wondered why we were both grinning as she showed us in to the waiting room.

Mr Roy Thomas recommended that I be fitted with a glass eye. Some weeks passed and I was given an appointment to attend the old eye hospital at Swansea. The same eye fitter from Neath was in attendance. She put some drops in my eye socket to lubricate it then fitted the new glass eye.

'You will have to be very, very careful with this eye. When you take it out stand over the bed, or make sure there is a cushion of some kind under you! This eye has come on licence from behind the Iron Curtain!' she lectured me quite severely. Unknown to her Mr Roy Thomas had come into the room and was standing behind her, resplendent in his morning suit and white carnation buttonhole and asked in his splendid Cardigan accent:

'How much are you able to see with it, George?'

12

We were officially informed that Gordon Terrace was to come down and we were offered one of the new flats with business premises. But first we would have to find somewhere to live in the meantime. All kinds of offers came up, none suitable, until councillor Mr Dan Lewis brought the key of Maple House to us. He was the former head teacher at Maesmarchog and had taught me. He had lost an eye as a very young child and he told me: 'George you'll always miss your eye. You'll get used to it not being there. But you'll always miss it. When I go fishing I've got to stay on one side of the river.' He pointed to his own eye. 'Or risk falling in.' He laughed and turned to Peg and spoke to her in Welsh.

'It's a lovely house Peg. Here's the key. Go and look!'

'Yes I will.' Peg, smiling, answered in English and took the key. It was a never-ending contest between the two. He determined to make her speak Welsh and she equally determined not to.

Maple House stands on its own in a large garden with a trout stream, Nant Cellwen, running the whole length of the garden. Peg's great-aunt had built the house and had sold it to the Evans Bevan Estate to house the under-managers of Banwen colliery. The National Coal Board had now taken it over. It was midsummer and a beautiful day. The privet hedges needed trimming. I put the key into the large lock and opened the door.

They say first impressions are all important. Maple House has fourteen windows and sunlight seemed to pour in through every one. The house had been newly decorated for Jefferys the new under-manager but his wife would not come to live in Banwen.

'This will do me, George. What about you?' Peg seemed contented as she looked around the large main bedroom.

'Yes. I think we'll be fine here!'

We called to let Mr Dan Lewis know we would be leaving 9 Gordon Terrace so the demolition could go ahead. The removal men made short work of the move. Only two men to carry Peg's German iron-framed Ehrmann piano. The front man had his back towards the piano, a wide canvas strap like a horse's harness across his shoulder and under his arms, then under the piano. The second man was facing the piano, wide canvas strap across his shoulders and under the piano, they just walked it out of the van into the big front room of Maple House.

I lit the fire in the back kitchen range and within half an hour there was warm water in the taps. I lit the fire in the big front room and the large chimneys warmed the thick stone walls of the house. Betty and her husband Ossi helped us sort out the bits and pieces. Betty and Ossi's daughters

133

Pat and Kathleen who had been babysitting brought Geraint home. He was sleeping. The fish and chip van came round and we all had fish and chips for tea. Peg drove Betty and her family home then put the car in the garage.

'You alright?' Peg asked.

'Aye, don't worry about me.'

Peg ran the bath. Owen had the first bath in Maple House. Tired out but clean we all went to bed. Sunday tomorrow; Peg had a lie-in.

After twelve years in 9 Gordon Terrace waking up in a strange house was curious, the things you were used to seeing when you first opened your eyes were not there like walking downstairs in the morning after twelve years of living in a bungalow. I had banked the fires before going to bed so the house was nice and warm. Maple House had a large old-fashioned pantry. Rows of sturdy brass hooks for the hanging of pots and pans; strong wide wooden shelving and two very wide stone shelves the whole length of the pantry. These were from the days when people kept and killed their own pigs. When the pig was killed and quartered it was salted and laid on the stone slabs to dry, then hung from the ceiling on large hooks. The remains of Maple House's pigsty was still at the top end of the garden.

The boys woke first. I went upstairs to carry Geraint down; he was still not steady enough on his feet to negotiate the stairs. We had breakfast as quietly as possible not to wake Peg, she was out of bed every other morning by half five.

Dai Richards called with a letter from Archie James, Secretary, National Union of Mineworkers, South Wales

134

Area, saying the NCB were offering the sum of £500 without admission of liability. The NUM had turned it down and had instructed their solicitors to proceed with the case. I told Dr Aubrey Thomas of the offer and he said, 'Are you really in need of five hundred pounds?'

'No.'

'Well let it take its course then.'

A letter arrived off Bob and Pat Bagley, asking if they could come down and see our new home. We were delighted; we had only seen them twice in the last ten years (just letters and cards at Christmas and birthdays), and they were no more than flying visits. By the time they'd driven down from Slough and had a meal it was time to start back again. They arrived: Pat, Bob and their daughter Sue. I had told Bob about the privet hedges so he came armed with new hedge clippers he had bought me. Pat had brought her sewing-machine.

Owen was going to the Gower with the Scouts. The contractors had brought loads of timber up from 9 Gordon Terrace when they demolished it. Bob set about cutting it into firewood for the Boy Scouts and loading it into Peg's new Ford van. The Scout Master could not thank us enough. He said there was plenty of wood there to do the cooking for the week.

Bob trimmed the hedges, Pat was busy making curtains. Maple House had fourteen windows and 9 Gordon Terrace only seven. The weather was glorious. We spent every afternoon either in Porthcawl or at Bracelet Bay. Sue was in her element wheeling Geraint around in his pushchair. Bob was working more or less at his own trade, fitting out cabin cruisers on the Thames. He was a cabinetmaker when he was called up. He had built a bungalow on the bank of the river and had named it Maymyo after the hill station in northeast Burma. They had been so happy when they left us. The three of them were as well-matched as three peas in a pod.

Some time later Peg came in from the paper round earlier than usual and obviously very upset. She sat in the easy chair next to the fire. 'Here! Read this!' She handed me the *Daily Mirror* opened to the centre page: 'Religious Revival Husband and Father Walks Out; Leaves Family For Church.'

The story was about Bob and Pat. Peg was in tears. There was no other woman or other man involved. Say nothing and hope and pray they'll get back together we thought was the best.

Owen was now going to Cadoxton School and was growing like a young tree. With an extra bedroom that was empty I thought I'd use it for painting. I wanted to get on with finishing the portrait of Peg, and I wanted to revise part of *The Fourth Device*. The weather was fine and I volunteered to take the Camnant parcel of papers down to Vera Clark, a fellow member of Peg's in the Pinafore Club; it was a very small parcel of six newspapers and I'd take Geraint in the pushchair.

A week later John Williams the manager climbed over the garden fence: our gardens ran alongside each other.

'Bit delicate George! Had a note through the door saying you were working! Don't panic. I know you're not. Anyway listen, I'm still entitled to a gardener – now you're welcome. Not to do the garden. Just tidy up about the place!'

'Thanks, Mr Williams.'

'Don't worry about it George. You're not the only one. Had a note telling me that the lad that has the taxi had stolen the corrugated sheets for his garage from the colliery. I had to inquire – he showed me the bill from the ironmonger.'

I didn't tell Peg. She was forever doing favours like picking up prescriptions from the chemist for the old-timers. She'd have been devastated if she thought one of the village people was trying to harm us. I told Dr Aubrey Thomas of Mr Williams's offer.

'He's a good old boy! But you can't George. Not until we get the better of this infection in the socket. You're still on Chloromycetin and Vitamin B.'

The cold weather was back, winter a few weeks away and the head pains started up. My nose ached; it felt as if it had been punched and my eye socket filled with mucus. Dr Littlewood called at the house and examined me. I told him about the ache in my nose and that the painkillers were upsetting my stomach.

'Try heat George, a hot water bottle. It could be neuralgia. Nerve ends when damaged take a very long time to heal. And stay out of the cold.' He got up to leave.

Peg gave him a bottle of brandy. 'Have a lovely Christmas, Doctor!'

'Thank you Peg. And a Merry Christmas to you all!'

Geraint's second birthday came. Peg bought him a pedal car, a replica of the Austin A40 she used to drive. It even had lights that worked, but the day before his birthday, Boxing Day, the water supply to Maple House froze.

David had come up to see us. He smashed the ice in one of the pools in the stream and carted buckets of water to the glass lean-to, to be used to flush the toilet. Got a three-gallon milk churn from the billiard hall and filled it with water for drinking.

We were lucky we had the stream in the garden. House after house in the village lost their water. People were hunting for water supplies everywhere. Thankfully there are fast-flowing mountain streams that didn't freeze over around the villages of Dyffryn Cellwen and Banwen. Peg replenished our drinking water supply from the bake-house. We survived.

Peg came in off the paper round and handed me a letter from the BBC from a man named Harry Green, telling me he had read my work *The Fourth Device* and would like me to come to London to speak to him. She was grinning.

'Well are you going to tell me?'

'When did you send it?

'Couple of weeks ago! Never mind about that! What does it say?'

'They want me to come to London!'

'When?'

I looked at the letter. 'The 9th of March!'

'Owen's birthday.' She was delighted.

'You going to let Dr Aubrey Thomas know?'

'Aye! I'll wrap up and take the letter up for him to read.'

The road was like glass; it took me ages to get to the doctor's house. His face changed to a broad smile as he read the letter: 'Read this Mair!'

Mrs Thomas read the letter with a look of disbelief on her face. 'George this is wonderful! Truly wonderful!' She stood up and kissed me on the cheek.

'Dafydd, will George be well enough to travel to London on his own?'

The doctor pondered. 'I'll think of something. I already have!' He shouted with excitement. 'I'll telephone Donald Alexander; he's working in London at the moment! Donald Alexander was at university with me George. He's a documentary film maker. I'll call him in the morning. He's a very interesting bloke. Worked with the likes of the great documentary maker John Grierson.'

Dr Thomas walked me home. Peg poured him a glass of whisky to fortify him on his journey back to his house.

I was only going to stay two nights in London. Peg had booked me into a hotel in Sussex Gardens, close enough to Paddington, and she insisted that she buy me a new topcoat. She went the whole hog. Went to Ralph Tyler's and bought me a JUNEX, coat makers to the King of Sweden. I was not able to wear my artificial eye so I'd have to wear the black eye patch, the one she had bought me from Boots and with this new coat she was determined I should look the part.

The big worry for me was the water had not come back. David said he would come up and carry the water from the stream to be used in the toilet. I was at the bus stop one hundred yards from the house, waiting to catch the bus to Neath, when Owen came running towards me shouting.

'Daddy! Daddy!' He laughed. 'The water's back!' He really enjoyed giving me the good news.

I lay awake in my London lodging trying to think what I was going to say to this man Harry Green. I had found out that he was one of television's most important writers. We had as far as I could work out nothing in common; we were

139

both Welsh and came from Neath and that was it. I wished Peg was with me.

I asked the hotelkeeper to arrange for a taxi to collect me and get me to the BBC Television Centre by midday. It was the biggest building I'd ever been in, the foyer it seemed to me was the size of a small railway station. I told one of the young ladies at the reception desk that I was there to see Mr Harry Green. I went to sit in a place so that I could see all the lift doors. Dr Aubrey Thomas had told me that Harry Green was a very slightly-built man; he had suffered from TB as a boy. People were in and out of the lift doors constantly. A man came striding towards me in a confident sort of way.

'George Evans?'

I stood up. 'Mr Green?'

'Harry will do, George.'

We shook hands.

'Tell me George is it still bloody blowing in Banwen?'

I laughed. There was no answer to that. Apparently as a young reporter for the *Daily Herald* in the thirties he had been sent to report on an explosion at Onllwyn No. 1 colliery. 'I got off the bus at the Onllwyn Inn and the bloody wind almost cut me in half!'

'Anyway how are you George?' He indicated to the patch on my eye.

'Oh, I'm getting there quietly.'

'We'll go for a bite to eat and talk about your work.' I followed him to the battery of lifts and we got into one. I recognized some of the faces from television. They were some of the cast of *Z Cars*, which Harry was working on at the time. He introduced me. The restaurant was palatial but then like the rest of the building it was brand new.

'George, I asked you to come to London to talk to you about your writing. You can write George. We get sacks and sacks of scripts and yours is the only good one I've read for ages. When you get home put it between two cardboard covers. In this place George they eat seed potatoes.'

Television was still in black and white and I had written, in my naivety, a drama that takes place in the pitch-blackness of a coalmine. Harry Green walked me back to the foyer.

'Remember what I said, George. You can write.' He gave me an envelope. 'That should cover your lodge and train fare. It was great meeting, George. And I'll be very disappointed if I don't hear of you in the future.' He smiled and held out his hand. 'Good luck, George.'

I stepped out into the car park and a voice shouted, 'George! George Evans!'

It was Donald Alexander. He recognized me he said because of the eye patch.

'How is Dafydd, and Mair? He told me all about you.'

'They are both fine. The weather's been the hardest thing they've had to cope with. Especially on Doctor's rounds!'

'I bet. You're pretty high up there.'

He was a tough-looking guy, quite different to Harry Green. We got in his car and we drove off to Hobart House, Grosvenor Place, the headquarters of the National Coal Board. It was a very posh address to say the least. Donald was in the middle of making a documentary for the Board. I thought it odd that the people working in this splendid place were entitled to the same concessionary coal allowance as a man working seven and a half hours a day laying on his side shovelling coal on to a conveyor belt.

I had tea with Donald and his wife; she was a book illustrator and the sister of Burl Ives, the famous American film star. He later drove me back to my lodging. There was a bit of tension in the hallway when I arrived, a young European girl was in tears and protesting to the hotelkeeper and his wife. The war had been over for eighteen years and there were still unfortunate girls, stateless, like this one. Reading about it in the paper or listening to a report on television was one thing. Hearing the weeping and seeing the tears was another thing altogether.

Dr Aubrey Thomas called the afternoon I got home. I told him what Harry Green had said and gave him Donald Alexander and his wife's love and best wishes.

'Got to have a second opinion, George! That's a must!'

We sat around the fire and talked. 'Let's send it to independent television!' the Doctor said. 'The biggest I think is Rediffusion; they're in London. Got a spare script and some stamps, George? Write a note to go with it. Head of Drama, Rediffusion Television, London! That will find them. I'll post it on my way home.'

The trip to London made its mark. When I woke up the following morning, I looked as if I'd gone fifteen rounds with Eddie Thomas. I decided to stay in the bedroom not to upset the boys. Peg telephoned the doctor; Dr Littlewood arrived. He took hold of both my hands and looked at them carefully, then turned my head to examine my neck. 'When did this happen, George?'

'Don't know Doc. It was not like this when I went to sleep. I woke up and felt my face swollen. Looked in the mirror – couldn't believe it!' He took the cotton wool pad off my eye socket and opened my eyelids. 'Very inflamed, George. I'll give you some antihistamines. And stay in bed!'

I had in my head that the injection they gave me in hospital was still having an effect. The following morning my face was back to normal.

I spent my time taking Geraint for walks in his pushchair. There was plenty for him to see; the lambing season was well under way and there was nothing better than watching one lamb start a frolic and as if it was contagious all the other lambs joining in and jumping all four feet off the ground at once, in their exuberance. The mountain ponies too had their newborn colts with them. I read in a book once that the Welsh mountain pony was the most beautiful horse in the world. Watching those timid highly-strung colts, their large Bambi eyes set in a perfectly sculptured head, their long, slight, shaky legs looking ever ready to bolt. They were truly very beautiful creatures.

A letter arrived from Kitty Black, Head of Drama, Rediffusion Television, saying she had read the script of *The Fourth Device* and would I come to London. I stayed at the same lodge I had stayed in a few months before. I had read in the paper that the great Spanish painter Goya's paintings were being brought to London and thought if I got the chance I'd try to see them. I saw the Spanish flags flying over a large building and thought this must be it. Climbed the wide stairway; at the top a uniformed attendant stopped me.

'Have you an invitation Sir?'

'No.'

'Then I'm afraid Sir.' And indicated with his hand the stairs. I walked down the stairs, glanced to one side and saw dozens of people dressed to the nines. Later I found out they were waiting for the Queen to arrive.

Took a taxi to the Rediffusion television studio; it was a big place but not as impressive as the BBC. Kitty Black was a tall very good-looking South African and had the look of an athlete about her. We shook hands.

'This afternoon, George, we are broadcasting an episode of *Boyd Q.C.* I'd like you to be there. We'll have lunch first!'

We were joined at lunch by Mary Revell, the American international long-distance swimmer, the first to swim the round trip of the Straits of Messina from Europe to Asia and back. Kitty Black introduced us.

'This is George, Mary, up from South Wales.'

Mary Revell held out her hand. '*How Green Was My Valley*?' she smiled.

'That's the place.' I smiled back. I thought looking at her she would be able to swim from the North Pole to the South Pole, she looked that fit and healthy. I had never seen or met a top athlete before.

I walked with Kitty Black to the main filming stage.

'In here George.' I followed her into what I found out later to be the main control centre of broadcasting. Above the stage it had a 180-degree view of the working area or the set. In the room technicians, five in all, sat on stools, some wearing earphones, all looking intently at the paraphernalia in front of them. The set was divided between a drawing room in a gentleman's apartment and a law court. There were lights and cameras everywhere. I was given a chair to sit on.

Signal lights began going on and off, the lights on the set blazed down. One man who was sat on a stool in front of me began barking orders into a microphone and the language he used would not have been out of place on a coalface. The actors were on stage, the leading man Michael Denison no less. All eyes in the control room were on the television monitors because the picture was going out live, being watched by millions of viewers. Everything went out live then. One camera was focusing on the butler's hands.

'Get that camera off that man's hands! He's got the ugliest fucking hands in the country!' In some ways it was like a conveyor face underground, middle of the shift going flat out.

Afterwards we went for tea and talked about my work.

'You could see, George, there's a great deal our cameras are not able to do? For instance, the floor covering, the linoleum – we actually have to paint the design on to the floor. The tools we have are very sophisticated but they have their limits. We have got to turn words into pictures, George. Which is much more difficult than putting words into a book.'

'Yes I see what you mean.' And wondered to myself why it is women seem always to be better at explaining fundamentals than men.

'What time does your train leave in the morning, George?'

'Ten off platform one!'

'Stay in your hotel. I'll pick you up and take you to the station.'

'Thanks.'

On the way to Paddington Kitty Black asked me had I thought about what she had said.

'Yes.' In fact that was all I had thought about. There was a crowd waiting for the Paddington to Fishguard train. Kitty Black gave me an envelope.

'That will cover your expenses, George. It's been lovely meeting you and I do hope you make a full recovery. And if you decide to come to London to work please let me know.' We shook hands and she turned to wave to me then disappeared. Before I boarded the train I went to Smith's the bookshop and bought the boys a book each and a box of Fry's dark chocolate for Peg. The train was full of Welsh and Irish, the Irish no doubt travelling to catch the Cork ferry. I opened the envelope Kitty Black had given me. There was more than enough to cover my expenses.

I thought about what Kitty Black had told me and as much as I wanted to write it was totally impractical for me to come to London to work: Peg running a business and looking after the house and two young boys, one two and a half and one eleven years of age. It was out of the question. I was beginning to feel like a scrounger sitting there, all togged up. Who the hell did I think I was sitting there like George Bernard bloody Shaw? And at the same time Peg was back at home working her socks off. Peg drove down to Neath to meet me off the train and I was glad to be back in Banwen.

The following day, after Peg had gone out to work and Owen had gone to school, I gathered up the scripts of *The Fourth Device*, took them to the top of the garden and set fire to them. I didn't tell anyone. Geraint was playing on the lawn; it was a nice day. I put him in his pushchair and we went for a walk. Lena my cousin was tending to her garden at Tafarn-y-Banwen when we passed. When all us cousins were in school someone said there's more of you lot than there are blades of grass on the mountain.

146

'Hello George, how are you? Bring him here, let's have a look at this boy you got.'

I pushed Geraint over to the farm gate.

'Hello my lovely!' Lena smiled at Geraint. Geraint smiled back; he had his mother's looks and disposition and people liked him from the off.

Dr Aubrey Thomas called and I told him everything Kitty Black had said. He thought the turning words into pictures was a very important bit of advice.

'I never heard it better put, George.'

'Doc is there any chance of me going to one of these training centres. So that I can go back to work?'

'George as soon as we can get the infection in your eye socket under control. Otherwise you'll you be back and forth to the surgery for evermore!'

I didn't tell him I had burnt the script.

13

Received a letter from T.D. Windsor Williams & Co, Neath, the solicitors the NUM had engaged to put my case. He was softly-spoken and had a good manner. The letter informed me that my case would be going to the Glamorgan Assizes at the Law Courts in Swansea. I had an appointment with Mr Roy Thomas the consultant the week before.

'I see your name is on the Assize list, George.'

'Aye. It is sir.'

'Are you worried about anything George?'

'Well there is one thing sir. After I had the accident I walked out, in all about a mile or more. Had a shower. Then drove down to the surgery. People will think I'm the bravest man in Wales or the daftest man in Wales. And I'm neither!'

'Don't worry George. That happens. When the wire went into your eye, there was a rush of adrenalin from your brain. That's what kept you on your feet. Don't worry now. And George do you mind if I come along?'

'No sir, I'd be pleased to have you there.'

Everybody was dressed in their very best. The policemen in their No. 1 uniforms looked very impressive. There was a QC's meeting. Windsor Williams took me into a side room: already in there were Alun Talfan Davies QC representing me and Mr Roy Thomas who winked and patted the seat next to him. 'Come and sit by here George; don't sit too close to that lot!'

The others in the room laughed. Roy Thomas was among equals.

The figure of £3780 was mentioned and the promise of a job. Huw Windsor Williams explained to me how they arrived at a figure.

'You are thirty-eight years of age. They look through the court cases in England and Wales, at all the cases involving a thirty-eight-year-old man that has lost an eye. There is a procedure called precedent and that is what they are using now. My advice is to accept, George.'

I did as Windsor Williams advised. He wrote me a cheque out for six hundred pounds and drove me back to Neath. I opened the door and turned to thank him.

'I'll let you know as soon as the rest of the money comes through, George.'

We shook hands.

The ride home in the bus was relaxing. It wasn't so much the money as worrying if old friends like Joe Tex would get into trouble for writing that second report saying that I had fallen. I wondered who had put him up to it? Knowing Joe he'd have been worried sick the minute he'd handed that second report in but I hoped we'd still be friends. The injury to my eye had been a tear. If I had fallen the injury would have been a stab wound. If John Williams had still been the colliery manager it would never have happened in the first place. Anyway, I was thankful it was all over. Peg was delighted with my news. 'Get you better now. That's the next thing!'

I couldn't work in the garden, I had made up my mind not to write, and for the want of something better to do one day I began fashioning a figure out of a wire-coat hanger. In the way you sometimes see clouds and you interpret the shape as what you want it to be, I saw the wire-coat hanger take shape. Perhaps there was a bit of autosuggestion involved in the creation of the image. I had watched a documentary on Scott of the Antarctic a day or two before and had been reading about the fate of Petty Officer Edgar Evans the Welshman from the Gower. He was the only non-commissioned person in the party and, as highly as Scott thought of him, I thought there must have been times when Evans was very lonely. In 1910, class was the benchmark by which men and women were measured.

I cut a pair of Peg's old tights into strips, mixed some plaster wall filler into a thin paste, dipped the nylon strips into the paste and wrapped them around the wire frame. The figure grew and became a recognizable identity. At the end of the week it was a man bent almost double battling against the elements with Herculean strength. I had created my Petty Officer Edgar Evans.

The following morning, working in the glass lean-to, I was putting the finishing touches to the figure when I saw PC Dai James coming up the garden path followed by a man I didn't know. I thought: Peg has had an accident in the car or is it that bloody dog! Dai and I got on well; we were both ex-servicemen and he was a good carpenter. He had served his apprenticeship before being called up.

'George this is Jon of the *South Wales Evening Post*, I've been telling him about your paintings.'

My paintings hung in the front room; he seemed reasonably impressed. We went back into the glass lean-to. It was then he noticed the figure standing on top of Peg's twin-tub washing machine.

'What's that?'

'It's a figure I've made of Petty Officer Edgar Evans.'

'Can I take it to be photographed?'

'Well I haven't painted it yet!'

'It does not need painting. I'll look after it!'

'Well alright, but bring it back when you've finished!'

The following day there was a large photograph of the figure on page 8, part of an article with a banner headline: 'Homage at last to an unsung hero.' I was very pleased. I received a very excitable letter the following day from a Mr Stanley Richards, Administrator, The Royal Institution of South Wales. The letter begins in Welsh then goes into English then back to Welsh, asking could they have the figure. I telephoned Mr Richards. I said yes; it was a great honour that they should want it. I had by fortunate coincidence made the model of Petty Officer Edgar Evans at the time Mr Stanley Richards was trying to make the people of Swansea aware of the fame of a local and national hero. The Royal Navy too: they had named the new accommodation block for chief petty officers at HMS *Excellent*, Portsmouth, the Edgar Evans Building.

The following week Bopa Mary Ann came up to stay with Geraint, as she always did on a Friday. They spent their time in the middle room. The television was in there, so was Geraint's toy cupboard. It was afternoon time and I was getting tea ready for Owen. Geraint started to shout.

'Daddy! Daddy! Come quick! Owen's pulling the shawl on TV! Daddy!'

I rushed into the room and there on the screen was my figure of Petty Officer Edgar Evans going around and around on a plinth. To Geraint it was his big brother Owen pulling a shawl because I'd asked Owen to pose for me bent forward with the shawl over his shoulder. My sculpture of Edgar Evans was placed with his skis at the Royal Institution, Swansea and later taken to Greenwich Naval College for display, then returned to Swansea.

At last I had found something to do that involved no one else. I got on with the portrait of Peg but only when she was not at home. I made the figure of a colliery horse being dragged backwards down the deep by a full tram. The tug on the left side had snapped from the horse collar to the shaft. I knew a horse had been killed like that. The horse was in agony until the vet arrived – underground the humane killer was a sharp spike driven by a very powerful spring.

Maple House has a large field next to it and in those days when the market for mountain ponies was good, there would always be a dozen or so mares in the field and in the spring the farmer would put a stallion in with them. Geraint was always with me when I was making a model. He was about four then. I was carefully shaping under the horse's belly model I was working on and Geraint tapped my arm. I looked at him; he had a dab of plaster on his nose.

'Dad, put a good cock on him Dad!'

'OK, Ger!'

The performance of the young stallion in the field had not gone unnoticed. When I told Doctor and Mrs Thomas they were in their doubles laughing.

'They don't miss a thing as young as they are,' chuckled Mrs Thomas.

Bert Coombes was delighted with the way I had emphasized the brute strength and the desperation of a colliery horse fighting for his life, and wrote about it in his weekly column: 'Its belly touching the ground!'

I was getting the hang of modelling, finding it easier than drawing or painting, now that I was monovision, to work on an object that was three-dimensional. The next figure I made was of Alby Thomas, Jack Llewellyn's small butty and my good friend. He epitomised the common sense, matter-of-fact attitude men of his ilk had to taking risks. If they didn't physically take risks the work would not be done.

Out of the blue Peg came home with awful news. 'Mrs Tabor came in now and told me, she'd heard Dr Thomas has had a stroke!'

It was hard to believe. Aubrey Thomas was the best scholar I had ever met in my life, a man who seemed to be able to keep going twenty-four hours a day. Kept the surgery open until nine at night if necessary. I remembered one morning at the billiard hall my mother called me. It was John Thomas the doctor's young son-in-law, married to his eldest daughter Branwen. The doctor had been called to an accident underground at Onllwyn No. 1 and Branwen was expecting her first baby. Things weren't going too well for her.

'I just want to let the Doc know Bran has been taken to hospital!' John said.

We got in my car and I drove down to the colliery and ran over to the lamp-room.

'Where's the doctor?'

'You can't bother the doctor now, he's on the face attending to W.S.!' The lamp-man was adamant.

'I don't want to bother him just pass on the message. Branwen's been taken to hospital and is OK!' Young Dafydd was born, the doctor's first grandchild.

Dr Thomas told me about that day a while after. W.S. was a collier in his fifties. The teeth of the coal-cutting machine had caught in his trousers and had taken his leg into the cut under the coal. A coal-cutting machine is very much like a chainsaw, only very much bigger and many times more powerful. Its large teeth are made of carbon-hardened steel and are extremely sharp. The Doctor told me it had taken ages to free W.S. The face was only two foot six high. They switched off the electric current. Then cranked the cutter by hand; he had to thread each of the cutter's teeth back into the wound it had made on the way in.

Thinking of that man, so unstinting in his efforts to help others, now struck down with the most disabling affliction was mind-blowing and tragic for him his family and the valley people.

We were going to have breakfast; it was Sunday morning.

'Mrs Thomas is coming up the garden path. The Doctor must be dead,' Peg whispered. She rushed to open the door.

'Peg! Peg I've come to ask. Will George come down to the hospital with me?'

'Yes! Yes! Anything!' Peg said.

'What's happened?' I asked.

'The consultant told us keep talking to Dafydd. Keep talking to him; don't stop. We did and you run out of things to say. Then Branwen looked up at the ceiling and there were some brown spots. "Look Daddy!" she said. "We'll go and fetch George, he'll come down and cover them up with a mural." And his eyes turned up to the ceiling.' I was already putting my coat on.

When we got to Morriston Hospital we went to ward six. I could hear this dreadful sound, the sound a pump makes when it's going on snore. The doctor was propped up on pillows. He was a powerfully-built man; it was easy to see why he had played centre at rugby. The awful sound was coming from a contraption on the floor at the side of the bed and a pipe led from it to a hole in the doctor's throat. I stood at the foot of the bed; he looked at me then at the marks on the ceiling. His daughters smiled. With my hand on the bed rail I gave him the thumbs up. I had seen some cruel sights in my life and that was one of the cruellest.

Dr Thomas was eventually brought home. I tried to pop in most days. Then the tendons in his legs started tightening. The physiotherapist called and showed Mrs Thomas how to hold the doctor's foot against her forearm, hold the heel firmly and press the sole and toes forward. I used to help her from time to time. Other times I'd sit by his bed and turn the pages of his book when he was ready. It was then I discovered why he was such an outstanding scholar. He took forever to read a page.

Dr Littlewood was the senior doctor now. He ran the place with the help of locums. I told him I'd like to try for a place in one of the Government training centres.

'Right George and the infection seems to have eased but keep using the Chloromycetin drops!'

I changed buses at Neath and noticed that Got James who I had seen getting on the bus at Seven Sisters was changing buses too.

'Where you off, Got?'

'Training centre, Port Talbot.'

Got James was quite a few years older than me. He'd worked on the coalface at Onllwyn No. 1 since he was fourteen, man and boy, and was now suffering from pneumoconiosis. He gasped slightly between each word. We got off the bus by the Grand in Port Talbot. Got could not hurry so I crossed the road with him. The level crossing gates were closed so we went by way of the bridge.

The reception area at the centre was quite full. A new batch of trainees were starting their six-week course. We were each issued with dungarees and allocated a locker and a workbench. There was an old black telephone on the bench in front of each trainee.

'Right ladies and gentlemen, there are tools on the bench in front of you. Take the telephone apart then put it back together again.' A bit like the army: first week at Brecon we were given such tasks: door locks, bicycle pumps, a kind of adaptability test.

On about the fourth day I noticed a very remarkable young man; his name was Peter. He was about eighteen or younger and I thought he was walking awkwardly. I found out why.

'See that lad?' Got nodded at him. 'He's had both his legs off at the knee.' He wasn't using walking sticks to get about: talk about Douglas Bader.

It was great being back in a workplace. We were taught carpentry, basic electrics, lathe operations and clerical work. We were assessed after a time and I was put in the office to assist the welfare officer.

That was when I got to know Peter better. One day I turned around and there was Peter and looking different; he was taller. They had fitted him with longer artificial legs but now his jeans were too short.

'You want to get your Mam to buy you a longer pair of jeans, Peter!'

'When she's got the money she will,' he laughed. He had had no compensation for the accident. He and some of his mates had wandered into this sawmill, switched on the big saw and that had been it. Got James used to carry his tea for him in the canteen because Peter did walk in jerks and spilt his tea, and Got became very fond of the boy.

'We must try and do something for him, George. You're good at writing letters. Write to Donald Coleman our MP, George.' I did and Donald Coleman happily got Peter some financial help.

Ernie Chanler started at the centre; like Got James he had worked at Onllwyn No. 1 and suffered from pneumoconiosis, plus he was very deaf. Ernie was a very accomplished artist and attended Swansea School of Art evening classes for many years but got off to a bad start with Got James. A minibus took the worst of the disabled from the centre to the bus stop at the Grand at the end of the shift. One place came free; it should have gone to Got James but Ernie grabbed it.

'Always been the same! Grabby bugger!' scowled Got.

I was told I was to go on an engineering storekeeper's course at Cardiff. Ernie was going on a silkscreen-printing course in England. My lodgings were in Cathedral Road with Mrs MacMarn, £3.10.0 a week full board. It was a magnificent Victorian house. There were sixteen of us lodging in the house, all ex-steel workers or ex-miners with bits missing. I shared the attic with Doyle; he had worked in the Port Talbot steelworks and was retraining as a carpenter. We were woken in the morning by the smell of bacon smoke. Mrs MacMarn's helper, Jess, had sixteen breakfasts to fry each and every morning, and she kept the frying pan very hot. Her face and arms were pitted with red burn spots.

Every day we walked through the beautiful tree-lined avenues of Llandaff fields past the TWW television studios to the Government training centre on Western Avenue. It was like learning a new language: every trade has its own language and mechanical engineering a very complex one. We had our midday meals in the canteen and our evening meals in Cathedral Road and they were always good. When we went out it was for a walk; we had no money to go drinking. We did go for one glass on Wednesday evening in The Halfway.

I had also found there was a studio where I could paint on Cowbridge Road as long as you bought your material in the art shop downstairs. I wanted to paint a picture for Dianne, my brother David's daughter. David was working in Cardiff for Turner's and drove me home every Friday. I had decided to paint a portrait of a Spanish woman with a gold earring. There were half a dozen other people painting. One evening the proprietor came up to the studio and told us there was someone coming from a hotel group and would be looking for paintings to buy, to hang in their hotels. There was one young man, an art teacher; he was painting an abstract of some kind but seemed to spend most of his time hanging out of the window talking to any pretty girl who came along. When the hotel rep stopped at his painting he asked how much and the young art teacher without a flicker of embarrassment said, 'Forty pounds'.

Doyle and I were in The Halfway when a bloke came up and tapped Doyle on the shoulder. Doyle was flabbergasted. They had been in school together and had not seen each other for years. His name was Will Morris, a senior engineer at the Welsh Office. He bought us a round but we refused to take another because we had no money to return the favour. We met up once a week after that with Will Morris and one time he said, 'Drink up. The wife has made you a meal. Come on!' We arrived at his very nice home alongside a lake in the Heath area of Cardiff and had a splendid meal. That went on every week for the rest of the time we were in Cardiff.

At the time they were building the Royal Mint at Llantrisant and were training machine operators at the training centre on Western Avenue. They brought the dies down from the Royal Mint at the Tower of London plus a supply of blanks. One of my jobs every morning was to weigh a bowl of blanks and take them to the machinist, in a room set aside from the rest of the workshop, where he would sign for them. I would collect the bowl at the end of the shift and weight it. The bowl now had in it brand new halfpenny pieces, the Queen's head on one side and a sailing ship on the other – the first coins of the Realm to be minted in Wales for a very long time.

David took me home on a Friday after work. Nurse Miller's son brought me back on a Monday; he was at college in Cardiff. I was happy enough during the day but at night in that attic, small and dingy compared with our bedroom back home, I was for the first time in my life homesick. In India, Burma or getting tossed about in force eleven gales in the Irish Sea, I was always quite happy to be where I was. I missed the boys but most of all I missed the physical presence of Peg, being aware that she was in the same room as me. I was away only from Monday to Friday and in that short time she wrote me two letters. I bought a Thunderbird toy for Geraint each week and a book for Owen to make up for not being at home.

When I had the time I'd pop in to see Dr and Mrs Thomas. Mrs Thomas seemed to be working herself into the floor. Tom Marston, their next door neighbour and a good friend of mine, went in every evening after work to help make the doctor comfortable for the night. Douglas Miller, another friend, had managed to get hold of an electric typewriter and the doctor had started writing 'A Taxonomy of Man's Approaches to Anthropology'. They were able to get him into a wheelchair so that on sunny days he could spend some time in the garden and he was writing letters on large sheets of yellow paper. The letters to Peg and me started with his sympathy for 'Poor, poor Peggy' having to put up with me.

PC Dai James lived next door to the doctor, and as I was leaving he called me: 'Come and have a look at the boat I've built, George.'

Resting on a pair of chucks in his back garden was a beautiful clinker-built rowing boat. Spot on! Perfect!

'Bloody hell Dai it's first class!'

'You like it, George?'

'Like it! I bloody love it!'

'I've been talking to Peg. She said you've finished in Cardiff and you're the only one I know who spent time on small boats. George if I take her down to the mouth of the river Neath to try her out, will you come with me?'

'Sure! OK Dai!'

The mouth of the river Neath. I should have thought longer and more carefully about that when I remembered reading that Gerald of Wales, when accompanying Archbishop Baldwin on his recruiting drive around Wales for men to go and fight in the Crusades, wrote fearfully about the crossing of the mouth of the river Neath: 'Horses and men being swept away'.

It was a lovely evening, wading through the mud was the only off-putting bit. We were not wearing lifejackets. We had none. It was top of the tide, slack water, and we were more or less just drifting.

I looked at the muddy water then out to sea and thought: George, you've got two young lads in the house. What the hell are you doing out in a boat with two novices Dai and Tom and no lifejacket either.

'Well it's not letting in water, Dai, that's one thing!'

Dai looked pleased with himself. 'Because I've left it out in the rain.'

14

Peg had sent some of my paintings to the 12th International Amateur Art Exhibition at Warwick Square London while I was in Cardiff. Two of my paintings were accepted for hanging, 'The Death of Silver' and 'Limestone Crop'. A letter arrived inviting us to a private viewing. We were not able to go.

The NCB started putting their houses up for sale, including Maesmarchog, the manager's house. They had not kept their promise of finding me a job although there were jobs going on the opencast sites. I never even had an interview. I think it was because Mr Justice Paul had given the judgement from the Bench at the Assizes and the newspapers could then report it.

I got a job as a Storekeeper in the Machine Shop with the Baglan Foundry and Engineering Company, a subsidiary of Duport Limited. I had to report to Mr F. Pokojski, ex-Polish Army man and foreman of the machine shop. Bit of a drop in wages compared to the colliery but I was back in work.

The main contract the works had at the time was making round cast-iron doors some six feet in diameter and stainless steel doorframes to renew Tokyo's sewage system. The order shipped out from Briton Ferry.

The machine shop was awesome. The only lathes I had seen before were the ones at the training centre and put alongside these they looked like Dinky toys. The lathes in this place could take ten-inch diameter steel bars, the huge bars moved about the machine shop by an overhead gantry. It was the only machine shop in Wales with a milling machine that had a moveable head. The rate of pay was set for the operator by the precision he had to work to. The miller in the Baglan machine shop was said to be the best in the country. One week, after being paid, he went to Hedges the local motor-bike shop and bought a Lambretta scooter for cash.

I got on well with the head storekeeper Fred Fear. Fred wrote poetry in English but stuck to a Welsh tradition: writing about people getting married, having a baby, or knocking off someone else's wife.

I made a mistake in an order for file cleaner; a roll of file cleaner arrived enough to last ten years.

'Don't worry about it George. It's not half as big a clanger as I dropped. They wanted six twelve-inch links from the chain makers Brown Lenox, Pontypridd. Two lorries pulled into the yard on Monday – with six fathoms of chain on board!'

At Baglan Engineering they had two foundries: one made cast iron, the other nonferrous metal. The cast-iron foundry made anchors for the shipping channel buoys in the Bristol Channel, hence the reason for the chains.

163

Christmas had a better feel about it now that I was back at work. Party time came around. That was something that never happened in the colliery. On the last Friday before the holidays we went for a drink in the Windsor club. I got on the bus to go home and realized I had left my working boots in the club. I was a clerk but because there was so much sharp and hot metal strewn about the place, wearing shoes at work was out of the question. Normally I spent most of my time in the tool room and machine shop but I had been working in and around the foundry for a day or two and developed what I thought was a stye on the lid of my right eye.

The works nursing sister Eira Evans was from Banwen.

'Hello George! Is everything alright?'

'Got a bit of a sore eye, Eira.'

'Sit down. let's have a look. Will you take the prosthesis out George.'

I did.

'It's not a stye.' She reached for a kidney-shaped bowl. 'Hold this against your cheek.'

She douched the socket with water, took the kidney-shaped bowl from me, carefully poured the water out of the bowl, then with the tip of her finger took some of the tiny specks of dust out of the bowl. 'There, that's the culprit.' She rubbed the tiny specks between the tip of her finger and thumb. 'Been in the fettling shop, George? This is cast-iron dust!'

An artificial eye is not fastened to the socket; there is a very small space at each side of the eye where dust could enter. But dust as heavy as cast-iron dust would not be washed out by tears.

'The socket is very badly inflamed. You'd best see the doctor, George. I'll let Mr Leitz the Personnel Officer know.' She dabbed some of the tiny specks of dust on to a small piece of lint. 'When you see the doctor, show the doctor how hard these grains of dust are!'

I didn't tell Peg. I went to the doctor as Eira had advised and gave him the piece of lint. Dr Littlewood gave me some antibiotics. 'Feels like emery. How does it come about, George?'

'Well whatever it is they're making in the foundry, when it comes out of its mould it is covered with a hard crust. And the fettlers clean it off with pneumatic chisels and that makes the dust.'

I went to work the following morning and was called in to see Mr Leitz.

'Nursing sister Eira has been to see me George Brinley.'

Mr Leitz still practised an old Welsh tradition of using both your names. The Dai Johns and William Davys are legion in Wales.

'This is bad news, George Brinley. No one could have fitted in better. And after you had uncovered those two twenty-foot, four and a half-inch diameter bronze bars under that pile of mild steel. They must have been there goodness knows how long. There's no record of them anywhere. It was a real bonus. Stay away from the foundry George Brinley. Stick to the tool room. Something's bound to turn up!'

That week a job did turn up. Mid Glamorgan Hospital Management Committee advertised for a Higher Clerical Officer of the main stores at Neath General Hospital. I told

Mr Leitz. He wrote me a glowing reference. I was interviewed and got the job.

At £853 per annum I had to wear my best suit to work and a clean shirt, and catch two buses every day. Between everything it was the worst-paid job I'd ever had but it was a job. Very busy and very interesting. Neath was then a Headquarters Hospital. A large part of my job was to sign requisitions received from other hospitals and make sure they were dispatched.

We used a Kalamazoo computer shared they said with the Coal Board; it was huge by all accounts. There were high-value goods and low-value goods and each item had a number, for instance butter was No. 12, an adult shroud would be say No. 70, and a baby's shroud perhaps No. 71. I was viewing life through requisition forms. I had often thought of the clerks and bookkeepers involved in ensuring that the Holocaust ran smoothly and effectively. The amount of paperwork must have been huge and the result shows how effective and efficient those bookkeepers were.

In the NHS if a low-value item such as porridge was issued, porridge came in 28lb packs and had to be marked 1, for one pack, on the computer card. The clerk had instead been marking '28' for a 28lb pack; consequently the computer was multiplying 28 by 28 showing that 784lb and not 28lb had been issued. They came down posthaste convinced that someone was supplying a pig farmer with feed.

I was told that a job was coming up with a local engineering company, Bewley & John, Neath Abbey. I telephoned and was asked to report to a Mr Bill Unthank the next afternoon.

I was shown into a small office in the main stores. Sitting behind the desk was a Yorkshire man with enough wrinkles on his face, as Jessie Jones would say, 'to hold a day's rain'.

'There's some foolscap on that desk,' he nodded at the desk in the corner. 'Write something about yourself.'

I sat at the desk and wrote the things I thought he'd want to know about me and handed him the foolscap. He read it.

'When can you start, George?'

'Well I'm still working at the hospital. I'll tell them this afternoon.'

The people at the hospital were great, helpful and kind, but I knew I wasn't cut out to be a Civil Servant. They were very good and told me if I really wanted to go they'd be happy if I worked to the end of the week. Owen wasn't happy. 'The first time I've ever liked writing father's occupation, Higher Clerical Officer'.

My job at Bewley's was to find out the cost on the bills of material that Bill Unthank had written out. Also working with us was George Jones from St Thomas Swansea as an engineering storekeeper. He had worked for all the notable engineering outfits. If you asked what's the next size down from 1/16 as quick as a flash 3/32. He was a stickler for the rules.

He had one son David who went sea fishing at weekends. On Monday when George came to work there would be three pieces of fish cooked to perfection by George's wife, whatever David had fished out of the bay on Sunday: dabs, cod, plaice. It suited me a treat: given a choice I have fish before meat always.

Bill had to go into to hospital and I would have to fill in for him. To my dismay one of the first orders I had to make up required four lengths of feathered steel. I didn't have a clue what feathered steel was let alone know where I could buy it. The embarrassment of not knowing kept me awake most of the night. The order had to be ready for Monday. On Friday morning I looked through every engineering catalogue in the stores and surprisingly George Jones didn't know either. By dinnertime I was in the depths of despair and Bill Unthank walked in. He had popped in to see if I was getting on OK.

'Feathered steel! Get hold of this bloke. Tell him Bill Unthank told you!' He wrote down a name and telephone number for a man in York.

Bill had been brought down from Press Steel Fishers, Oxford to set up the assembly lines for the new washing machine factory on the outskirts of Swansea, which became the Ford factory. During the war he had been in charge of the welding of tank turrets and he always maintained that women were better welders than men. 'You see a woman knitting. She puts the knitting down to answer the door then comes back and picks it up and starts knitting again. And when the garment is finished you can't see where she stopped or where she started. And that's it! Same pressure on her fingers! She does not even have to think about it!'

It was then, working for Bill Unthank, that it really dawned on me that the cleverer your boss is, the easier he is to work for.

He had a touch of the republican about him too I thought. Titles for instance: even someone conferring upon themselves the title of Mr. I remembered one unfortunate who, when Bill asked him his name, said, 'I'm Mr John Whatever'.

Bill in his heaviest Yorkshire brogue asked, 'Were you christened Mister then mate?'

About a month later I was called in to see Mrs Bewley at the Head Office. It was obvious that there was a woman in charge. The office was sparklingly clean, polished and gleaming. Mrs Bewley was an attractive brunette about my age. She explained that the man they had employed to look after their office on the massive BP Baglan Bay site was leaving and asked me to go out there to take charge of the office work. She was very anxious about this new site; Bewley & John had invested heavily in it, forty-four wheeled Lincoln welding sets, miles of welding cable in Bewley livery.

For me it was to prove the best move I had made to date. The following Monday in the site office I met the pay clerk. A stunningly beautiful blonde, Beryl Hill was a widow with three children. Her husband had been burnt to death in Port Talbot Steel Works. My office was next to the Field Engineer, the boss Paul Hughes who could have passed himself off as Ronnie Barker; he was the comedian's double but a very capable engineer.

He liked telling stories about his young son. 'My mother is a devout Catholic. Took the young spark to see her one day and like all grannies after she had stopped kissing and cuddling him asked. "Who's that up on Nan's wall?" She was pointing to Christ on a crucifix. The lad looked at it and said believing he had worked it out. 'Tarzan!'

'Another time she pointed out two nuns to him. "Look, Nuns." "Nobody can be a nun Nan, they got to be something!"'

It was one of the highest paid sites in the UK, certainly the highest paid site in Wales: a pound an hour for craftsmen and fifteen shillings an hour for labourers. A fitter and turner, a highly paid craftsman outside, was lucky if he earned £17 or £18 for a 40-hour week. As well as a top rate of pay, craftsmen were issued with a brand new full tool kit. People were coming from all over to work there, welders from as far away as Glasgow. They had to be coded. I issued each one with a punch that the welder would stamp his work with, like a hallmark, and if his work failed the x-ray test the welder was sacked.

There were at the peak of construction about five thousand men on site. They were building a gigantic chemical plant. A stack 600 feet high and cooling towers 350 feet high and the largest steel pipes ever rolled, 94 inches in diameter. The welders had to stand on scaffolding inside the pipe. Beryl and I went to the topping-out ceremony of one of the three hundred and fifty foot cooling towers. It was a beautiful day. The sky blue and against the blue this gigantic brilliant-white curving structure, it made your head spin just looking up at it. One young man had died in the building of it. One of the timber struts from the thousands of feet of the timber lacing spanning the inside of the tower fell and killed him. Downhand welders turned up who had worked on the thirty-eight inch diameter line they had brought down from the North Sea to the Baglan site. The amount of money shown on their P45s was mind blowing.

My mother became ill. She had had a fall whilst shopping in Neath. My sister Ceinwen had taken her to hospital. They treated her and Ceinwen brought her home. A week later she fainted when she reached for her cardigan off a coat hanger. At the hospital they had failed to notice that she had broken her collarbone in the fall. By now she was in her seventies and never properly recovered. She was at home in her bed for a few months and was then taken to Cimla hospital. The end came very quickly. Owen and I were sat at the side of her bed. She indicated she wanted to whisper something to me. I bent my head towards her.

'Take Owen out of this old place George. Please!'

'Ow! We'll pop out and let Dad come in for a bit.'

My father was stood leaning against a fence post. There were seats nearby but he was comfortable in the stance of his generation, standing up. Bosses sat down. He sat down to eat his food or he'd put his feet up on the open oven door and go into a deep sleep for just ten or fifteen minutes, wake up then go straight to his work.

What he was going to do without Gwladys? She was small and kept her house, herself and family spotlessly clean. Clutter was something she was disciplined against, having worked as a maid for eight years in London. If there was milk on the table it was in a jug not a bottle. The only thing she regretted was talking my father out of buying Tynwern Farm in 1936. He had been born on a farm and if there was one thing he knew something about it was farming.

My memory of her would be of her calm, steady, grey eyes looking at me and telling me to be a good boy on the morning I set off for Burma and the scent of Ponds Cold Cream when I climbed in to bed with her when I was a small boy, of teasing me about Peggy and on Saturday afternoons wiping Vaseline and coal dust from the corners of my eyes before I went out to take Peg to the pictures.

They were flying lads up to Newcastle to test them to see if they were capable of welding aluminium. The gas being pumped ashore was too cold to be transported through a steel pipe. I had to send out to Woolworths for children's balloons; the lads blew the balloons up and forced them into the end of the pipe to stop the heat of the weld pulling air through the pipe.

Dr Thomas once told Peg that the swallows born at Maple House would fly off to Africa, come back the next year and build a swallow's nest in the eaves of Maple House, not a thrush's nest or a robin's nest but a swallow's nest, although they had never seen a swallow's nest being built: 'It's called inherited memory, Peg!' Strange as it may seem most of the lads who passed the special welding test to work on the aluminium pipeline came from the Swansea area: Llansamlet, Landore, Morriston. Perhaps these lads too had inherited their grandfather's and great-grandfather's skills – skills honed in an area once known as Copperopolis.

As well as shipping gas over from Rotterdam to the river Neath a small tanker carried a cargo of contraband, much to the delight of the workforce. Litre bottles of Dutch advocaat at one pound, a box of fifty cigars one pound, everything at a pound and a plentiful supply of Swedish pornography. Those of us who had served in the forces overseas had seen pornography before. The faded sepia photographs, usually featured plump middle-aged women doing whatever with men, dogs or donkeys. The Swedish magazines however were high-quality coloured glossy magazines and the people in them looked like students.

There was one very large vessel fabricated in Holland, too big to be shipped, which was towed over and beached.

Wynn's the haulage firm hauled it aboard one of their huge wagons and brought it to site with a police escort and, so the story goes, once the police escort had left, the blank flanges were taken off and the vessel was packed with contraband. On Friday payday the road over the sand dunes to Baglan village was lined with traders' vans, fishmongers and butchers. It must have played havoc with the local shopkeepers. It all made me realize what a sheltered unworldly life the life of a coalminer was.

I learned too how brutal the law of our country still was towards women. Until Beryl's compensation case for her husband's death came up in the High Court I sincerely believed that men and women were equal in the eyes of the law in our country. Beryl told me the following day that the youngest of the children had been given the biggest award of the children and the eldest the least. Her award was reduced by the judge; he thought her chances of remarrying were good because she was so attractive. It was 1970: I could not believe what I was hearing. Nor did he did allow her to have all the money she was awarded; it would be doled out to her a bit at a time. In my own case, on the other hand, I was given all the money. They had no way of knowing if I was going to go straight to a betting shop and blow the lot and let Peg and the boys whistle.

I was walking back from the canteen and someone was calling my name. It was Doyle who had shared a room with me in Cathedral Road.

'George how are you?' Doyle beamed and offered his hand.

He was now a foreman carpenter.

'And how are you?'

'Great! Got married!'

'Well done! Who's the lucky girl?

'I told you when we were in Cardiff that when I was in North Africa my wife went off with a Yank. And left the kids with my mother! Well she married the American but he died about four years ago. She wrote and asked me could she come to see the children. I could hardly say no and I thought the kids perhaps would like to see their mother. Anyway cut a long story short we remarried!' Doyle looked a bit sheepish. 'What do you think of that George?'

'I think that's the nicest story I've ever heard!' I shook his hand. 'All the luck in the world to the both of you and the kids!' But I wondered could I have been as forgiving and as courageous?

Like all good things, the contract at BP Baglan came to an end. I was brought back to the main office. Ted Heath had clamped on a pay freeze. You could have a pay rise if you changed your job. They changed my job title and I got to share an office with Ken Curran, the Contracts manager. Ken was a very hard-working and very capable engineer. Plus he was a very good-looking six-foot-three blond. When he was working every woman in the building would find some excuse to be in our office. Mr Bewley stopped by to talk to us one day; he was just back from Paris after seeing the rugby. The top rugby men were often calling in the yard: Mr Bewley was very generous to Neath Rugby club. Glyn Shaw, Welsh rugby iron man, popped his head around the door one day.

'Hello, Mr Evans!'

'Glyn. What are you doing here?'

'Mr Bewley's given me a job.'

I knew Glyn had started playing for Neath. He was the same age as Owen; they were classmates. He was that strong, a crew repairing a big gas cylinder in the steel works were waiting for tackle to lift the oxy and acetylene bottle to the roof of the cylinder when they realized Glyn had already carried both the oxy and acetylene cylinders up on his shoulders.

Had a phone call from Des at Neath Hospital. There had been a power cut in the night and my father had fallen down the stairs and with some force, smashing a hall table. He'd never been in hospital as a patient in his life. He was lying on a trolley in a busy corridor with his hand over his face. Des was with him. I stood next to Des; it helped the old man be less self-conscious of his situation as he was a shy man. Since selling the billiard hall he had lived with Des and Ceinwen and had taken on two allotments; he was there from morning till night. An old workmate of his, Emlyn Morgan, called me one day.

'George is the old man going simple-minded?'

'Maybe! Why do you ask Em?'

'He was coming off the mountain the other day, a rope tied around his shoulders, dragging a bloody big air pipe. People will be laughing at him George! He's eighty for goodness' sake!'

Bewley and John were awarded the contract to convert the annealing furnaces at Trostre sheet metal works, Llanelli, from oil to North Sea gas. Cyril Preston, an old mate of mine from Banwen who had also served in the Far East, would do the work; I would go with him to check that the replacement components matched the amended drawings that were supplied by Salem of Chicago. The speed at which the shining continuous sheets of tinplate were rolled into a reel big enough to be shipped out was amazing.

I dropped a clanger shortly after coming back to the main office. Martin Rees the safety officer fell out with Jeff Morris the works manager. They asked me to cover for Martin. I said yes, not thinking there was that much to it. I was hoping Martin would not pack it in altogether: we were good friends. He and his wife Vera had given Geraint a beautiful black Labrador pup, and I had painted a portrait of Vera's favourite Boxer dog from a photograph. They used to come up on Sundays. Peg loved listening to Vera's stories especially the one about the laverbread.

Martin was working in Aden at the time. Vera was going out on a visit. Martin telephoned her: 'Go down the market. The Welsh Guards are out here, buy some laverbread and bring it with you.'

'I did, a vanity case full. Things were a bit iffy in Aden then. The plane landed. No Martin or Welsh Guards in sight! Just Arabs! They're going to think I got a bag full of plastic explosives! Then thank God Martin drove up in a jeep full of Welsh Guards.'

My first job deputizing for Martin was to go into the huge Llandarcy Oil Refinery to check on some of our lads. Len Heath was there. He was an expert at hot tapping. Len would drill into a pipeline while gas or oil was being pumped through it and fit a branch line.

'What you doing here then George?'

'Covering for Martin Rees.'

When I got home that evening David my brother was there.

'What are you trying to do? Land up in jail! If you want to be a safety officer there's a course going on now in Neath. I can get you on it tomorrow! They tell me you were in Llandarcy today acting as a safety officer. One of the most dangerous sites in the country!'

I explained to him how it had come about.

'I know how good the Bewleys have been to you but unless you are qualified it is against the law and if someone gets seriously hurt or killed they'll throw the book at you!'

I guessed what had happened: Len Heath had got in touch with him – they had been in school together. David was then the Chief Safety Officer for Turner and Sons, Wales's biggest and most prestigious builders, restoring the blitzed Saint Mary's in Swansea and the blitzed Llandaff Cathedral in Cardiff; he was also chairman of the South Wales Construction Safety Group. Thankfully Martin Rees and Jeff Morris patched things up and I was relieved of the odious post of stand-in Safety Officer.

Christmas came around and as usual the Bewley Christmas do would be at The Dragon Hotel, Swansea, evening dress to be worn.

'Well I can't come, I haven't got a suit!' Ken said.

'Well you've got plenty of time to get one,' said Mr Bewley.

'I can't afford one! I got two sets of twins and a bloody mortgage!'

'Put your coat on! We'll go in to town and get a suit!' Mr Bewley ordered Ken. He took him to Ralph Tyler's the top menswear shop in town. When they returned Ken was fully kitted out, down to dress shirt and tie. So it was to everyone's shock when Ken Curran announced, in the spring, that he was leaving. He had been offered a directorship with Roadvale Engineering of Newport. He was going to be badly missed. When it came to organizing a site there was no one better. When he was in his early thirties he had supervised the construction of the mass of complicated pipe work at Queen's Dock and always kept the workforce on his side.

Now I was back in the main yard and back enjoying the treat with Bill Unthank of fresh fish for Monday lunch, caught by David, George Jones's son, the night before, and cooked by his mother and there was the extra pleasure of one of George's stories, of the time he was stationed in Singapore and was given the job of moving some furniture into an officer's billet. He was carrying a basket-woven bedroom chair on his head, with the back of the chair down in front of his eyes. He put the chair down.

'And there they were. Her, plump and her plumpness wobbling like a jelly, her skin a patchy pink, in her thirties, a British nurse! Not a stitch on! On her knees and him performing like a Bull Terrier! For a moment the three of us froze. He sprang at me snarling. He was crazy, shouting "You stupid Welsh bastard!" He was bollock naked and he chased me out onto the street! Never got on with him after that.'

By the sound of it George Jones and British Officers didn't get on. In fact, he brought a newspaper cutting into to work to prove it. He had done time in the glasshouse for smacking one of them in the mouth.

178

The investiture of the Prince of Wales was coming up. I thought I'd make something for Peg, to commemorate the event. Dr Aubrey Thomas once told her, 'You're the only communist I know Peggy who believes in Royalty.'

How right he was. If the Queen was on television and Peg was not working she'd be watching her. I made a relief sculpture of the head of Prince Charles in plaster and took it to Dynevor Engineering, Neath. Its foundry made six brass and six aluminium relief copies. I bought some jeweller's rouge on the advice of Bill Unthank and spent every spare moment polishing one brass relief (the one that looked as if it needed the least work) and set it in a piece of anthracite coal.

There was an article in *The Observer* newspaper about an appropriate monument to Sir Winston Churchill. I thought the pose he was depicted in, the photograph I had seen of the statue in London, was nothing like I remember seeing in newsreels; he always seemed to be smiling. It was the biggest piece I had attempted to date. When it was finished I was pleased with it and so was Peg. I had read quite a bit about Churchill, especially his time as a Liberal with Lloyd George. He brought in the minimum wage and had a law made to stop employers forcing their employees to work excessive hours. Plus although at the time he only had his earnings as a journalist and MP, he repaid all his mother's debts on her death. They were large debts but he adored his mother. That struck a chord with me remembering some of the bad payers who were so blatant about it. One I remember who put on airs and graces who would be tucked up in bed while Peg was out in the pouring rain or freezing cold delivering her paper. This bad payer felt she was entitled to an account as she was the lady of the manor and never ever paid what she owed.

179

Whatever else Churchill was, he was a hardworking man, writer, artist and a first-class bricklayer who worked twelve to fourteen hours a day: he and Peg had something in common. I took the statue to the NUM's exhibition of arts and crafts held in the pavilion at Sophia Gardens, Cardiff.

'What the fucking hell's he doing here?'

'He's here because he got you the minimum wage!'

When Dai Francis saw him: 'A very good likeness George!'

When he looked at the portrait of Peg he muttered. 'Peggy Jones!'

He had known Peg all her life and he didn't know Peg was standing behind him. She tapped him on the shoulder.

'Peggy! Peggy! How are you Peg bach?'

Dai like most Welshmen was emotional and was squeezing Peg's hands. She told me afterwards her engagement ring had twisted around and Dai was squeezing it into her finger. 'He almost had me crying too.' Peg was very fond of Dai Francis – they had been neighbours for years. *The Coal News* reported: 'the Prince is a model "visitor" at the exhibition like the two-foot statue of Winston Churchill and model of former pit mate Alby Thomas.'

Jeff Morris, who I had always got on reasonably well with, seemed to be getting rattier by the day. Jeff was the Works Manager and a director of the company and Mr Bewley's brother-in-law and I was an employee. Ken Curran's departure I suppose had caused his workload to increase quite a bit, and it didn't help when Mr Bewley showed him up in front of me. His attitude towards me definitely changed after that. He showed his irritation with me each time we had anything to do with each other. There was the time I explained to him that the Iron Fairy cranes should have Lang's lay wire rope.

'And what's Lang's lay?'

'It's rope made up of triangular strands.'

'And how can you have a round rope made up of triangular strands?' he shouted loud enough for everyone in the office to hear.

'Have you ever seen a box of Dairylea Cheese?'

I suspected he knew what Lang's lay rope was but was trying to make me feel stupid and uncomfortable in front of the others.

I went back to my office; the Bewleys had been the best people I had ever worked for but I was angry at being made to look stupid and thought to myself, I'll look even more stupid if I don't do anything about it. I got up from my desk, put my coat on, knocked on Jeff Morris's door.

'Mr Morris will you put my cards in the post please!'

I closed the door and walked down to say goodbye to Bill Unthank.

'I've finished that painting for you Bill. Pop up one weekend to collect it.' I had painted a rock pool with a large wave crashing into the rocks. I was pleased with it.

'Thanks George! How much do I owe you?'

'Nothing Bill! It's a thank you for all the help you've been to me.'

We shook hands and I was off home.

15

The problem now was how to explain to Peg why I had given up my job with Bewley & John which had been the best employer I had ever worked for. When I told her she thought I had gone completely daft.

'You're forty-five years of age and you give up a perfectly good job? And for what! Because? Why?'

'I just told you!'

'No you haven't. You got into a bit of a huff and walked out! A good example to set Owen!'

One of Peg's most endearing characteristics was that she'd be blazing mad for ten minutes. Rows never lasted very long. Then she'd say the same thing every time. 'You friends with me now?' She'd excuse her temper by saying. 'It's the Irish me.' By bedtime she would have persuaded herself perhaps it was all for the better.

Around this time there were two great losses. One day Peg had some very sad news. Dr Aubrey Thomas had died. They had gone to stay near their daughter Hedydd in Powys. He had been such an important part of so many people's lives; people truly felt he would pull through and be there to look after them for ever.

Some happenings in a life are so horrifying that, even recalling them years later, they still feel unreal. Peg shook me awake.

'There's someone hammering on the backdoor!'

There was and there was urgency in the hammering. I rushed downstairs and opened the door. It was David, Dianne's husband, in floods of tears.

'Uncle George! It's Dewi! Please come right away!'

'You go David I'll be right behind you!'

I got to the billiard hall bungalow. There was a police car there and Doctor Khan's car. Dianne was weeping inconsolably; Ceinwen my sister was holding her. David was in the bedroom, tears streaming down his cheeks, looking down into the cot at his dead baby son, who for all the world looked as if he was still asleep. An appalling blow, traumatizing and stupefying, that had struck like a thunderbolt, and a blow that Dianne and David never got over.

Received a letter telling me that the well-known author and historian George Ewart Evans would like to call and speak to me. I had met him before: he and Dr Thomas were lifelong friends and he was regarded as the top oral historian in the country because of his work in East Anglia. I jumped at the chance of meeting such a famous scholar.

He arrived, quietly spoken, immaculately turned out, and was going to write about the anthracite miners of the Western Valleys. He was very deaf and used a tape recorder and wanted to know the ordinary daily routine of a miner working in an anthracite drift mine.

He interviewed a dozen or so besides myself: John Williams the manager, Jeff Jeffries, and others. Later he wrote and asked me would I make some sketches of a coalface and the general layout of a drift mine. I did and he used them in his book published by Faber and Faber, *From Mouths of Men*. He had read some of my work and wrote to me saying. 'You should return to your writing even if it gives less time for your painting. You have a feeling for words.'

It was Sunday night, almost time for bed, and someone was knocking on the front door. It was Ken Curran.

'I was in a club in Porthcawl and somebody there said you had told Jeff Morris to stick his job up his arse!' He laughed and pushed into the house past me. 'Peg!'

Peg was on her feet and he was kissing her.

'No I didn't tell Jeff Morris to stick his job up his arse. I just asked him to put my cards in the post.'

'Why do you stay with him Peg? Listen Peg I'll take him off your hands. I want him to come and help me at Morganite, Peg!'

'I'm looking for a job closer to home.'

'Where? There's nothing up here?'

'I haven't looked yet! And Morganite is an hour or more by bus!'

'Get to site as soon as you can! Just be there! Come and go when it suits you!'

'Ken let me make you something to eat.'

'No Peg I'm ok!'

'Yes I got some beef there. I'll make you some sandwiches.'
And off she went to the kitchen.

One and a half hours later Peg had taken sides with Ken
and was coaxing me to go and help him.

'Ok! Ok and who will I be working for?

'Roadvale Engineering of Newport.'

I arrived on site about nine o'clock. Morganite was a huge
works moved down to Morriston, South Wales from
Battersea, London but more than one hundred years ago it
began life in Brecon. What a contrast my new place of work
was to the office I worked in at Bewley & John. A shed full
of pipe fittings of every description, boxes of welding rods,
tool boxes, working clothes, working boots and a desk in
the far corner near the window. It had on it a mixture of
cardboard boxes, old newspapers, empty bean tins and a
telephone. There was a work crew that varied in number
from one day to the next except for John Williams the
foreman and the two craftsmen Jackie Smith the fabricator
and Eddie Jones the coded welder.

I once had to take Eddie's welding to the Engineering
Department at the University to be tested, not just x-rayed,
machine tested too. It was because of Eddie's expertise that
we had the contract to work on the very special presses.
When a welder welds, the rod melts and so does the parent
metal each side of the weld rod. Eddie's work passed with
flying colours: they had actually sawn the weld in half and
it was impossible to tell where the parent metal ended and
the welding rod metal began.

Roadvale Engineering's main work was to assist with the dismantling and removal of the great Bussman presses from the old works at Battersea, London, and installing them at the new works in Morriston, Swansea. The product manufactured at the works was very high-tech. Morganite produced special carbon for customers all over the world – carbons impregnated with all sorts: gold, silver, even sugar.

The workforce had their urine tested every so often to ensure their bodies had not ingested and become contaminated by the lead in the atmosphere. There were warning notices everywhere. 'No Eating, Drinking Or Smoking In This Area'. One engineer at his periodic medical was told to stop biting his nails or he would have to leave.

Breakfast time in the office-cum-shed was always a bit of an event. Stories from the night before, horses they had backed that had won but most often lost, women who had led them on or had completely taken over. Blokes from the time they are small kids like telling embellished stories. Ken would not stay in the shed if Jackie was having his pea soup for breakfast. Jackie would open the tin of soup first thing, put it where it would not get tipped over, on top of one of the furnaces and by breakfast time the soup would be warm enough to eat. Ken would leave. Jackie kept his spoon in his toolbox; he didn't wash it, just threw into the toolbox when he had finished. The result was that the spoon had a tyre of hardened pea soup where Jackie's lips had reached. Ken couldn't stand the sight of the spoon, let alone Jackie eating with it.

Nevertheless they could not manage without Jackie. He was that good a fabricator that an American company would take him to the Caribbean when they would be servicing one of their oilrigs. Working out angles for Jackie Smith was as easy as breathing. I had often wondered when passing the steel works about the intricate pipe work. It was, as they say, as tangled as a pig's guts. People like Jackie Smith, masters at geometry, would measure up and work out the angles. The pipe would be cut and the flanged branches welded on, a crane would lift the pipe, now with its many limbs and all the bolt holes would slide over all the bolts: craftsmanship of the highest order.

One day Ken Curran asked me to come and have dinner with him off site. He told me he was going to start his own company.

'And I got a name for it – Gemmak Engineering! I want you to call at these solicitors tomorrow morning.' He handed me a scribbled note. 'They're in the same street as the library in Neath, Proctor, pick up the key and sort the office out. Carpet, desk and chairs, I got a drawing board sorted.'

By the end of the week Gemmak Engineering head office was in place and ready to go.

On Monday, Wednesday and Friday I went to the Market for dinner, to the famous faggot and pea stalls. I remembered them from when I was a boy. Each stall had a big coal fireplace in the corner on which they did their cooking. Each stall was white limed out and absolutely spotlessly clean and the smell of the food being cooked made people ravenous. Bus trips were organized from as far away as Hereford to eat at the faggot and pea stalls. My cousins drove down from Cray, now that the trains had stopped, to savour Neath's famous faggots and peas mindful of the happy train rides of their childhood. June, Ken's wife, telephoned me and asked me would I take her for faggots and peas after she had done her shopping. She was a bit self-conscious of going on her own. The seating arrangements were a bit intimate; you sat on benches. In times gone by people sat next to each other and thought nothing of it. Peter Jones my nephew had become an accountant in the Midland Bank, Neath; he too would sometimes keep me company on my faggot and pea outings.

Things were going very nicely. Owen was doing well at Grammar School and playing number 14 for the school rugby team and Peg told me that Owen was going out with a girl from Gorseinon and he had asked if he could bring her with him on our forthcoming weekend trip down West. We stopped to pick her up outside a very nice detached house. She was a tall brunette, quite a stunner. She sat in the back with Peg and Geraint. Her name was Patricia Williams. She and her Mum lived alone; her father had died when she was two, her sister Jennifer was a school teacher in London and about ten years older than Patricia. That night Peg and I talked about Owen's young lady and we thought Owen had found himself a lovely girl. We were both very pleased. Young men, if they're not courting by their late teens, start looking for fights on a Saturday night. Owen was looking for a place at University too. Peg waited anxiously on his return from Manchester, Kings and Imperial College.

There was one interview he was especially pleased with. The professor at Kings had shown him a box of small stones and had pointed to one. 'What would you say that is Owen?' 'A diamond I said. And I was right!'

Owen settled for an honours course Bachelor of Science degree in Engineering at Lanchester Polytechnic, Coventry.

What I think made up his mind was that it was a sponsored course and he would not have to ask his mother or me for money.

A letter from the NCB estate office arrived offering Maple House for sale. So we bought it. Had George Howells to put in central heating. George put the large copper tank from the old system in the garden. They began working on the Maesmarchog Mineral Railway. The lads told me they were going to strengthen the railway bridge crossing, the Roman Road, and that would mean taking off the nameplate Evans & Evans Engineers Greenwich 1866. And where could they put it? Made of cast iron, measuring a yard by two foot and half an inch thick.

'Put in a front loader and bring it up the side of the house and put it in the garden.'

I got home from work one day and Peg asked me had I given the forty gallon copper boiler to anyone.

'No.'

'Well it's not in the garden!'

We both went out to look. It was gone. So was the cast-iron nameplate off the bridge.

The house was empty for most of the day, someone had had a word in the ear of one of the rag and bone men and a copper boiler worth a few bob and a priceless nameplate, as far as I was concerned, were gone. People extol the virtues of village life; in my experience there are as many thieving twats to the dozen in a village as there are in any town or city.

Mary Miles the music teacher had persuaded Geraint to sing solo at the school concert to be held at the cinema in

Seven Sisters. Patricia came up for the weekend. The four of us were sat in the front row in the balcony. The master of ceremonies announced, 'And now Master Geraint Evans!'

Miss Miles accompanied him on the piano with 'The Little Road to Bethlehem'. I had been living with this boy for eleven years. I had no idea he could sing, and sing so well as this. What a difference a first-class teacher makes. His Aunty Vi was in the audience, the Aunty who had named him after Sir Geraint Evans. She had him at the Half Way Inn having singing lessons the following Monday and enlisted in a concert group by the end of that week. One of the concerts was very memorable for Peg. It was at Adelina Patti's castle that had been turned into a hospice for old miners. After the concert a young man came over to Peg and Vi and asked would the young boy come to sing to his father who had been too ill to come to the concert and was still in his room upstairs.

'Yes! Yes certainly! Won't you Ger!' Aunty Vi answered for them.

The old collier, Peg said, was propped up in bed, oxygen mask on, frail but managed a smile.

'Now then Ger bach!' encouraged Vi, holding her tuning fork up, then brought it down gently on the bedside table. Its musical pitch filled the small quiet room. And Geraint began to sing Dafydd y Garreg Wen (David of the White Rock).

'Maybe it was being in that room. Or the old miner, worn out by a lifetime of hard work, listening to that haunting melody, with tears rolling down his cheeks. I almost burst into tears myself.' Peg was close to tears telling me the story.

Peg bought herself a new car, a Vauxhall, very smart in its new metallic sea-green paint: first time we'd ever paid a thousand pound for a car.

'We're going to see Owen on the weekend,' she announced on coming in from work.

'How?'

'In the car, how do you think!'

We had never seen a motorway, let alone driven on one. Come Saturday morning we were on our way. We had just left the M50 and were travelling along the M5. Geraint was sitting in the back, no seat belts then, head between his mother's seat and mine.

'Well done Mam. You're doing a ton!'

She looked at me and grinned and slowed down. She told me later: 'I was just following the bloke in front.'

We arrived at the street where Owen was lodging since leaving the Hall of Residence.

'You stay here with Ger!' Off she went with Owen's address in her hand. She stopped about three doors away, climbed a few steps, knocked the door, the door opened and Peg went in. About a quarter of an hour later she came out with Owen carrying his bag. Peg was all smiles, shaking hands with the woman of the house. Peg never quarrelled with, or was ever rude to anyone.

'I told the woman he was coming home. You should have seen it George. Cooker tight up against his bed! No ceiling rose for the light just the wires twisted together. And the College people had approved it!'

Peg would not speak Welsh but had a very Welsh attitude to life. She drove Owen to his new lodging. It was with an Irish couple; he was a bus driver and they had two children.

Although the children would never get to meet Peg, from the day Owen came to live in their house until the day he left they would receive a parcel of comics in the post each week.

Geraint had started at Llangatwg School in Cadoxton and played rugby with quite a bit of flair, so Peg said. The boys calling at the shop had told her he was another Barry John, of which she had no doubt. She washed and ironed their jerseys and nicks, polished their boots, even washed their bootlaces, but she would not go to see the boys play. Her uncle Ivor Thomas the Lamb and Flag, who had played for Neath in the 1920s and 1930s, had told so many stories of the brutality on the field and why Neath wore a black shirt to commemorate the death of a player in a game it made an everlasting mark on his young niece.

Owen and Patricia decided to get married and live in Coventry, taking rooms with the Irish couple Owen was lodging with. He graduated with honours. Peg checked what Owen had to wear for the ceremony. She sent off to Chancery Lane in London for a black gown, hood of gold, lined with turquoise blue, and a black college cap.

We had seen photographs of Coventry Cathedral and seen it on film. Now we were in the magnificent building, the organ playing and reading the order of service.

David Owen Evans, Neath Grammar School for Boys, Bachelor of Science, Honours Degree in Engineering.

Peg had embarrassed her mother years before by telling me one of her mother's dreams while she was in the room. 'She saw you in a huge building like a church. Didn't you Mam?' In the Cathedral watching Owen, the sun shining on his fair hair, she said, 'It wasn't you my mother saw, it was Owen!'

Seeing Peg around the two boys, she seemed to devote ninety per cent of her time fussing over what she could do next for them. I brought it up as discreetly as I was able one day.

'Listen George! Owen and Geraint are my sons. You are someone else's son!'

It was at about that time the idea for the story 'Boys of Gold' began to take shape in my head; the songs men had written through the ages in praise of their mothers. In the first talking picture *The Jazz Singer*, the highlight of the film was Al Jolson singing 'Mammy', a song that went on to sell more than twenty three million copies worldwide. Writers have written over and over again of the indestructible bond between mother and son. At school we were taught about the mothers of Sparta who told their sons before they went into battle: 'Come back with your shield or on it.' The Spartan mother handed over her son to be brought up by the military when the boy was just seven years of age but her love and pride in him lasted until death. I still was not a competent typist; one finger was the most I could manage, but I found the time to complete the bit of scribbling I had begun.

Dai, Peg's brother, was taken ill and was taken to Morriston Hospital. His lungs were very damaged by now. The TB was never ever cured; it lay there dormant – a slight cold would set it off again and that was what had happened. It was November and he was older and weaker and he died. He was eighteen years older than Peg. She would feel it strange not to have her big brother around.

16

Banwen was surrounded by slagheaps, aerial tips, opencast tips: not a blade of grass from Banwen to Glyn Neath. Even so, standing in Maple House's garden you could see Pen y Fan, the highest point in southern Britain, more than twenty miles away. The water in the trout stream that ran the length of the garden, Nant Cellwen (the stream of the pure cell), was crystal clear as it slid gleaming in the sun over its smooth pebbles and flowed into the Afon Pyrddin (the river of the pure man – people believed it was named so to mark the place where Saint Patrick was born). If I was going to tell a story what better place to start than on the banks of this historic stream, so I wrote 'Boys of Gold'. How to get it published I had no idea. They do say it's not what you know but who you know. I sent it to George Ewart Evans in Norwich and, thanks to his influence, it was published in *The Anglo-Welsh Review*.

Owen, who had been posted to Coventry mine as an engineer, saw an advertisement for a Senior Mechanical Engineer holding a degree at the Opencast Executive of South Wales. Owen applied and got the job. Peg was landed. George Wimpey & Co. Ltd. were going to open another opencast site in Banwen. I applied for a clerical post and was asked to come to Maesgwyn Opencast Coal Site to be interviewed by the area office manager Mr Fitzpatrick. I drove to the office; we could see it from our house.

People had cursed the opencast site and cursed the men who had worked on it, conveniently forgetting that it had kept the loss-making deep mines open with its profits, thereby sparing the workforce of the deep mines, myself included, the humiliation of being sent down the road, in 1957, on fourteen days' notice with just two weeks' pay in their pockets. Opencast mining was started out of desperation. People were dying because of the bitterly cold

winter of 1947. A million houses had been destroyed, another million were damaged in the bombing. Houses with their slate roofs blown off were left with a sheet of tarpaulin thrown across. A pane of glass for a broken window could not be got for a King's ransom. People in East Anglia were queuing knee deep in snow at 6am for half a hundredweight of coal. The Labour Government of the time would have dug up Buckingham Palace if there had been coal underneath it. Like it or not, history will I am sure say that opencast mining was a godsend and a blessing to the people of Britain.

The interview went well as far as I was concerned. Mr Fitzpatrick was Irish and a bit old-fashioned. I was comfortable with that; it suited me. On April 3rd, I had the letter telling me I had got the job. I reported to Mr Fitzpatrick. 'You will start in the Onllwyn site office. George – Glyn Widlake is the office manager. He'll show you the ropes. You have a car?'

'You can see my house from here, Mr Fitzpatrick. I don't need a car!'

'You are entitled to a car allowance; goes with the job.'

I met Glyn. I was to find out that he was quite a bit of a star but at his work first class. He had to bring out a balance sheet every Thursday that showed every penny spent on site wages, down to the cost of the last unit of electricity. The NCB had named the site Onllwyn knowing full well the site was on the Drum mountain and called the site on the Onllwyn mountain the Drum. Nothing the NCB ever did seemed to be straightforward.

The Onllwyn site was, according to the lads, the deepest hole in Europe. I was working on site when they hit a million ton. Friday night free bar in the Price's Arms.

A Wimpey minibus took us home. Back then mountain ponies still roamed all over the place. I got out of the bus; it was two in the morning, and tripped over a pony laying on the piece of grassland between Maple House and the road. I said 'Sorry!'. The following Monday people were ringing up asking to speak to Doctor Dolittle.

Wales were playing England at Twickenham in the Five Nations, 1980, and the Welshman Ringer was being sent off. A protester was running on to the field. He looked familiar: it was Glyn. Two burly English stewards bundled him off. The following morning it made the front page of the *News of the World*. When Glyn came into work on Monday he had shaved off his beard. He told me the boys, his sons, had got hold of the paper first and had come running into the bedroom shouting, 'Look at Daddy! Look at Daddy!' 'That's when I knew the beard had to come off.'

Maesmarchog site office was ready. It had a glass-fronted corridor running the whole length of the front of the office, with the best view of any office anywhere, looking out over the Carmarthen Fans. Maesmarchog means Field of the Mounted Knight. This area was once a large Roman settlement. With the five hundred men garrisoned at the fort and perhaps another two thousand in the Marching Camp, with one packhorse for every six Roman soldiers, not hard to see why the name has stuck for two thousand years.

The first office was for Reg Jones the site agent, the next office was mine, a room for the telephone switchboard, the lavatories and wash room, the engineers' office, and dining room with access to the canteen. All the furnishings were new. It was something I would learn over the years, that my new employer would be the best employer I would ever have worked for. No road vehicle was kept on the road more than three years. There was a book of rules locked in the safe of every Wimpey office and amended at intervals and security would check to see they were amended. What had happened to me after my accident I doubt could happen in this strict set-up.

Mr Fitzpatrick arrived one afternoon with a very pretty young blonde.

'George, this is Mrs Joyce Jones who will be working with you.'

It turned out I knew her husband and his family very well, known them all my life in fact; her father-in-law was a great friend of my father. They had worked as colliers in the same district for years. Danny Bach Jones, the very backbone of the Banwen Rugby Club. I pointed to where I lived. What a godsend it was to be working close to home again. The NCB had promised me a job as part of the settlement at the Assizes. Over the years since, I had sent in perhaps a dozen application forms but never had an answer let alone an interview.

I couldn't ask her age. So I said, 'I bet you I can tell you on what day you keep your birthday.'

'I bet you can't.'

'February the third,' I said: my father's birthday. She was flabbergasted.

'How did you know?'

I never told her it was a guess. We got on famously from the start.

Over the weeks the Maesmarchog workforce grew to one hundred and twenty. Each week I had to bring out a balance sheet to be ready for Thursday to be approved by the site agent before the figures were sent to HQ at Hammersmith to be published, along with other duties. We got into a bit of a flap sometimes. The pays came by security van. We would pay out nightshift starting at about 8pm. In the winter and in the dark the lads would be so wrapped up you really didn't know who you would be handing the pay to. There were times when one of us would forget to tick the list when a pay was handed over; the following day there would be twenty pay packets in the box and twenty-one still on the list. That's where the panic came in!

My father became ill and was taken into hospital for radiation therapy. He came home and stayed mostly in his room. The last day I spoke to him he asked how things were going at work and would I cut his nails. I cut his fingernails. 'My toenails too please George.' The following morning Des walked down and told us that my father had died.

He would be buried from Maple House, with British Legion bearers and his coffin draped in the Union Flag. He, like my mother, could not stand clutter: everything in its place and everything shared out equally. He had even arranged for his funeral to be paid for. His younger sister Janet, she was ninety at that time, told me about the morning their mother Mary died at the age of just thirty-eight. They lived then in the Neuadd, one of the oldest farms in Heol Senni, Neuadd meaning Hall because when it was built it was just one very large room. She remembered my father, her brother Davy, picking her up out of her crib and carrying her past the bed on which their dead mother lay, 'with his hand covering the side of my face and he was only twelve years of age at the time and it was his mother too. I've always remembered that, George,' she said.

Geraint had moved to Dwr-y-Felin school, Neath, the old grammar school. Owen and Patricia were moving to Haverfordwest, Owen to work for the Water Board and Patricia would be giving up her job with a local paint manufacturer. Peg sold their bungalow for them and got a good price for it.

Haverfordwest brought Peg the biggest bonus of all: a grandson. Noel David George was christened at St Justinian's church, Freystrop, by the Rev George Pembleton, one-time Commanding Officer of RAF Brady. It was the most enchanting church I had ever been in. Reputed to be over one thousand years old. If it had a congregation of thirty it would have been packed out. Set in a gentle hollow, the churchyard carpeted by primroses, it was a fairy tale setting.

Noel was all Peg talked about. We would come in from a Saturday night out with Ron and Renee and our other friends and Peg would ask me, 'Did I talk a lot about Noel?'

'Yes.'

'It's your fault, you should have stopped me!'

Hughie Maguire the General Foreman had things running like clockwork in the field and made a good match for Reggie Jones the Senior Site Agent. They were both very intelligent quiet men, a first-class combination. It was a very nice place to work. By Christmas time they had dug a hole big enough to put most of the town of Neath in. The huge Euclid trucks hauling sixty ton of rock and shale a time to the top of the mountain but not without controversy. The Euclid truck tyres, nine feet in diameter, costing nine hundred pounds a time, were being worn out on the steep climb from the cut to the top of the mountain. It caused people to come down from London to investigate.

There was a first-class reason for the hole to be dug. Plans had been drawn up for a lake to be created from Banwen colliery for a mile alongside the inter-valley road. It was to be a quarter of a mile wide and not more than four feet deep. The twin Maclean slag tips of Banwen colliery, more than a hundred feet high and a half-mile around the base, were to be pushed into the hole. A million bushels of peat dug from the massive peat bog that had covered the site was stockpiled at F stocking ground. That would be used as dressing around the lake.

Then a local farmer who owned the tip stopped them. All those millions of pounds gone to waste; why had someone not found out before or why had not the council offered to buy the tip off the farmer? We will never know. In 1980, £10,000 would have done the trick and we would now have a sailing and rowing facility that people from all over would be queuing up to use. Draglines could have been used, there would have been no need for the fleet of Euclids and millions would have been saved.

Wimpey site canteens were the best works canteens I had ever come across in my working life, open twenty-four hours a day. If a man came to work early he could have a full breakfast. Mid-morning the Hurry-up-cart went out. The lads would have placed their order before going out to site. The main fare was a Wimpey double-decker made with Dyffryn Bakery bread. First a thick slice of butter-soaked toast, an egg fried hard on top, another thick slice of butter-soaked toast, two rashers of bacon, another slice of butter-soaked toast and a birthday candle if one of the lads had a birthday. It was a very rough ride in the Hurry-up-cart; the girls were provided with straps to hang on to as the Hurry-up-cart careered around the site. The Hurry-up-cart also serviced the nightshift. Great care had be taken in the winter on the Maesgwyn site; at one time, at its deepest, the high wall was 545 feet and a mile long.

Geraint did well with his A-levels and got himself a place at Cardiff reading chemistry. His professor was an Australian who had come to Wales to teach and look for the wreckage of his father's fighter plane. His father had been killed defending Liverpool flying a fighter plane and he had found the wreckage and had a part of it on his desk. He used to tease Geraint that he had never met anyone who had ever heard of Banwen. One weekend when Geraint was at home he received a letter from the professor, who was in New York, giving him instructions and Geraint showed me the P.S. at the bottom of the letter. 'And I still have not met anyone who as ever heard of Banwen'. The headline in the *News of the World* that Sunday: 'Entire Banwen village rugby team locked up in a West Country jail'. Geraint cut it out and sent to his professor.

Peg drove up to Cardiff twice a month; there were seven students sharing the house and she took enough Welsh cakes and a pie she bought at the Bakery for each of them. Argentina invaded the Falklands and the first we knew of it apparently was a bloke in North Wales. A radio ham sitting in his shed waiting for his missus to call him for dinner picked up a May Day from South Georgia. Whatever else it would do, the Falklands would save Thatcher's bacon.

A few weeks later one of our drivers came dashing into my office.

'Peg asked me to tell you that the *Sheffield*'s been hit! She stopped me to tell me.' When I arrived home Peg was very upset, close to tears, waiting to talk to me.

'David! David Howells – he's on the *Sheffield* and it's been hit and it's the Radar room that's been hit! And that's David's job!' She began to cry.

I caught around her. 'How do you know all this?'

'Well you were there! When Geraint and his friend Eurfyl came back from their hike around Europe we met them on Neath station. And who else was on the station? David! And two of his shipmates and on their tally band it said HMS *Sheffield*!'

I remembered. Geraint and Eufryl looked downright scruffy and shabby, and David and his two shipmates looked as smart as a lick of paint. There was kissing and back-slapping all round. The first time I had met David was on a brilliantly sunny afternoon. There was a knock on the door. I opened it and there was this fresh-faced boy.

'Hello does Geraint Evans live here?'

'Yes. And who are you?'

'I'm David Howells I live in Glyn Neath and I got the tallest tree in Glamorgan growing in my garden.' The sentence came out in a torrent with a big smile.

His uncle used to get tickets for Geraint and David to go to all the international rugby matches at Cardiff. He would sleep over on Friday night and they'd catch the bus to Neath for the Cardiff train. Then the train back to Neath and the bus back home to Maple House. He would sleep over and Peg would drive him back home on Sunday morning.

Peg didn't sleep that night and could not watch the *Sheffield* burning on the television news. A day went by and another driver came dashing into the office all smiles. 'Peg's told me to tell you David is safe!'

Only one family of tinkers still sold tin boilers around the valley. They had a small three hundredweight truck always well kept painted in dark oak household paint. It belonged to the Gypsy Marie's husband. He would offload a dozen or so boilers on to our front lawn, plus Marie, who always seemed to have a baby with her. After Marie had sold her boilers she'd put the baby to sleep on one of the easychairs and have tea with Peg and tell her fortune. When I got home off shift Peg was beaming. 'Marie was right! She told me if I was worried about someone I care about to keep turning their photo around, keep touching it and holding it. I did that! And David was kept safe!'

What had happened was that HMS *Cardiff* was a radar operator short and David was transferred from HMS *Sheffield* on the way to the Falklands.

Geraint gained an honours degree in chemistry and found work with Inmos in their Space-Age looking factory on the outskirts of Newport, manufacturing microchips. Peg helped him find lodging near the factory. He had started courting Jayne Culpan. I knew Jayne's maternal grandfather well; we had worked on the same coalface and I had worked with her mother's brother Derry. At Geraint's graduation ceremony Cardiff city was full. It was a lovely July day. We found a place to park next to the Castle. Peg had hung his gown on a hanger and had bought him a white dress shirt and he was wearing my black bow tie. Dressed in his full regalia Geraint strolled across the city with his mother and Jayne to the

University. Patricia and Owen had brought Noel with them to the ceremony. Geraint dressed his mother in his cap and gown and stood her between himself and Owen to have their picture taken. Peg enjoyed every minute of that day.

I started to suffer eyestrain so the doctor recommended I should do something at work which did not require reading. I was transferred to work on the weighbridge. The weighbridge was electronic; no scales. The vehicle ran over a steel plate and was weighed. The operator scribbled the number of the vehicle on a ticket and the weight then handed it to the driver. A thousand tons a day brought one hundred lorries over the weighbridge in a shift. Each time a driver came in he almost always had a story to tell.

I was enjoying the easygoing life in the weighbridge when Mr Fitzpatrick sent for me. He said he'd like me to come up to the main site office and look after the cost office. It was exacting work, accounting for every penny spent on site each week. From a Monday morning to the end of Sunday nightshift the method used worldwide on Wimpey sites had been devised by a man called George Michael at the end of the First World War, known as 'theoretical costs'. Maesgwyn had a balance sheet that amounted to £100,000 to £150,000 a week.

Margaret Thatcher put a man called Ian MacGregor in charge of the NCB. He had the reputation of being a ruthless operator. He put forward plans that would cause the loss of twenty thousand coal mining jobs. The President of the NUM was Arthur Scargill, in speech and method a seemingly fierce man, honest enough but as a strategist he would be found wanting. Over the next twelve months terrible hardship would be brought on to the mining communities of

Great Britain. Strikers were never paid welfare benefits but the women and children had always been allowed to claim; Thatcher stopped that. She called the mining community 'the enemy within'. It was an outrageous thing to say considering the massive contribution the mining families had made to the wellbeing of our country in wealth and in its defence, South Wales alone at one time producing fifty-eight million tons of coal a year, in war providing some of the finest infantry regiments in the world to shed their blood on the battlefields of the Somme and across the world to Burma. The same woman had no qualms about losing a quarter of the British Navy in the defence of the Falklands. A community whose contribution to the democracy we enjoy in Britain according to her wasn't worth half a cup full of piss. Some Yorkshire villages had a heavier police presence during the strike than French villages had during the Nazi occupation. One Yorkshire miner, who had never been in trouble in his life, was beaten so badly it left him an epileptic. A veteran councillor from the Rhondda summed up Thatcher's patriotism after hearing her on the radio saying, 'during the war we always had Spam for tea on Monday'. The old councillor and grandmother said, 'No family of four would have enough points to have Spam every Monday. But then her father was a grocer. They must have been eating some other poor devil's food.'

The magnificent effort put in by the women's support groups throughout Britain, to stop Thatcher and MacGregor literally starving the men, women and children of Britain's coal-mining communities into submission, will be a lasting testimony to their courage and integrity, and will have a far-reaching effect on the lives of the communities in the future.

17

The garden looked good. Peg had just bought me a new Flymo. She had spread a shawl on the grass and had brought out two cups of coffee.

'Come and sit, I've got something to show you.' I sat down next to her. 'Look at this. Feel it.' She lifted her arm and held her thumb on a spot under her armpit.

I felt it. I could feel a lump. Before the days of antibiotics one way of telling if a wound had turned septic was to feel for a lump under the armpit.

'Best see the doctor! Better than worrying. Perhaps for nothing?'

She saw old doctor Morgan. 'Muscular spasm Peg.' Peg came home happy and relieved.

Peg very rarely went to the surgery but a month or two later she had to go again. This time she saw Dr Khan and came home looking frightened.

'Dr Khan wants to see you, George. And he's in the Coelbren surgery.'

I drove over to the surgery feeling uneasy and anxious. I suppose it was because I had never seen Peg frightened before.

'Dr Morgan told her it was a muscular spasm?'

'George, Peg is a very strong-willed woman. She'd convinced herself there was nothing wrong with her. And very likely convinced old Dr Morgan too.'

I knew what Dr Khan was talking about. She was always first up in the morning and last to bed every night. Never missed a day's work except the week when Owen was born and just one day when Geraint was born.

I wish she had listened to Dr Roseian Davies. Dr Roseian used to call on a Sunday for snippets of news for the Welsh-language paper and had come into Maple House when Peg was stretching herself off the stair rails. She would reach up as far as she could, holding on to the stair rails, standing on tip toe and stay there as long as she could bear it.

'What are you doing Peg?'

'I got this pain in the bottom of my back and this is the only way I can ease it.'

'Peg you really want to go for a thorough checking up.'

'I've been and had an X-ray, everything.'

'No! I mean go privately, from head to toe, Peg!'

Friday the 13th July 1984: Peg had an appointment with a Mr Williams, the consultant at Neath General Hospital. Peg was put on Tamoxifen and while she was getting dressed the Sister told me Mr Williams wanted to talk to me.

'I have not got good news for you Mr Evans. The cancer is well-established. Mrs Evans I am afraid will not get better.

The treatment will make life easier for her. I'm sorry Mr Evans.' He held out his hand. I told Peg I had to go to the dispensary for her tablets.

'Ask them will I be able to drink Guinness when I'm taking them.' Peg drank a bottle of Guinness every night. I did ask and they said yes.

We got back home and I told Peg I'd have to pop to the office for a while just to tidy up. Ron MacNeil was waiting to hear what had happened. I told him it could not be worse. I was filing some of my work and my telephone rang. It was Elton Morgan the director. He asked me to come to his office.

'MacNeil has told me about Peggy, George. I can't tell you how sorry I am. You take all the time off you need.'

'Thank you Mr Morgan.'

Peg put her Newsagent's business up for sale on the Monday and by the Friday it was sold to an accountant from Caerphilly. He split the business in two and he sold the top half as we called it – Onllwyn, Dyffryn Cellwen and Banwen – to David Pasco. The following Monday Peg suddenly remembered: 'The billiard hall till!' When my father had sold the billiard hall and the land to the Co-op he had had David my brother to take the till in his car to Peg's shop; it was too heavy to carry. It was a very ornate, very attractive brass and copper-fronted contraption usually seen in Italian shops in the valleys. Griff Morgan had bought it very likely in the twenties or thirties. I called in the shop: it was gone. The lad from Caerphilly had a keen eye.

Ever since I can remember I've seemed sometimes to be able to separate myself from what is going on around me. It manifests itself in how I react very often to the simplest things.

I don't like handling money so most of the time I never count my change. I'm a first-rate snob in as much as I can't stand anybody criticizing my work; I will go to any length to get it right, taking work home and working for hours on it or going without meals to finish one of my own paintings. That was the way I was trying to handle Peg's illness. I hadn't told her what the consultant had told me nor had I told the boys. This idea that people should be told the truth no matter what I have always thought is a load of bollocks. We all know we're going to die so why make a song and dance about it.

Peg and I never ever spoke about the meaning of life, or why we were here in the first place. We lightly touched on it sometimes. I remember her saying once that someone in the shop had told her, 'You and George have done well for yourselves!'

'What do you think George? I think we've just been scrambled from one day to the next! Don't you?'

'Yes.' We were here and that was an end to it and we tried never ever to make plans.

For the first time in her life she had time to watch television. Music had always been an important part of her enjoyment. She would hear a tune once or twice then she would be able to play it on her piano. The part she liked in the theme tune of *Eastenders* was when whoever it was started whistling: I had never noticed anybody whistling.

Geraint and Jayne were married in Onllwyn Chapel and they bought a new house in Heritage Place St Mellons, a nice brand-new, one-bedroom house. Jayne had been transferred from the DVLA to the Welsh Office and was pregnant. They had good friends at church in St Mellons where Geraint was the church registrar.

Peg's radiation therapy began at Singleton Hospital, Swansea. The radiation burns were very painful and looked awful. Pat Bowden drove her down each day. Owen and Geraint called to see her as often as they were able. The hospital was very pleased with the way she was reacting to the Tamoxifen; it was still a new treatment. Radiation therapy over, Peg was back on form, cleaning the house, washing and ironing, and every day when I got home the field gate was open, the garden gate was open and the garage doors open, and my dinner on the table, and she was back driving.

A new man moved in to the next office to mine: D.I. Williams, retired head geologist of the NCB, in his sixties and according to him had picked up £60,000 in redundancy pay. Here he was with a new Wimpey car and all the perks. It didn't go down well with some of the Wimpey old-timers. 'What the hell do we want a geologist for?' was their main crib. A geological survey had been carried out on this part of the coalfield in 1881 and it was as near as dammit spot on. Plus he never came into work before breakfast time. The girls had to take him a full breakfast on a tray to his office every morning.

Reclamation was starting on Maesmarchog. It was a spectacular sight to see: the huge earth-levelling machines travelling, one behind the other, making a giant figure of eight. These were based on the design of an ordinary carpenter's wood plane. Where the ground was proud the massive blade planed it into a box that was capable of holding fifty ton and where the ground was shy it allowed soil out. Maesmarchog site office was closing and the staff moved up to share the main office with us. Joyce Jones saw an advert in the paper wanting coal miners in South Africa. She wrote to the mining company for her partner, David, and he got the job. She wanted me to come to her farewell party. I couldn't; I wouldn't go without Peg.

Anne Brown the telephonist rang me. 'Peg's left a message, George. They have taken Jayne into University Hospital Cardiff and Peg is asking will you come home.' It was bitterly cold and we caught the train to Cardiff then a taxi to the Hospital. We eventually found the maternity ward. Geraint was already there, and so were Jayne's parents, Peter and Val.

We travelled home with Peter and Val. Peg said to me, 'I feel a bit guilty. I've been wishing for a girl and perhaps Val and Peter wanted a boy.'

Emily arrived on her first visit to Maple House, and Pastor John Mansfield, a friend of Jayne and Geraint's, held a small service to bless her.

Peg seemed to be gaining ground by the day. The Royal Welsh Show was a must. Peg drove us to Builth Wells. Owen had been transferred to Hereford and he, Patricia and Noel were living in a flat rented off Mr Roberts the City Engineer, whilst their new house was being built. Noel had started to talk and called Mr Roberts just Roberts and Mr Roberts called him just Evans.

The weather was at its best at autumn time in the South Wales valleys. The sky clear, you felt you could reach out your hand and touch the tops of the mountains, leaves turned from green to yellow, from yellow to red-gold then to dark brown, and the purple heather hugged the ground. Peg wanted to drive to Tal y bont and walk along the canal. Marie and Dilwyn came with us. Peg did all the driving. We stopped at Bishops Meadow for an evening meal. Marie and Peg walked arm in arm back to the car. Marie was delighted; she really felt her little sister was getting better.

The anti-smoking campaign was underway and Mr Elton Morgan was its leading champion in our office. I was smoking about twenty a day but very often the cigarette would be burning in the ashtray. Elton Morgan would walk into my office.

'Good gracious me George! How can you stick it in here?'

One Saturday there was an accident in the cut. Elton Morgan was in work; he never came in on a Saturday. I could hear him talking to Ron MacNeil in the corridor. 'George in work, Ron?'

'Yes Mr Morgan and by the way he's stopped smoking, Mr Morgan!'

I hadn't stopped smoking. MacNeil was trying to drop me in it. Right, I thought, I will stop smoking, and I did. It was effortless. If I'd known how easy it was I could have stopped ages before and saved a fortune. I started smoking when I was about eleven years of age, on the sly, but on the day I started work my Tommy box was on the kitchen table and a packet of five Woodbine cigarettes on top of it. People had thought that in some instances smoking helped, in times of stress for instance. The American government took over the tobacco company Passing Clouds and issued free cigarettes to American servicemen all over the world during WW2. Captain Belton had entered me in a diving competition diving for A section in a swimming gala. I won and the prize was a couple of hundred Woodbine cigarettes. It was my fault that Peg smoked. We'd be watching TV and I would light two cigarettes. 'George!' Peg would protest but she'd smoke the cigarette.

One day Anne Brown came to tell me Peggy was on the phone.

'George, the hospital has been on the phone. They want me to come in and bring my things with me?'

'Don't worry. Expect there are some tests they want to do. I'll come home now.'

I telephoned Pat Bowden at her farm and she arrived at the same time I did.

'I want to go shopping first Pat. I want to go to Debenhams!' said Peg.

'You say what you want to do and we'll do it!' laughed Pat.

Peg bought herself a new bed-jacket and other bits and pieces then we went for a meal. They hadn't said why they wanted Peg back in hospital; she looked really well and was getting around her housework with ease.

After Peg was settled into her ward Pat drove me home and I telephoned the boys. They wanted to know had she become worse. 'No, as far as I can see she looks great.' Jayne and Geraint brought Emily down to see her but Emily was not allowed into the ward because of the risk from radiation. Peg got out of bed and spent the visiting hour in the foyer nursing Emily. They could not get over how well Peg looked but Peg had her hair done every time a hairdresser came anywhere near the ward. It was a fetish she had had all her life. her hair was her pride and joy. Owen and Patricia

214

and Noel came down from Hereford and they too had the same impression, that if anything Peg looked better. Jayne said after the second or third visit: 'Do you think Peggy's tummy is swelling?' The following day they put a drain into Peg's stomach that fed into a plastic container. Peg called it her petrol can. At visiting times she still came out to the foyer to nurse Emily.

Peg had been in hospital twenty-one days. The telephone rang. It was seven o'clock in the morning. It was the ward sister. 'George you had best come down right away!' I telephoned Pat Bowden and Peg's sister Marie. Marie told Dilwyn when he came into the room, still in his pyjamas. He flopped down on the couch horrified. Dilwyn couldn't believe what he was hearing. He was a ginger with a temper, but the one person he never ever fell out with was Peg. He had no brothers or sisters and whenever he went away he always brought a present for Peg: she was the closest he had to having a sister.

They had moved Peg into a room on her own; she was on a drip and awake. She looked at Marie. 'Who's with Dilwyn?'

'Dilwyn is alright, its you I'm worried about!'

'I'm ok. You go back and look after Dilwyn. Take her home Pat, please.'

'I will in a bit.'

Marie had turned seventy and Peg was genuinely concerned for her.

The sister came in and told me the consultant wanted to speak to me.

'Hello Mr Evans.' He offered his hand. 'I'm afraid the end is near. We will move Mrs Evans to Tŷ Olwen this afternoon. I'm very sorry!'

215

'Thank you all very much for all that you've done for Peg.' I shook his hand.

Marie was waiting outside the consultant's door. I told Marie what the consultant had said. 'So just as well do what Peg said and you go home to Dilwyn.'

I sat at the side of the bed, the end of my tie folded on the bed. Peg wrapped it around her hand.

'Shall I tell the boys?'

'No!' Her eyes were closed. 'No you stay by there.' And gently tugged my tie. And that's how we sat, not saying a word.

She was doing what my mother had done: found a way of getting Owen and me out of the room when she knew she was dying. Peg didn't want her two boys Owen and Geraint to see her die. I sat holding her hand and she had hold of my tie. Her eyes were only half open most of the time. She didn't look worn and haggard; her cheeks were still pink and her hair still shining. The sister popped in from time to time to check the drip and take Peg's pulse. Pat Bowden returned in the late afternoon and sat on the other side of the bed.

'What about the boys?'

'Peg said no!'

Then there came a kind of purring noise from Peg's throat. Pat went to fetch the sister.

I was half standing. Peg still had hold of my tie.

The purring stopped.

The sister put the tips of her fingers against Peg's throat.

'Peg has gone, George.'

I bent and kissed her.

Pat Bowden had phoned Clem her brother-in-law and he had told Val and Peter and they had phoned Geraint and Jayne and Geraint had phoned Owen.

Pat Bowden drove me home. Maple House felt empty although Owen, Geraint, Jayne, Marie, Dilwyn and Pat were there. No one had anything to say because there was nothing to say. Pat offered to make some tea but no one wanted it. They all left for home except Owen. He stayed the night.

That was my blackest moment of despair: realizing that I would never hear Peggy's voice again, that I would never ever speak to her again. Never ever again would she squeeze my hand each night before going to sleep and say 'Goodnight George', never darling or any other name, always just George.

Peg and I never made plans. On one Saturday before Palm Sunday we were attending the family graves in Onllwyn cemetery. It was bitterly cold. We could barely feel our fingers.

'We won't give the boys this awful job after us! We'll be cremated!' Peg was emphatic. Her funeral took place at Margam Crematorium; her former paperboys, now very large young men, her bearers. Patricia was heavily pregnant; Jamie was born on the 23rd December, eleven days after his grandmother died. Carol and Pat Bowden took the £373 donated in lieu of flowers to ward six at Singleton Hospital.

I went back to work grudgingly, but after a time realized what a blessing it was. I found the house without Peg felt like a prison cell. Having no one to laugh with at a joke on television. No one sitting opposite you at meal times and no one to whisper goodnight to in bed. You felt you no longer belonged to the same tribe. You were an outsider.

Because of the nature of my work, doing sums of one kind and another all day demanded my full attention. It was a very cold January. The cold killed most of the Welsh Black honeybees and Peg's wallflowers and, I heard on the television, put paid to Sir Leslie Joseph's famous wallflower garden in Porthcawl.

Something else happened, something that I had read happened to other people but never ever thought it would happen to me. I had had a telephone extension put upstairs when Peg had become ill on the landing windowsill. It was January, two o'clock in the morning and the telephone rang. I got out of bed; it was bitterly cold; worried in case there was something wrong with one of the children.

'Hello?'

'I need screwing right now!' It was a young woman's voice.

I put the phone down and went back to bed and racked my brain trying to work out who the hell could it be? Who the bloody hell was it? This went on for about two weeks, not every night, and the calls became more obscene. On one occasion I stupidly asked her name. I never mentioned receiving the calls to anyone, but years later I found out that other bereaved husbands and wives had been subjected to the same weird behaviour.

18

Redundancies were happening everywhere, pits and factories being closed. One of the NCB lads, a coal inspector on site, was made redundant and had more than £20,000, so they said, in redundancy payment. One of our lads was made redundant; he got £3,800 and he had been driving the 38 front loader and must have filled more coal than anybody in Wales, nine hundred to a thousand tons a shift. Never missing a shift, 100% reliable. The coal inspector had had a shed on site with a table, chair, fire and dartboard and would when he felt like pop to town shopping in a NCB Land Rover. I wrote to the *Western Mail*, not mentioning the NCB man's name, and they published my letter much to the annoyance of my neighbour D.I. He slammed the *Western Mail* on my desk.

'This demeans your argument George! The reference to the NCB bloke having been paid £20,000 in redundancy.'

'The only one being demeaned D.I. is the driver of the 38,' I retorted.

I wrote to Mr Donald Coleman, our local MP, and as usual had a prompt and sympathetic reply. The problem he thought was that the opencast miners at the time of the negotiations for the setting up of the European Coal and Steel Community had little or no trade union involvement.

I knew a friend of mine, Freddy Creswell, who had written applying for membership of the NUM whilst employed as an opencast miner and had been turned down. And the irony of it was that each and every opencast worker paid into the European Coal and Steel Community. Everyone from the canteen women to the site managers: a contribution was made every month for each of them, based on output that was outstanding, turning in profits of millions of pounds, and attendance, which was an outstanding record of 98%. I knew that because I filled in the forms every month.

In 1957 the collieries of the Dulais Valley made a loss of £9m. Under normal economic rules the collieries would have been forced to close and the workforce would have been entitled to fourteen days' notice with pay and that would have been all and I would have been one of them. The huge profits made at Maesgwyn opencast coal site and the Central Washer saved us in the deep mines of the Dulais Valley from that fate.

There were many who saw the injustice that was being done to the opencast miners. I even received a telephone call at work from a Mrs Eileen Fawcett at the European Social Fund in London, who said she agreed wholeheartedly with me that the opencast workers were being treated most unfairly.

The important points everyone seemed to be missing was that the opencast workers' place of work was inspected by HM Inspector of Mines; a point missed by a BBC industrial correspondent, a pretty brunette who dismissed the opencast miners' claim with a curt: 'These men are not working down a mine!'

Another unfair result was that opencast engineers' and managers' redundancy pay would be based on 30 weeks at £164 = £4920, after bringing in massive profits, year after year. Meanwhile British Coal managers and officials who very likely had never turned in a penny profit in their entire careers walked off with a barrow full of money, in some cases equivalent to winning the football pools.

There was a message on my answering machine when I got home; it was Dianne, my brother David's only daughter, telling me that her Dad was in hospital having suffered a heart attack. Des and I went to the hospital. We took his eldest grandson Ceri with us. David was sixty-three years of age but still well-built and looked ten years younger. He was in a bad way, attached to wires and monitors and an oxygen mask on his face. He was struggling. Des and I kept having to put the bedclothes back over him. He was naked. Ceri was upset seeing his grandfather so vulnerable and exposed but no one came to help. A nurse was bent over talking to her friend, her arse stuck up in the air and kept glancing back at us but carried on gabbing and never offered to help. Len Heath his old school mate was in the bed opposite and he told me later they didn't even take David to the intensive care unit.

David died two days later. He left his family well provided

for but at his funeral Joan his wife would not pay for an order of service. The vicar upset Dianne by referring to David as Mr Thomas. David's name was David John Thomas Evans and seeing as David had made sure the church had had a plentiful supply of coal during the miners' strike Dianne thought the vicar should have remembered her father's name, if only out of good manners.

At work, Joyce had moved to South Africa. There were two Annes working there: Anne Brown the petite blonde and Anne James the petite brunette, whose sister Ruth was at university with Geraint. Anne Brown was a bit of a rascal. Once, the senior director Mr Frank Rose had gone out on site without telling her. The rule was you let the switchboard know if you went out. Mr Rose came in and passed the switchboard.

'Mr Rose you are supposed to let me know when you're leaving the office!' Anne dished out a severe reprimand. Anne in her stockinged feet was about five foot two inches tall, Mr Rose about six one. Mr Rose went out again in the afternoon and put his head through the hatch.

'Anne I'm going out on site again Anne! And in my Land Rover!' Giving as good as he got, he thought.

'I didn't think you'd be going out on your bloody horse, Mr Rose!' Anne always had the last word.

She was also an accomplished artist producing beautiful images of Welsh castles in ink on to large limestone pebbles she picked off the beach. Hetty Pritchard, now a Gwillym, Peg's old school friend, was made canteen manager. She made the best bread and butter pudding in Wales. The lads would come into the canteen and shout 'What's for sweet Het?'

'Bread and butter pudding!'

'We've had bread and butter pudding once this week already!'

'Well George wanted bread and butter pudding! So there!'

As was always the case Ron was first out of the office at finishing time and always poking his head around the door of my office. 'Come on then! Don't you want to go home!'

At seven that evening the telephone rang; I thought it was Owen or Geraint. 'Hello?'

A voice said, 'Stores here. MacNeil is dead. Dropped dead in the house!'

'Hello?' But whoever it was, was gone.

What a bloody stupid way to pass on such a message. I never did find out who it was. Old Ron could be quite abrasive and this twat must have thought he'd found a way of getting back at him.

The following morning in work Roy Morgan the nightshift agent was there.

'George you knew Norma better than any of us. Will you come down to the house with me?'

Norma told us that Ron had been sat on the settee and had called her to come and watch the wedding on Coronation Street. 'I sat down with him. He coughed! I looked at him and I knew that he was dead, George!' Norma was still numb with shock.

Roy took some details and told Norma if there was anything she needed just to ring him. It knocked the stuffing out of everybody. Ron and I had worked together for the best part of ten years. He was an ace at his job, the most numerate person I had ever met.

One Thursday, walking back from Mr Morgan's office, he asked me: 'That tip George,' pointing to Banwen colliery tip. 'Is there much coal in that?'

The farmer and a coal recovery firm DSF had a barrel wash on site and were trying to reclaim coal from the slagheap.

'I wouldn't think so. All that was filled out as muck. Now those!' I pointed to the massive aerial tips that had dominated the village since 1932. 'All that was filled out as coal and if for instance a piece of coal the size of your thumbnail had just a sliver of shale on it, the washer would turn it out. That's where the coal is!'

'Can you find out who owns the tips George?'

'I'll try and find out this weekend!'

That weekend was the YMCA carnival weekend. This was one of the highlights of Peg's year. She was a founder member of the Pinafore Club, the group that raised money to keep the YMCA going. Every year the squad she belonged to dressed as Dad's Army, Chelsea Pensioners or whatever. They would dress in our house, chicken in a basket from the Pant and a few bottles of wine and they'd be away. I hadn't intended to go to the carnival now that Peg would not be there. I did go and met Councillor Moira Lewis.

'The aerial tips Moira who do they belong to?'

'To us George!'

I told her about the conversation I had with Elton Morgan. On the Monday I told Elton Morgan that the tips belonged to the council. Within a few weeks Wimpey Laboratories were on site taking samples.

Mr Elton Morgan asked me would I like to be transferred to Ffos Las site to work.

'Well I'm sixty-four, Mr Morgan. Thanks all the same but it's a bit of a long way to travel. Especially in the winter!'

'I'll get in touch with Hammersmith and let them know. They'll sort something out for you. Is there anything you want George in particular?'

'Well if I could have an English version of that training film you had made for those Chinese engineers?'

I had seen the film when Mr Morgan popped his head into my office and asked me would I go to the canteen and keep our visitors company. There were about a dozen Chinese young people, men and women, all trainee mining engineers. The film was for their benefit. I stayed and watched it with them. It was made by Wimpey World Wide Films on site at Maesgwyn and I thought what a wonderful historical document it was.

'I'll let Nottingham know, George! They will let us have a copy I'm sure.'

The personnel officer came down from Hammersmith. I was pleasantly surprised by the retirement settlement they had worked out for me; after all, I had only worked ten years for what was now Wimpey Mining.

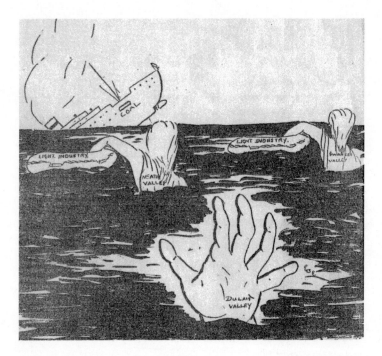

BOOK THREE

19

Doug Millar called to see me. He was a retired head teacher and long-time friend and we were both founder members of Cwmdulais Historical Society. He had come to persuade me to join a course on writing at the DOVE (Dulais Opportunity for Voluntary Enterprise), an organization formed by the wives and daughters of striking miners. It was based in a building that had belonged to the Opencast Executive. A bare austere building, the only concession to creature comforts a kettle for making tea and central heating. In front of the DOVE a large coal-washing unit working twenty-four hours a day. Locos, shunting trains of coal wagons, from early morning until late at night: an unlikely place for scholarly pursuits.

'The tutor is a top man George, Alun Richards.' Doug persuaded me. I had heard of Alun Richards and read one of his short stories, 'The Former Miss Merthyr Tydfil'.

There were people in the class from as far away as Port Talbot and Sketty, very interesting people like the writer Barbara May Walters and her husband David, one-time sailor, coal-miner and a talented musician, so much so he had played in the band at the Savoy Hotel in London. Alun Thomas, former manager of the British and Irish Lions and his wife Margaret, daughter of a very well known Swansea family who manufactured industrial clothing; Angela Ifold who had won the gold medal at the miners' Eisteddfod at Porthcawl for prose writing and was the widow of the well-known artist Cyril Ifold. Or just listening to Doug Millar who'd been a Captain in the 19th Welch, nonchalantly telling of an experience on a beachhead in Italy. There had been a bit of a lull in the fighting so they brought some mail ashore. He had two letters, one off his mother and the other off Glamorgan County Council, informing him that if he didn't start repaying the loan he had received to go to Teacher Training promptly, it would go against him when he started looking for work in the county. The following day he was ordered to take a patrol out. They hadn't gone half a mile when a sniper shot and broke his leg. There was no going home if you were wounded then; they patched him up and the Colonel told him, 'You can ride in the armoured car Millar!'

The first impression you got of Alun Richards was that there was a lot of him and that he was a happy sort of bloke. 'Nitpickers I can't stand.' It could have been tattooed on his forehead. A session lasted from about half nine until lunchtime with a tea break at eleven. The first session we talked about Somerset Maugham, a writer who wrote I thought with genuine human sympathy, the same compassionate concern that Dr Aubrey Thomas showed to his fellow humans. He could be witness to the most brutal act of cruelty and write about it without becoming hysterical. His description of the execution in 1930 of a Chinese boy, of how the boy kneels in a puddle of water and the executioner asks him to step forward to a drier place and the lad obediently does. A bullet in the back of the head. Suddenly the group of witnesses – a judge, a journalist and the vice-consul – smile at one another, say goodbyes. Repair to the club and someone asks: 'Everything go alright?'. 'Yes, he wriggled a bit!'

A week or two earlier, the Neath branch of the Burma Star had agreed to write and ask for an amnesty for the young men shot by firing squad in the First World War and to allow their names to be placed on the war memorials. The German Army executed 48 men in the entire war. The British Army and the French Army together executed 18 men a month, in all 946 men. Not one officer, not one from a public school; if one of theirs broke down he was whisked off to hospital. That dreadful attitude fostered in the public schools of our country, to treat the lower orders like shit, still prevailed in the British concession of Shanghai into the 1930s, as Somerset Maugham had witnessed.

After the third session I knew I had made the right decision listening to Doug Millar. It was opening the door to a world that I had been skirting around the fringes of for most of my life but my life had been so full. Working at times, between trying to help run a clutch of businesses – the fish and chip shop, the ice cream round, helping my father with the billiard hall and Peg with her newsagent – and holding down a full-time job meant working sometimes a full 24 hours without going to bed.

Alun Richards was four years younger than me and rode a very large motorbike to work. He called me aside: 'Why didn't you tell me you had a story published?'

'Just one story and that was ten years ago now!'

'But in *The Anglo-Welsh Review*, George! The top magazine! I'd like to give it to the group to read if it's OK with you?'

'I don't know if I could sit there and listen to my work being pulled to pieces.'

'I won't tell them whose work it is!'

Alun Richards had ten photocopies of 'Boys of Gold' made and distributed them among my classmates. The following week dragged and yet I didn't want the day of judgment to come. I said a nervous good morning to everyone. No one except Doug knew it was my work. Alun came into the class and sat down. 'Good morning everybody! And how did the story I gave you go? Did you like it?'

'We spent the weekend in Hay-on-Wye, most of my time looking for a back number of *The Anglo Welsh Review*.' Alun Thomas smiled at his wife Margaret. 'She was sitting on the bed crying as she read it.'

'One thing, the word *'sbaddu* is wrong, it should be *disbaddu!*' put in Doug. I had used the abbreviated Welsh word that working people and boys used for castrate, but then Doug was an ex-head teacher and I suppose felt bound to pull me up. Doug's family and mine had worked together as shepherds for generations and had come into mining at the same time and there were marriage ties too, so we were as thick as thieves and we enjoyed the latitude that gave us.

Ron Williams and I started evening classes in geology at the DOVE, and the man we had as our tutor was none other than Professor Richard Owen, the top geologist of his day. There was no more satisfying way of passing an evening away than listening to that brilliant scholar explaining how the very fabric of the world was put together. Most of the class were ex-miners and together we had spent our time taking that fabric apart. Jeff Jeffries Camnant started work underground at 14 years of age, Lesley Jones likewise except he had done five years in the army in WW2 and had lost two brothers, Wynford at nineteen and Will in his forties, killed in the Grey's district of Banwen colliery.

Ron and I enlisted in the astronomy class as well. Our tutors were the men who had built the twenty-inch telescope at Swansea and it was then, in my late sixties, that I found out where the planet Mars was in the night sky. One of the tutors took us outside the DOVE. It was pitch dark: he shone an ordinary torch up into the star-filled sky.

'Now look along the beam!' and there it was, not silvery like the rest, just a slight, slight touch of orange.

At one session with Alun Richards they discussed Bert Coombes's work and Doug Millar told the class that I had been a good friend of Bert's.

'Were you George?' Alun asked.

'Yes! I knew him from the time I came out of the army until he died.'

'People have been wondering at the university where his work is and if they could get to see it?' Alun said.

'Well his grandson Viv Davies lives at his grandfather's farm now. Would you like me to ask him?'

'If you would please George!'

I drove over to the farm, Nantyfedwen. I hadn't been there since driving Bert home after his shopping trips to

Banwen on a Saturday. Viv agreed to get everything down from the attic. The following week I drove Alun over to the farm and he was pleased and surprised how close the farm was to the site of the Caer, the Roman Fort. He had read about the Fort and now he could see the commanding position it held, with its three hundred and eight infantrymen and one hundred and twenty cavalrymen.

Viv and Val had worked hard; there was a very large stack of papers, manuscripts and books that had not been touched since before Bert had died in 1974. Alun explained that although he was taking the papers to the university they would still be Viv's property. They were taken to the library at University of Wales Swansea to be catalogued. Later we were invited out to a meal with Alun Richards and Professor Hywel Francis as a thank you.

With Dust Still in his Throat, an anthology of writing by B. L. Coombes, was published by the University of Wales Press in 1999, edited by Bill Jones and Chris Williams. Reading Professor Chris Williams's work gave me a better understanding of the way Bert saw the world, of why Doctor Dafydd Aubrey Thomas had said Bert belonged to the 'tidy left', after the hardships his family must have faced as shopkeepers and why he always had a sympathetic ear for Peg when she complained about being owed money by bad paying customers. 'Bad payers Peg are really thieves by nature!'

The dig was starting on the oldest tips that had towered over that end of the village since 1932, right next to Miss Bryan, the school headmistress's house. Moira Lewis now the Mayor of Neath was sat in the cab of a brand new

Wimpey JCB. Newspaper reporters and TV cameras at the ready, Elton Morgan was there and other dignitaries waiting for the Mayor to take the first shovelful of the tens of millions of tons of the aerial tips to be removed from the landscape they had dominated for generations. The tips where during the Second World War the Home Guard practised their shooting skills. The bullets went through the targets and buried themselves in the soft culm.

Alun Richards gave me a copy of *Cambrensis*, a magazine of short stories, edited by Arthur Smith. 'Have a go at writing something for this bloke George. He's a bit of a stickler mind.'

I wrote a short story, 'The Man Who Stayed a Miner'. The principal character in the story was Bert Lewis Coombes and of my memories of him. Arthur Smith published it in issue no. 27. The cover of the magazine was coloured green and brilliantly illustrated by Dewi Bowen with the head of St Tydfil.

At our next session of lessons we had a new tutor, Neal Mason. Neal was then the resident writer for Neath Council and was a Peterloo Poet (Poetry Publishers). His knowledge of the poets was immeasurable, making me wish that I was half as disciplined as he in seeking out the whys and the wherefores. There was a very beautiful young lady attending our class too and one morning Norman Burns handed me back the LP tapes of *Under Milk Wood* that I had loaned him.

'You've got that?' inquired our beautiful classmate.

'Yes you can borrow and copy it if you want to!'

She laughed. 'I'm in it!'

Indeed she was; she was Carole Morgan-Hopkin, Gossamer Beynon no less, and sister to Mary Hopkin the world-famous singer: and, as the conversation went on, related to Peg's Aunty Viv the Blue Riband singer, daughter of Peg's stepgrandfather, the choirmaster William Bowen. Music surely did run in the family.

Neil had the article I had written on Banwen being St Patrick's birthplace published in a locally produced magazine, *Black and White*. My maternal grandfather Thomas Williams farmed the smallholding of Tafarn y Banwen that according to legend was the birthplace of St Patrick. I had written a letter to the *Daily Mirror* claiming this and much to my surprise had a thank you letter from the Archbishop and Primate The Most Rev Illtyd Thomas DPM of the Celtic Catholic Church thanking me for keeping interest in our beloved Celtic Saints alive.

The persistence of the legend is perhaps due to the place names here about: Ton-y-castell, the land of the fortress, Ton-y-fildre, the place or town of the soldiers, Waunmarchog, a moor or field where soldiers would turn their horses out to graze. For every six Roman soldiers there would be one pack horse plus the cavalry horses. The large military presence was due to the fact that iron was mined here; all metal mining came under strict military control in Roman times.

The place would have acted like a magnet to the Iron Age Celts and the marauding Irish in search of La Tene craftsmen. Looking east Craig-y-llyn not three miles away as the crow flies at the foot of which is Llyn Fawr where the 600 BC Iron Age Hallstatt sword was found.

Also as the result of the letter to the *Daily Mirror* I received a letter from a Mr Iolo Lewis, Welwyn Garden City, telling me he had gone to school at our village school and went on to name his school friends but the one he was most concerned about was Vernon Edwards. Iolo wanted to know if I knew where Vernon was buried. He'd addressed the letter to Mr George Evans; obviously he'd not worked out who I was.

I telephoned him. 'Iolo Lewis?'

'Mr Evans?'

'Don't call me Mr Evans, Iolo. My father used to have the fish and chip shop next to London House!'

For a moment there was silence. 'George! I can't believe this! It must be fifty years since I last spoke to you.'

'And more,' I reminded him. I was the same age as his younger brother Calvin. Iolo had been back to France on the anniversary of D-Day to look for Vernon's grave but couldn't find it. I told him that Vernon's family were long dead. Vernon's mother died shortly after Vernon was killed. He was her only child. She had given up her career to marry. Female schoolteachers were not allowed to marry in those days. Vernon was not only a good boxer but good at just about everything; at school, *Cymanfa Ganu*'s he always walked away with at least one prize. The conclusion people in the village came to was that Vernon's mother died of a broken heart.

I read an advertisement in a local paper by a Tracey Walton of Peterborough asking writers to submit short stories for an anthology that would be called 'Shorts from Glamorgan'. I wrote the story 'Icons'. I wanted to write a story in which I could say how dear and precious Peggy had been to me and that I understood that even men, like the Japanese prisoners we had on our boat 373, who just a few weeks

237

earlier would have quite happily put a bullet in my head, had, I was sure shared the same yearning and carried an image in the front of their brain, in their forehead, an icon of someone loved and adored by them as I did. It was accepted and published and so was a story from a young lady who lived in Cwmgwrach, 'Seasons Greetings', by Claire Roberts, a young lady who ten years from then would become a very dear friend.

In the meantime Peter Weavers, Regional Manager, British Coal, South Wales Region, called to see me on a Saturday afternoon.

'George sorry to disturb you on a Saturday! And I know you are retired. But I've come to ask for your help. We're going to start restoring Maesgwyn site. And I'm hoping you will help me.'

Maesgwyn was vast, the largest opencast site in Europe, covering the whole of the mountain between Banwen and Glyn Neath. There were 28 miles of road on site.

'What I'm hoping to do George is create a huge nature reserve that will serve the people of Neath, Swansea and Aberdare and the people of the valleys as well, with the DOVE as the learning centre.'

'Brilliant! I'll be more than happy to help!'

I walked with him down to the gate, we shook hands, and I thought what a change this young Englishman had brought to the job from the arrogant old twats that had been in charge. There was one, a Welshman, sat in his office in Aberdare far enough away from the noise. When D8s, with no silencers, worked within two hundred yards of the village 24 hours a day, he called the people of the village a bunch of bolshie moaners. One of the so-called moaners a young mother in tremendous pain dying of cancer.

I had heard Tom Marston often talk about the standing stone known as *Maen Dau Lygad yr Ych*, 'the stone of the Ox's two eyes', the Roman burial post and the ninth century Hirfynydd Slab: a fragmentary slab with a standing male figure carved in low relief with a girdle and plaited tunic, holding up the arms in prayer. The oldest Christian monument found in the Neath area. I thought if I could have replicas made and placed at Clwydi Banwen they could be one of the focal points of the reserve.

I asked to see someone at Swansea City Museum. The interview did not go well; I got the feeling that they thought I was an ex-miner getting above myself. When I suggested that perhaps we could make a mould of the stones, that was turned down flat. A week later I received a letter from the museum, the tone of which was unhelpful. I wrote to Professor Hywel Francis at Swansea University and thankfully he agreed to help and roped in help from other influential people.

Then out of the blue I received a letter from a young lady called Bobbie Williams, down from Reading, inviting me to the Museum for a meeting. Present were Igor Cusack, Projects Leader British Coal, the sculptor Terry Briers, Carmarthen College of Technology and Art, and Roberta Williams, City of Swansea Museum. This Ms Bobby Williams was a female Bill Unthank but a thousand times prettier mind and I'm sure Bill will forgive me for saying that. She was a natural organizer and go-getter. A meeting took place at Clwydi Banwen, the Banwen Gate on the Roman Road right on top of Mynydd Cefn Hir, the Long-Backed Mountain, where the replicas would be placed. Terry Briers brought with him a minibus full of his students to help choose the stones to be sculpted. The stones were then taken to Terry's studio at St Clears.

Once the replicas of the Hirfynydd Slab and the Roman burial post were made, they were still in Terry Briers' studio in St Clears. How was I going to get them to Banwen? Not on the bus that was for sure. Thankfully the newly-formed company of Celtic Energy offered to transport them from St Clears and Walters Mining offered to carry out the tidying up of the site. Walters Mining also arranged for a small outfit from Penclawdd in the Gower to do the tidying up. It was very cold and snowing, just the two Penclawdd lads and myself. I wanted some protection for the standing stones once they had been erected from the motorbikes that roared around the mountain and the four-wheel drives. There was a massive slab of rock must have been the best part of four or five ton.

One of the lads said: 'What about this, George?'

'Your machine will never lift it!'

'Don't need to lift it. Just tumble it!' and that's what they did.

Not without mishaps though: a hydraulic pipe burst, sending red hydraulic oil squirting over the white snow. Michael Cross, son of an old friend, was a crack hand at repairing earth-moving machines and he had it fixed for the following day.

The stone replicas arrived and the plaques, then a photographic session on site by the *South Wales Evening Post*. In the photograph were Huw Edwards of Walters

Mining, Lynette Newington, Dulais Valley Partnership Project Manager, Alun Morgan of Celtic Energy and myself.

Within a week the stones were vandalized, sprayed all over with blue paint and rubbish strewn everywhere. Ron Williams drove me in his new car to the top of the mountain. We both sat there in dismay staring at the mess, flabbergasted. Wondering who the bloody hell would come all this way to do such a thing? Ron carted all the rubbish away in the boot of his new car then helped me scrub off the paint.

What with field trips with the geology class and being able to attend the Cwmdulais Historical Society again, of which I was a founder member, going on holidays for the first time in my life with Val and Peter, Jayne's mother and father, then with Ron, Renee and Eunice, and keeping my promise to Peter Weavers to help with the restoration of Maesgwyn, I was finding very little time for writing or sculpting. I rewrote the television script, *The Fourth Device*, the script that had got me my interview with the BBC, into a short story and sent it to Arthur Smith, editor of *Cambrensis*, who published it in issue No 36.

Reflecting back on the shambles the NCB had become and how sad that was for the men who had fought so hard to bring it about, one old-timer, Gwilym Jones, wrote in the *GLO* magazine: 'I would say that rather than being nationalised we were Powell Dyffrynised.' I supposed he meant the same bosses were in charge and went on to award themselves all sorts of goodies like sick leave, pay which was never awarded to the rank and file. The very men who had struggled and sometimes paid a very heavy price to bring the mines into public ownership. Some of the benefits the rank and file did share in, like pithead baths, the introduction of cap lamps for all and the employment of rat-catchers. In dry districts such as the 18 feet at Banwen the place swarmed with rats causing the dreaded Weil's disease carried in their urine. A severe illness affecting the liver and the kidneys, it caused jaundice and in those days was fatal.

The people who were picking up the perks were the very people who had in the bad old days kept the bodies of miners that had been killed on shift wrapped in bradice, tarred hessian, underground until the end of the shift so as not to disturb the flow of coal. The owners got the blame. 'But it wasn't the owners that were at the pit was it? They were away on their yacht or at a grouse shoot,' growled old Gwilym.

In the same issue of the *GLO* entitled 'NC Bloody B' they asked me to write an article. I wrote: 'Dreaming sometimes is not enough.' With hindsight emphasizing the total lack of training and preparedness there was in 1947. Brooding about that caused me to create the figure, *Aros am Golau*, 'Waiting for Light'. It was a practice carried out in a drift mine, especially on a sunny day or if there was snow on the ground. When you entered the darkness of the mine you would be blind, so you'd turn into a manhole, about seven manholes down turn off your lamp and sit in the darkness for a while until your eyes became used to the dark. The figure in my sculpture is sat down, his lamp on the ground between his feet and he is blindfolded. I wanted to say: 'And where the hell do we go from here.'

Professor Dai Smith in a television programme he produced had a young actor read an address a miner had written to his friends at a meeting. The time was in the 1930s and in his address the young miner had warned against nationalization. As close as I can remember it went. 'If we do nationalize the mines, in any dispute that follows we'll be up against the Government no matter of what hue! And up against the Government means up against the police. What we want are Co-operatives!' How right he was.

Then there was the arrogance shown by Lord Robens not turning up until the very end of the inquiry into the Aberfan disaster where 144 people were killed, 116 of them children. Then, according to one television journalist, Lord Robens having to be told by Sir Edmund Davies QC to stand up when he was giving evidence.

I began another piece of work. A collier-cum-chapel deacon, Mr Samuels, people called him Iachog but not to his face. They said that when one shovel full of coal landed in the tram there was another one on its way in the air and his shovel already driven into the pile of coal on the floor. He dabbled in stocks and shares and set his son up as an optician in a leafy suburb of Surrey. I once heard Professor Gwyn Alf Williams (my favourite Welsh scholar, whose sympathies were always with the ordinary people of Wales) say: 'There are two kinds of people. Those with *trefn* and those without *trefn*'. Translated into working-class language, them that work and look after their families, and those with no discipline who piss it all up against the wall then blame everyone and everything for the plight they are in.

Mrs Thatcher privatised British Coal and the restoration of Maesgwyn was only part finished. The site with 28 miles of good road and a million and a half young trees, some of which like the Japanese spruce would one day become very high quality timber and worth a lot of money. The massive site went on public auction and our local council never went near the event.

Received shocking news: Dianne, my brother's only child, had died – she was just forty-nine. The best scholar in our family, she had flown into Neath Grammar School for Girls. The worry now was for her youngest son Dean in his final year at Cardiff. Thankfully he got a First.

The Neath branch of the Burma Star had arranged to go to London for the fiftieth anniversary of the end of the war in the Far East. We travelled the long two hundred miles in a minibus. I was the youngest I think and I was seventy. We got out of the minibus a dozen very crumpled old men. Walked onto Horse Guards, the fine sandstone pebbles raked to perfection. We would form up in a column of men from Wales and the West Country, another column would be the South of England, another London, the Midlands, and so on, the North East and North West and Scotland and Northern Ireland. Our column would march off behind the band of the Irish Guards. There was the boom, boom, the beat of the bass drum and an Irish Guard's RSM, a giant of a young man, came striding down our ranks, his kilt swinging, barking at us as if we were new recruits.

'Right Lads! Look to the front! Shoulders back! Chests out and heads back! Stand at ease! Column! Column shun!' He was stood front and centre, his back as straight as a ramrod.

'Column will move off in column of route! Column! Column will move to the right in threes! Column right turn! Column by the right quick march!'

The band struck up 'Men of Harlech' and the crumpled old men in the blink of an eye, medals shining in the sun, un-crumpled.

The generation gap made itself very plain on one occasion that day. Mr Havard Jones, an eminent orthopaedic surgeon and our President, was laughing coming towards me in the Red Cow pub after the parade.

'George! Some young girls asked me: 'why were all you old gentlemen wearing medals?' I told them we were commemorating the end of the Japanese war. "Who won?" one of them asked.'

The DOVE began a course on video film-making and asked me would I help. They wanted to record someone who attended school in the 1930s to take part. There were four young women in the film squad. The camerawoman was Sonia Wheeler, a young woman who had come to live in Banwen from Henley-on-Thames. She was extremely hard working, had jet-black hair and looked French to me. She did an excellent job of filming the children in the primary school and the big Winder at Cefn Coed pit and the miners preparing to go underground. I thought it would be a good idea to make a film record of the whole area as it was then. We had four very large opencast mines all in sight of each other. Among them was the massive site of Maesgwyn that would by completion yield eleven and a half million tons of best anthracite coal. I asked Sonia if she would help me; she said yes and a first-class job she made of it.

I managed to put another short story together, by going over the emotions I had felt on Horse Guards. I wrote 'Ships that Pass', with dead bodies scattered about the place, and one body that had been decapitated lay close by. There was a little girl selling peanuts; Bob and I bought peanuts from her and continued to see her from time to time over the next two years. I thought of her as we stood in front of the Cenotaph and wondered if she was still alive? If she was she would be in her mid fifties, probably a grandmother, and wondered would she still remember Bob and me.

Arthur Smith wrote to me saying that he and Richard Lewis Davies the writer and publisher were putting together an anthology of short stories and would I like to try my hand at putting one of my stories forward, one that had not been published. I knew Richard was a prize-winning writer but I had never met him. I thought about what Hywel Jeffreys (Jeff Camnant) had told George Ewart Evans. What the fireman had told him on his first day underground. '*Mae dy haf bach di wedi paso*.' 'Your best (literally, Indian Summer) has passed'. I set about writing the 'End of Summer' with the main character in the story called Hywel, in memory of Jeff, a very old and dear friend.

The anthology was entitled *Mama's Baby (Papa's Maybe)*. I went to both launches, one at Waterstones in Cardiff. Geraint, Jayne and the girls came too and met Richard and the pleasure of meeting Leonora Brito, author of the story 'Mama's Baby Papa's Maybe'. Gaynor and Tom came with me to the Swansea launch at the Dylan Thomas Centre, where I met Arthur Smith for the first time. There were fifty-five stories in the Anthology. 'The End of Summer' had some very flattering reviews. From that moment on everything seemed to take off.

246

Owen, Patricia and the boys had gone to California to visit Peg's cousin Marion Wilson. They took the boys to Yellowstone National Park then Sequoia Park and there they bought me a 'giant' sequoia tree; it was barely twelve inches long in a special plastic tube. Patricia told me there were times trying to get through customs when she wished she hadn't let the boys buy the tree. There was a customs officer 'must have been a relative of Captain Mainwaring of Dad's Army. Thought I was going to be stuck there for ever trying to get past him!' I could not plant a giant sequoia tree in my garden; they grow to be three hundred feet high and have a trunk diameter of thirty-six feet. I spoke to Lynette Newington the Project Leader of the Dulais Valley Partnership, and said I'd like to give it to the Valley to mark the coming Millennium.

Lynette called to see me. I had planted the tiny tree in a pot and took Lynette's photograph with it. The ultra-efficient Lynette arranged everything including seeking permission from Mr and Mrs Byron Jones, Ton-y-fildre Farm, to plant the tree on their land. Byron thought that planting the tree near the old fishpond would be good idea. It was where the village families had picnicked for years. That was stopped because the land was part of Corsllwyn, land designated as an Area of Special Scientific Interest. Byron found another spot in the shelter of some mature trees. Edgar Pugh, the oldest surviving miner in the Valley and my cousin through marriage, had the honour of planting the tiny tree. Present at the planting were Lynette Newington who had done all the organizing, Fred Day, Tom Marston and myself, Byron and his son Andrew the Valley warden, who had erected a fence to protect the tiny sapling.

A young woman – Stephanie Jones – came to lodge with Carol and John at the Bakery. I answered a knock on the door; a pretty fair-haired young woman stood there.

'Hello! Are you Carol the Bake House's uncle George?'

Stephanie had come to the Dulais Valley to write a thesis for her doctorate, on what effect the complete shutdown of its main industry, coalmining, was having on the community. I was to spend a great deal of time with Stephanie over the next eighteen months. She hailed from Haverfordwest and Tim Davies, her artist husband, one of Wales's most talented, hailed from Solva, Pembrokeshire.

After gaining her doctorate, Stephanie became a Research Fellow at Aberystwyth at the Centre for Advanced Welsh and Celtic Studies. She wrote to me asking would I accompany her to an exhibition being put on by her boss at Aberystwyth, Peter Lord, at Cyfarthfa Castle, former home of the Crawshay family. An exhibition of paintings commissioned by Francis Crawshay from the artist WJ Chapman of worker portraits and the launch of Peter Lord's splendidly informative book, *The Francis Crawshay Worker Portraits*. There are twelve portraits of ironworkers in the book. The portrait I found most interesting was portrait number 10 *David Davies Fineries Hirwaun*; he appears to be suffering from a cataract of his left eye: a grim reminder that there was no eye protection provided at work in those days. It interested me because in my time with Bewley & John and Gemmak Engineering one of my duties was to see to it that there was always a supply of dark lenses in stock for the welders.

Stephanie told me that there was a Professor John Harvey at Aberystwyth, Head of the School of Art, and that he was thinking of putting on an exhibition of the artwork by Welsh coalminers. I wrote to him; Professor Harvey arrived at Maple House and was pleased with what he saw, so he and his assistants spent quite a few hours wrapping everything up in bubble wrap.

'Is there anything else George we can see?' He asked during a break in the proceedings.

'There's this one.' I took the unframed painting out of a drawer. It was of my brother David getting out of the bath and the girl next door has come in to borrow something and is looking at him and him at her; her reflection in the mirror and my mother in the pantry fetching whatever it is the girl has asked for.

'We'll take this if we may, George!' The professor was very enthusiastic. The painting had never been framed because Peg thought it may offend David because he was completely naked standing in the bath.

The exhibition would take place first at the National Library of Wales on the 11th of March 2000. Geraint and Naomi drove me there. The weather was fine, Cardigan Bay looked at its best and the imposing edifice of the National Library looked magnificent, standing overlooking the Bay and it made me sad thinking that more than half the people of Wales, because of the appalling transport, have never even seen this national treasure.

The exhibition was held in the newly refurbished main gallery. If you had hung an old coat on the wall in that place it would have looked grand. A band played in the corner, people were wandering about dressed to the nines, sipping glasses of wine. An attendant handed me the catalogue,

Miner-Artists: The Art of Welsh Coal Workers by John Harvey. It measured nine and a half inches by thirteen and a half inches, a truly luxurious publication, and my painting of David in the bath was on the front cover – the highest praise my work had received ever. Professor John Harvey and his wife came over.

'What do you think, George?

I tapped the cover of the catalogue. 'What can I say?'

Naomi stood under the portrait of Peggy the Papers telling everyone that stopped in front of the painting: 'That's my *Mamgu!*'

The *Western Mail* carried a half-page photograph of my painting *In the Bath*. S4C made a half-hour programme on the exhibition. The three of us were very pleased with ourselves on the way home but I had a little bit of a nagging feeling of guilt because Peg was not there, not just the exhibition but to enjoy our lovely grandchildren. The two youngest that she never even knew, Naomi and Jamie. Children she had all the time in the world for. The boys had been able to bring all the friends they wanted to home. Philip Evans when he was five and six would stay on holidays with Geraint although he only lived five hundred yards away in Roman Road. Peg would make chips for them all, in the garden on school holidays, and steak cooked in stout when Geraint and his friends from university turned up after waterskiing on Llangorse Lake. I remember her saying that she wished she'd been like Aunty Hanna and had a houseful of children.

There was one story she loved telling about young Barry Evans, who no doubt was the prettiest little boy in the Valley. He had the kind of face you see painted on the ceilings of cathedrals, the face of a cherub but wearing glasses. Barry and Geraint were about four years old at the time playing in the garden, digging into the bank of the stream, pretending to be working an opencast site, loading the dirt into their toy tipper lorries. Peg had made them chips and pop for lunch. Peg said, 'I called on them but they took no notice but kept working away. So I walked down to them. "Geraint! Barry! You coming for chips and pop?"' Peg said Barry looked up at her, then this angelic face looking up at her said, 'Tell her to fuck off, Ger!' They both carried on digging like two old colliers.

The exhibition opened in the Glyn Vivian gallery in Swansea on 20th of May. Owen, Noel and Jamie came down. The BBC and ITV made programmes with John (Chopper) Davies being interviewed and a commentary by Professor John Harvey. The *South Wales Evening Post* had a photo of the portrait *Peggy the Papers* on the front page and inside articles on Cyril Ifold and myself and photographs of our work.

On the 22nd of July the exhibition opened in the National Museum of Wales Cardiff and was very well attended even though the lorry drivers were stopping supplies of petrol getting through. I was asked by Helen Waters, Assistant Curator of Modern Art, to speak at the exhibition on one afternoon. I was surprised from how far and wide the audience had come. Talking to individuals afterwards the reason was obvious. Seventy years before there had been a million miners on this island and these were some of their descendants. Received a fan letter from my dear friend Margery Burns telling me she thought my paintings were the best in the exhibition.

In the meantime I heard from from Richard Lewis Davies of Parthian, Cardiff, once again, this time by letter, written on the 27th of December 1999, Geraint's birthday. In the letter Richard said he enjoyed reading my stories and was now aiming to publish a series of books called Parthian 7, which would be seven collections of seven short stories by seven writers, each individual writer getting their own collection. He was hoping I would be interested in the project. Interested! I was flattered that they had even asked me. Richard came along to the exhibition and said they were starting to put the book together. I realized he was younger than both my sons and felt a great admiration for him; he had done so much with his life. Bestselling author and now one of Wales's most successful publishers. We agreed to meet in two weeks' time at the National Museum tea bar.

I asked Eira Roberts, who had worked for Peg for years when she was a girl and would help out when I had visitors, to accompany me to Cardiff. I was seventy-five years of age and getting deafer by the day. I drove to Aberdare and we caught the train because I didn't feel confident enough to drive in Cardiff. Age not only stiffens your joints, it takes away a lot of your confidence. We stood on the steps of the Museum and Richard turned up on his bicycle. I was in for one of the most pleasant surprises. Richard produced the proposed cover for my anthology of seven short stories *Boys of Gold*. The cover was a very dark green with gold lettering and a photograph of my painting *Coggin Four Feet* and underneath in white lettering my name. On the back cover a very flattering photograph of me taken in Rangoon in 1945.

Boys of Gold was launched at the DOVE workshop to, as reported in the *Neath Guardian*, a sell-out crowd. Alun

Richard, the *raconteur par excellence,* enchanted the audience with his tales. The staff of the DOVE put on a buffet fit for a king. Richard and Gill were busy selling books and me signing books and having my photo taken. The next launch was in Cardiff at Waterstones The Hayes, on a night pouring with rain along with Gail Hughes's *Flamingos* and John Sam Jones's *Welsh Boys Too*. Geraint, Jayne the girls and Eira were there. What the girls found most entertaining was the sight of a little old man who had come in to shelter from the rain and at every opportunity kept darting forward to take another glass of wine and as many Welsh cakes as he could.

Waterstones placed the sculpture of *Alby Thomas the Rider* in their shop window looking out on The Hayes in the centre of our capital city. Wondered what Alby Thomas the rider would have made of that? Or his six-foot odd mate Jack Llewellyn, that Alby had laid low every winter by coming to work and spreading his flu germs. A week or so later, the *Western Mail* and *South Wales Evening Post* carried the headline: 'Retired miner outsells Dylan'. Sales of *Boys of Gold* had outstripped Dylan Thomas and Alexander Cordell. Waterstones selected it as one of their books of the year.

That summer there was the Hay-on-Wye Festival. We took a community bus of sixteen and the ladies from the DOVE made their own way, making sure I suspect that I would have reasonable support. Happily indeed the event, 'Welsh Miner Writers', was so oversubscribed that they had to move the venue from The Turning Leaf Marquee to the Salem Chapel. Taking part would be Alun Richards, Professor Dai Smith, Professor Chris Williams and myself, chaired by Jon

Gower, Arts Correspondent of the BBC. Afterwards I spent a pleasant hour in a downstairs room of the chapel signing copies of my book, made more pleasant by a middle-aged man who said his name was Brenig. He smiled, 'Remember me George?' Then he said his surname, Carret. I had known him since he was a boy. He had gone to university and had become a lecturer at a university in England. I knew his mother and father better; his father had been the manager's clerk who had tried to comfort me the day that Morris the agent had torn a strip off me, humiliated me by shouting loud enough so that everybody on the surface of Onllwyn colliery could hear. 'That I was a disgrace to my family! And didn't I know there was a war on!' I had dashed off mad as hell and joined the army.

Missed lunch by having to take part in a photographic session, the subjects Dai Smith, Alun Richards and myself. Endeavouring to somehow fit the bulk of Alun in with Dai and me tested the patience of the American lady photographer. When we got to the pub there was a dish of cooked mussels in a buttered sauce on the table and Alun started eating them.

'Those are not yours Al,' said Professor Smith.

'I know. I'll only eat a few.' They were Richard's, but by the time Richard sat down it was to a bowl of empty shells.

They gave each of us participants at Hay a beautiful white rose. I gave mine to Naomi. I was also given a case of six bottles of M Hostomme Champagne. Headlines on the *Western Mail* arts page the following morning: 'Historians revel in fiction by ex-miners.' Former US President Bill Clinton was at Hay-on-Wye on Saturday the 26th of May and I was there three days later, on the 1st of June. Banwen is a mining village in the South Wales valleys; they interpret events to suit themselves. The talk was that Clinton had been warming up the audience for me.

Jon Gower came to Maple House to interview me for BBC Radio Wales. Eira arrived armed with a biscuit tin full of newly-baked Welsh cakes. I enjoyed being interviewed by this very large, quietly spoken Cambridge-educated young man. Eira spent a lot of time gossiping to him while he enjoyed her delicious Welsh cakes. Radio Wales dramatized parts of the story of *Boys of Gold* and they did it really well I thought. The part I liked the best was when the young actor was barking out orders, taking off the regimental train officer at Rangoon Railway Station.

Had another very pleasant surprise and honour in the post, a letter from Mr Peter Finch, Chief Executive of the Welsh Academy, telling me I had been elected a full member of the Academy of Writers for my contribution to literature. There were book signings to go to, official and impromptu. I visited a Waterstones bookshop with my old comrade Fred Day. Fred had served in the RAF regiment and had taken part in the first wave of landings in the attempt to recapture the City of Rangoon. He was a radar operator on a bage that had no engine that had been towed twenty-six miles up the Rangoon River by the Navy and left there. I often wondered what would have happened to Fred if the Japanese had decided to re-cross the river. He returned to mining after the war as a mining surveyor, and married Betty Edwards who lived opposite Peg's paper shop. Peg and Betty were good friends. We four often went picnicking together. Fred asked the young bookshop manager: 'Do you know who this is?' Fred had a copy of *Boys of Gold* in his hand and pointed to my name. 'He is the culprit!' then pointing at me. The young manager asked me to sign some copies. I was only too pleased to.

20

The landscape at the top of the valley was changing as you looked at it. Ron Williams and I went for a walk around the small lake they had made as part of the restoration. The Barrel Wash was still working on Banwen colliery tip. We walked over to what could be call the main cut and looked down and there it was! The brickwork of the main Fan Drift. They were taking the coal from the barrier that was always left at the side of every main airway to act as a seal, not salvaging coal to wash out of the old tip. We wondered who exactly could be involved in this very profitable scam and no doubt picking up a tidy bit of loot? The coal they were mining, not salvaging, was best Welsh anthracite.

The DOVE along with the Dulais Valley Partnership was getting involved in promoting tourism in the valley. They had organised a Valley Festival and asked me to write something about the history of the place. Over the years I had heard stories and tales about the fairy-haunted land of the Banwen Pyrddin and thought that would be the theme. Enough of coalmines, iron works and Romans. I called at the Neath Museum, then housed in the Mechanics' Institute, to see the Curator Marion Woodham and ask for her help. I could not have gone to a better person. Marion obtained for me D. Rhys Phillips's *History of the Vale of Neath*. The story that caught my attention was Edward Lhuyd, regarded by many as Wales's first travel writer, writing about the very stones that I had spent the last eighteen months having copied. Edward Lhuyd had seen the originals in 1695 and conjectured that the monument could be there to commemorate the slain party of a duel, fought between two warriors, as in Irish legend. When the stones were taken to Lady Mackworth's garden at the Gnoll to become part of an elaborate park in 1790, a violent storm wrecked the grotto and the base of the stone was broken. The superstitious pointed to this as proof of the anger of the fairies against those who had taken the stone from the fairy-haunted land of the Banwen Pyrddin.

I had to add the story of Yspaddaden, a monster giant that all others paled before, because we have a farm called Ton Yspaddaden (The Land of Yspaddaden). It was said his daughter Olwen was so beautiful 'Whoso saw her would be filled with love for her. Four white trefoils sprang up behind her wherever she went'. She was won by the knight Culhwch with the help of King Arthur. Then Maesgwyn named in the Nedd-Tawe region. Maybe the heaven God of British mythology, son or foster son of the Goddess Don. His son Gwyn ap Nudd appears in the Nedd area as King of the fairies. He haunts the summits of hills and in a dialogue which graces the Black Book of Carmarthen, he opines: 'I am called the enchanter. I am Gwyn the son of Nudd, the lover of Creiddylad, the daughter of Lludd. This is my horse Carngrwn, the terror of the field; he will not let me parley with you; when bridled he is restless; he is impatient to go to Drum, my home on the Tawe'. This is the man Shakespeare writes about in *King Lear*.

Reading these amazing stories made me realize that the mundane, day-to-day happenings of our present-day lives we count as adventures don't hold a candle to the characters that came out of the dreams and imagination of the people who inhabited this hallowed place in the ages gone by.

On our next walk, some months later, across the ridge above Roman Road, Ron and I were greeted by a much more pleasant sight; the ground was covered by tens of thousands of young tomato plants. It was the result of the whole area of the mountain being sprayed with raw sewage. What had been called the biggest opencast coal site in Europe was turning into an undulating lovely green landscape. Tomato Mountain.

I was invited to take part in a Children's Art Day. Galleries all over Britain were to be involved. Sharon Ford the Education Officer at Big Pit and Ceri Thompson the Curator came to my house and took my work to the Collections Centre, Nantgarw. Three schools had been asked to send sixth form Art students. Ceri came to collect Eira and me. Security was very tight; half the treasures of Wales were stored there. I spoke to the youngsters about my work and then they were asked to draw any object they chose. They were brilliant. I was very thankful they did not ask me to draw.

Some months later Tom Marston telephoned me. 'Switch on the TV; go to teletext.' He gave me the page number.

'Iolo's put a message for the village on it.' Iolo had been back to France and he had found Vernon Edwards's grave at St Marie Cemetery, Le Havre. Vernon had been killed in action on the 13th September 1944 aged 21 taking part in operation 'Astonia'. The fighting was heavy, tanks and flame-throwers had been used, three infantry regiments had been involved: the South Wales Borderers, the Gloucesters and the 2nd Essex in which Vernon was serving. The thing now was to have Vernon's name put on the local war memorial. The Commonwealth War Graves Commission informed us that Vernon's name could not be added if it was on any other memorial. It was not. By November of that year the Neath branch of the Royal British Legion had Vernon's name engraved on to the Seven Sisters War Memorial and had arranged a memorial service at St Mary's church. Taking the service the Revd Steven Barns and the Revd Stan Zeal. There were four ex-Maesmarchog pupils present: Iolo Lewis, whose dogged persistence had brought the event about, with his wife Gwladus, Glyn Thomas who like Iolo had served in tanks, Billy Pritchard Royal Welsh Fusiliers and professional footballer playing for Leicester City, and myself. It was a sombre day but Billy, Glyn and Iolo had a tale to tell that made everyone smile. The war had only just ended and it was decided that there should be a football match between the British Army and the German Army.

'That British goalkeeper looks familiar!' said Glyn to Iolo.

He was; it was Billy Pritchard. There were three Maesmarchog ex-pupils at that historic football match on ground that had been a battlefield just a week before. Iolo had had a rough old war, wounded twice and one of the first into Belsen, and it left its mark. Iolo is an accomplished poet. I include two lines from one of his poems, 'Belsen Silence':

'Remembering comrades, young men all,
Who died to reach this awful Hell.'

Also at the service were members of the Essex Regiment in which Vernon had served, the Royal British Legion, and members of the Burma Star Association.

Parthian had arranged for an exhibition of my work at the Gwyn Hall, Neath. Robert Merill, Curator of the museum, and Clive Reed called to see me and arranged for my paintings and sculptures and other bits and pieces to be picked up.

I was thrilled to see what a splendid job the staff had made of the layout of the exhibition. It was then that I first really got to know Claire Roberts, The Assistant Curator. I didn't know at the time but we had both had stories published in the same anthology, *Shorts from Glamorgan.*

The exhibition was opened by Dr Hywel Francis MP for Port Talbot; present too was the Mayor of Neath, Des Davies, and also his lady wife. I could not believe that my work would attract so many people. My work, that was intended only for the walls of 9 Gordon Terrace, was on show for everyone to see. As ever, I wondered would Peg have approved? Dozens of my friends, amongst them Dr Tom Davies and Dr Roseina Davies, had turned up to see my work. Dr Tom's brother and I had been cub scouts together. Dr Tom once asked me to go with him to Aberpergwm House. The vandalism that the NCB had committed on that beautiful Elizabethan mansion was criminal. They had actually drilled holes through the fluted ceiling of the

261

magnificent long room, created by Italian craftsmen, to fit electric light fittings that could quite easily have been fitted to the wood wall panelling, and had even knocked a hole in one pine end wall of the house to pass an electric cable through. I left the great mansion hoping that if there really was a ghost at Aberpergwm that ghost would one day take a terrible revenge on those vandals.

Jon Gower interviewed members of the audience at the exhibition. It was Alun Richards' remarks I remember and value the most: 'George's work has a clarity about it! His prose, his painting, his sculptures. George knows what he sees and records it accurately.' Later in the week I went to the museum for a photo taking session for the newspapers with Claire. I had a photo taken of the painting she liked the best, 'Stone Tiles', and had it transferred to a china mug as a small thank you for all the hard work she had put in.

A BBC researcher came to speak to me about an art programme called *Double Yellow*. Within a week there was a film crew in Maple House. Eira as usual came up to help with tea and Welsh cakes. Luce Donahue was the producer, the interviewer was the stunning Welsh actress Rakie Ayola. The weather was at its best. You could see for miles and the film crew wanted to make the most of it. We went right to the top of the mountain and it was colder than they expected it to be; on the first day Rakie had to wear one of my windproof jackets. On the second day she brought her own woolly coat. We were both leaning against the plinth holding the plaque that described the magnificent view before us of the Brecon Beacons and the Carmarthen Fans. A young actor was reciting extracts from *Boys of Gold*. He did it splendidly with Fan Hir, the peak of the Lady in the Lake, as a backdrop.

Sonia Wheeler had made a video film of the area when there was not a blade of grass between Banwen and Glyn Neath. Ten years later I had asked Elaine Parry, a good friend, now that she had a video camera would she make a film of the area returning where possible to the same locations that Sonia had filmed. She did and made a super job of it. Lynette Newington got to hear of it and made inquiries at the Glyn Vivian Gallery asking could they make a feature out of the two videos to be called 'Then and Now'. I went with Lynette to the Glyn Vivian. I gave the technician the two videos and they worked for most of the day on it. The amount of work was unbelievable but the end result was well worth the effort.

I made the mistake of playing it for the crew of *Double Yellow*. One of the researchers seemed spellbound by it and begged me to lend it him, promising faithfully to return it. Eira whispered to me not to give it to him but he seemed a nice straightforward young man. I should have listened to her. That was the last I saw of the video.

There were two more standing stones I wanted to see in place at Banwen: one as a memorial to all the men, women and children who had been killed or injured mining coal in our valley. The first record of mining was in 1564 by a William Jenkins. He was given permission to mine from Nant-y-cellwen, the brook that runs through my garden, to Onllwyn. The memorial would also show the name of Katie Jones working as a collier boy to her brother John in Maesmarchog colliery. Her name appears on an old plan of

263

the mine. The memorial was unveiled by Edgar Pugh the oldest surviving miner in the Dulais Valley, the Rev Stan Zeal officiating.

The other standing stone I wanted to see would commemorate Tafarn-y-Banwen as St Patrick's birthplace. Three magazines had published my article putting forward the proposition that St Patrick was born in Banwen: the quarterly magazine of the Celtic Catholic Church *The Visitor*, the magazine *Cambria* in its first anniversary edition, and the local magazine *Black and White*. Andrew Jones had been appointed Valley Warden and was making good progress in drawing people's attention to the fact that people had been living and working in this part of the world for tens of thousands of years. Andrew turned up at the house one morning to tell me he had obtained permission to erect a standing stone at the side of the Roman Road.

'Do you know where I can get a stone big enough George?'

While Andrew was there I telephoned Robert Jones, a site agent for Celtic Energy and son of Reg Jones my old boss at Wimpey. Within two days the Maen Hir standing stone was delivered and erected, unveiled by his Worship the Mayor of Neath and Port Talbot, Councillor Peter G Lloyd, on St Patrick's Day 2004. The Rev Stan Zeal officiated. On that day too the BBC made a live broadcast from New York, speaking to the American scholar and writer Thomas John Clark who had been researching the life of St Patrick for the past ten years. For him Banwen was the first choice as St Patrick's birthplace and he wrote a book in which St Patrick was born in Banwen: *The Chronicles of Saint Patrick*, published by Black Lab Books, New York, foreword written by the Head of Celtic Studies at Harvard University.

Received a letter off a Mr Barry W.G. Plummer, an art history lecturer who was in the process of editing a book on the paintings and drawing by the distinguished Swansea-born artist Evan John Walters BA (1893-1951). The aim was to publish the book to coincide with the 2006 National Eisteddfod opening at Swansea. Enclosed with his letter a photograph of one of Evan John Walters' best known paintings, *A Welsh Miner*. I was very flattered to be asked for my opinion on the work of one of Wales's most famous artists. I wrote:

'Evan John Walters probably saw the subject for his painting, *A Welsh Miner*, in the bar of his mother's pub, having a pint and a Woodbine on his way home after a shift on the coalface. The collier is from the time when they wore soft caps and no kneepads, long before the hardhat and orange boiler suit came into fashion.

'His hand that holds the Woodbine says as much about the man as the collier's face. It is the portrait of an anthracite miner, a miner who, to save a few pence on gelignite, works the coal with a mandrill, a lightweight pick-axe, kept razor sharp by the colliery blacksmith, to bring down the glass-hard slips of coal.

'The work of driving the blade into the fissures between the coal slips, with all your might, day after day, day in day out, from the day of your fourteenth birthday, gave you hands the size of dinner plates. The massive thumb, bent like an eagle's talon, is the lynchpin that holds the fist together when the torrent of full-force blows are struck, freeing the slips of glistening anthracite coal.

'He is a good-looking bloke. Scrubbed and hair shining stuck down with Brylcreem. He could pass himself off as a chapel deacon or the local Casanova. Perhaps like many a good-looking anthracite miner he was both.'

I went to the Glyn Vivian Gallery on a Sunday and was thrilled to see what I had written was included in the book resting on a plinth below the portrait.

Having your work published I found brought all kinds of pleasant bonuses. Richard asked me to help in the launch of a new book to take place at the Dylan Thomas Centre Swansea – ten writing workshops for disabled people across Wales; 86 people took part. The book was *Hidden Dragons* published by Parthian Books. To meet these authors was truly a humbling occasion. Their happy easy attitude towards life even when faced with the most appalling disability had to be witnessed to be believed. There was the young, lovely Lella Bedd from Mynydd-y-Garreg. Her mother had bought her the most beautiful evening gown for the occasion; I mentioned it to Gail Marsh the newspaper photographer. She took Lella to stand near the splendid arched windows at the town end of the old Guildhall that the Luftwaffe had failed to destroy and to Lella's delight she was photographed a dozen times. Afterwards Lella read her poem and the audience was entranced by the love and beauty this young woman saw in her world. Then Andrew Hubbard read his poem, *The Invisible Blind Man* was very powerfully written, making all present with the gift of sight feel guilty.

A very tall Australian came to see me: Jonty Claypole, a television producer from the BBC. They were making a programme *Beautiful Britain*, including paintings of landscape from all over Great Britain by greats such as Constable and

Turner and Richard Wilson, one of the founder members of the Royal Academy. The programme was to be hosted by David Dimbleby and filming on the very same locations the artists had painted from. Jonty Claypole asked me would I be willing to take part. I really didn't know what to say. I think I muttered, 'OK!'

David Dimbleby arrived with the film crew. It was pouring with rain. It never fails to surprise me the amount of mechanical and electronic equipment that is required to make even a small amount of television film. Owen my eldest son is a Chartered Mechanical Engineer whose big gripe is the lack of credit engineers are afforded. His throwaway line always was, 'We engineers have more than likely saved more lives than doctors'. He could have added, 'And there'd be no film industry without us either'. Waiting for the rain to stop it was most enjoyable listening to David Dimbleby tell the story of how his grandfather, while working for David Lloyd George in the early 1920s, became the first spin doctor, the Alastair Campbell of his day.

The one landscape I had painted that always seemed to gain people's attention was of the Cribarth – a massive limestone outcrop on the western side of the Swansea Valley and raising behind it the impressive Fan Hir at 2366 feet. The whole area was steeped in the legend of the Lady of the Lake. It was a view that had fascinated me for as long as I could remember. More so after attending a geology course and being told by our tutor, Doctor Geraint Owen, that these cliffs of limestone towering over the upper Swansea Valley once lay, for hundreds of millions of years, under a warm tropical sea and were the transformed remains of billions upon billions of sea creatures. It had gained a place at an International Amateur Art Exhibition in London in 1957. David Dimbleby had a chat with me by each of the paintings that interested him, while the cameraman filmed us, but the rain never let up. Nevertheless we dressed in our raincoats and trooped up to the small lake just two hundred yards from Maple House. It was useless; visibility was down to a hundred yards. The episode filmed at Banwen was never used in the main series.

Jonty Claypole the producer very kindly sent me a DVD of the Rhondda sequence that included the work of three well-known valleys painters, Walter Evans, Cedric Morris and Archie Rhys Griffiths, and rounded off the sequence with David Dimbleby talking to me and looking at my best known painting (*In The Bath*).

People have often asked me. When and why did I get this urge to paint? I always found it easier than writing. They do say a picture paints a thousand words. And because I found out early in life I could draw and being no different to any other young boy, any opportunity to show off was jumped at.

I remember trying to explain it to David Dimbleby when he interviewed me. We were talking about the painting, *In the Bath*, the painting on the cover of this book; that I thought some boys could sing, play the mouth organ, that everybody I thought could do something. Then with hindsight it began to dawn on me many of my cousins on my mother's side of the family were very talented pencil drawers: Billy Brec the Farm, then Melfyn Morgan and his younger brother Ray. I remember Ray doing a pencil drawing of the film actress Rita Hayworth; her hair on the pillow looked so real. You thought if you blew the hair would move.

Ray went on to become Dr Raymond Morgan and Principal of Eaton Hall College, Cheltenham.

I drew cartoons if I was angry enough that the local paper the *Labour Voice* would publish, and then two of my paintings were accepted for the 1967 – 12th International Amateur Art Exhibition in Warwick Square, London, after Peg sent them. That was the first time I was involved in art publicly and it grew from there.

21

Around this time I returned to Burma for the first time since the Second World War. The story of that trip is told in the Epilogue to this book. When I returned I started on a new book, which I had given the title 'Before Counselling' because it seemed that whatever happened, the people who were witness to the incident, large or small, were given counselling. Yet I remembered as a boy along with my friends, standing at the side of the road watching a dead miner, a man we knew, being carried home on a stretcher. We knew he was dead because they carried him shoulder high. Then on the newsreels at the cinema we had seen children coming out of an air raid shelter and seeing human remains stuck to a wall and no one had the time to even talk to them, let alone counsel them, but they lived on and no harm seemed to come of it. Or so we supposed. If something awful happened to a family in those days, the rest of the family would gather round, the doctor would call or the vicar or chapel Minister, and that would be it. Then remembering a conversation I once had with Dr Aubrey Thomas skirting around this subject, because I was talking to an expert and the best scholar I had ever known, he said: 'And who is going to psycho-analyse the psycho-analyst? Is that what you're asking George? Lots of people ask that. I find George people seek comfort wherever they can, in something or in someone: Psychoanalysis, Witch Doctor or even chucking salt over their left shoulder!' he grinned. Dr Dafydd Aubrey Thomas once told me that whenever he could he swam in the ice-cold waters of Llyn y Fan Fach in the first week in August. The legendary lake from where the mother of all the doctors of Wales supposedly came. I had spent more than half my four years in the army on the Irrawaddy River, or the 'Road to Mandalay'. So I changed the title of my new work to a line from Rudyard Kipling's famous poem, *Mandalay*, 'Where The Flying Fishes Play'. The story would begin in Banwen and end when I left the army.

I wrote the book, the autobiographical novel as Bob Roser, reviewer for the America Newspaper *Ninnau*, described it. I wrote in the third person because I suppose, being in my late seventies when writing it, I was very self-conscious. Brought up in a society where weeping and wailing in public was thought of as vulgar and, if indulged in, it should be done behind closed doors. All funerals were strictly men only, even children's funerals. I was the product of that society.

Life in an anthracite coalmining village in the 1930s, with hindsight was about as good a life as a British working-class family could have. My father with his brother Jim were the first coalminers on that side of the family and on my mother's side it was the same; her brothers Jim and Tom were the first miners. They had both served their apprenticeships as bakers in Brecon and in those days apprenticeships had to be paid for. Most of my relatives still lived in the country on farms; my mother's father farmed Tafarn-y-Banwen and the adjoining smallholding Coedcae. He also had the lucrative contract of empting the earth lavatories of the sixty-four Evans Bevan-owned houses in Roman Road. My father and my uncle Jim helped him, starting the work at midnight on a Saturday night. Because every house had an allocation of 13 ton of coal a year, 19 ton if they had apartments, maybe a married son or daughter living with them, the lavatories contained sixty or seventy per cent ash. The ash used to flush and stop the flies. Nevertheless I used to wish my grandfather would give the job up and I complained to my mother.

'George our family have always been farmers, cleaning up after cows, horses, pig and chickens. It's a job that has got to be done. Some people are so filthy! Someone has got to clean up after them! Take the nurses in hospital, taking away the bedpans, where would the hospital be without the nurses?'

That made me feel a bit better about it but I still didn't like it. My father still went shearing; one of the farms he went to was the Varteg high on the side of the mountain looking down on Ystradgynlais, Maggie his youngest sister's farm. It was the only farm I went to that had its own coal level, a seam of best Welsh anthracite. There would be ten or more men shearing. David, my brother, because he was bigger and stronger than me, helped to pass the struggling sheep out of the pen. I was given the job of 'doctor'. I had a tin of clean axle grease and a flat piece of wood. A sheep would jerk to try to break free from the shearer's grip and the razor sharp shears would take a slice of flesh.

'Doctor!' the shout would go up and I would have to race over and apply a good helping of grease to the wound, enough to protect the wound from the flies. Before the sheep were turned out they were branded with hot pitch.

Afterwards a feast; my Aunty Maggie and her friend and neighbours would have made bread, cooked beef, pork and ham and apple and blackberry tart. Her father-in-law was very old and had a special mug that was shaped to keep his moustache out of his tea. The feast and kisses good bye over, we would walk down the mountain to the Traveller's Rest, a small pub very appropriately named, standing at the side of the road after a long steep climb out of the Swansea valley up into the Dulais Valley. My father would have a few pints with Mr Gardener, hoist me up onto his shoulders, his shearing clippers in a leather holster on his belt. It would be pitch dark, with David walking we would cross the Crynant Common and wait for the bus to Banwen.

I enjoyed writing the book. Being made to remember is sometimes very pleasant: having to recall being the only soldier with a squad of ATS girls working in the kitchen of a grand old mansion just outside Alfreton and how they used to enjoy themselves teasing me because they weren't sure was I a virgin or not and I wouldn't admit one way or the other.

Researching into the activities of Army Motor Boats was an eye opener. When I asked Captain Belton when did the Army first have boats?

273

'Not sure Taff, think it was after Dunkirk!'

I read a letter in the Burma Star magazine, DEKHO! signed Vic Stone, The Boats. I guessed he was one of ours. It was Vic Stone of C section now living on the Isle of Sheppey and he sent me a book entitled *The Army's Navy: British Military Vessels and their history since Henry VIII*. How wrong can you get? I read that one Company had been sailing captured Italian schooners under the cover of darkness under the noses of the enemy, from Bari to Manfredonia, then on to the island of Vis with ammunition and supplies for the Yugoslav partisans and the British who were fighting with them. Undertaking tasks such as that it is not that surprising the Corps lost more than ten thousand men from 1939 to 1945. The great majority of the dead were drivers. Then I suppose if a pilot was out on a raid shooting up enemy lines he'd go for the lorries, not a few blokes huddled in a field. After all bombs did cost money.

At a talk I was asked to do at Neath Library I said that our boats were made of deal.

'They weren't bullet proof then?'

'At a thousand yards they were!'

Lucie Prescott a researcher for Indus Films contacted me asking me would I take part in a documentary they were planning to make on art and the Welsh coal miner. Professor John Harvey of Aberystwyth University had given them my name. I said yes immediately, still not quite believing why I was being asked. The day before the Indus film crew arrived I was so ill I had to telephone the doctor. I had asked a friend Vic Hales to bring me some of the concentrated chicken manure from the garden centre. The lid of the plastic container was so tight-fitting I had to struggle to get it off. When I did, it came off suddenly and I gulped in a mouthful of the dust that flew up. Not long after I began vomiting violently. The last time a doctor had had to be called to attend to me was in the 1960s. It was Dr Jones, an attractive brunette and a very nice young woman.

'Have you eaten anything that has upset you?'

I told her about gulping down the dust from the chicken manure. I had to keep a towel in front of my mouth in case of a sudden spasm of vomiting. It was really very embarrassing. She examined me. 'Take plenty of liquids. I think that should see you better.'

I must have drunk about a gallon of water and had stopped vomiting by the time the lads from Indus Films turned up the following morning. They wanted to film me painting and talking to them at the same time. Indus Films sent me a DVD and a note telling me it would be broadcast on BBC Two. Naomi was not too pleased because of the untidiness in the kitchen when they were filming me painting. 'Everybody in Wales saw your untidy kitchen, Gramps! Why didn't you tidy up first?' What they had not told me was that I would be the anchorman as far as the miners were concerned. It featured work by the Welsh pre-war greats Evan Walters, Vincent Evans and Archie Rhys Griffiths and modern-day artists Josef Herman, Nicholas Evans, James Donovan (a young non-miner), and Valerie Ganz, whose beautiful paintings captured the togetherness of the bond between men as they faced the threat of death each working day. She expresses that special quality of the comradeship in her work.

The commentary on the paintings was by the eminent art historian Peter Lord and Professor John Harvey, the man responsible for bringing the art work of Welsh Coalminers to the attention of the public, when he organized and launched the exhibition *The Art Of The Welsh Coal Worker Miner-Artists* in the year 2000. The storyteller in the documentary was Eve Myles, the star of the TV series *Torchwood*. Tom Marston brought a visitor to the house, Ceri Thomas, Research Fellow, Ernest Zobole Art Collection, University of Glamorgan. Ceri said he had wanted to meet me for a long time and gave me a gift, his book *Ernest Zobole: a retrospective*. A while later Ceri Thomas invited Tom and me to the launch of his book in the new art gallery Oriel Pen y Fan in Brecon. There was a painting hanging there I would have bought if my brother David had still been alive, *The Dock Gate Cardiff*. David had blown them off their hinges when he worked for Turners.

Richard of Parthian asked me to come and stay in Cardigan so that we could put the finishing touches to *Where The Flying Fishes Play* together. Mandy Orford the librarian at the Banwen branch of the South Wales Miners' Library arranged for me to stay at the Black Lion, one of the oldest hotels in the country, where her uncle and aunt were the proprietors.

Where The Flying Fishes Play would be launched at the DOVE then at Big Pit then book signings at WHSmiths, Swansea, the new Waterfront Museum Swansea, the Borders Book Shop on the Morriston Business Park, and the Borders Bookstore Llantrisant. The DOVE put on their usual first-class celebration and arranged for Mr Rob Humphries, the head of the Open University in Wales, to host the launch. I was very aware of the honour being paid to me by having Rob there to launch the book. I had known Rob many years before and we were good friends.

I was very mindful and sad of the fact that Alun Richards was not there. Alun had died suddenly in the summer of 2004. Owen and Patricia had come down from Hereford. Geraint, Jayne and the two girls were there. The girls were dressed in their Burmese dresses and looking absolutely lovely. My sister Ceinwen was there too. Eira was there and as usual helping Gill, Richard's wife with the sale of the books.

The book signing at WHSmith, Swansea came next. It may have been run of the mill to Rose Widlake and Lucy Llewellyn but to me at eighty years of age, walking in a large shop and seeing photographs of myself on large posters hung around the walls was odd to say the least. Billy the Kid must have had the same sensation I thought when he saw pictures of himself nailed to a wall.

Then on to Borders in Morriston Business Park and Ron Williams turned up dressed immaculately as usual, holding up a copy of *Where The Flying Fishes Play* persuading, coaxing, cajoling members of the public to buy a copy. Eunice and Renee were there too and we all had our photo taken at the table while I was signing books. Reflecting on it, it was very nice; three of the people who had helped me through the bleak, black winter of 1985-86 were there, especially Renee who had been one of Peg's dearest friends.

The book signing at Neath was very much in the public eye in the main doorway of WHSmith – on the pavement almost; I was waving to shoppers I knew as they walked by. Llewellyn Jarvis a lifelong friend stood in front of the table. 'Hello George!' Llewellyn had served as a paratrooper, one of the originals, and had been severely wounded in North Africa. Standing alongside him was John Williams the accountant who had looked after Peg's books. He put his hand on Llew's shoulder. 'I'll pay for this gentleman's copy George!' he smiled. Llewellyn had been bayoneted through the thigh close to his crotch and lay in a ditch close to a badly wounded German; they were both later picked up by a field ambulance. Llewellyn told me he was appalled at the verbal abuse aimed at the wounded German by one orderly. 'I told him,' said Llewellyn. 'You gutless bugger. Leave him alone!'

The next launch was at Big Pit and the heavens opened. Carol was there, the young teenage redhead who had very kindly typed the script of *The Fourth Device* all those years ago, now a grandmother. Also present was someone I had met just a month or two before, Ron Dudley and his mate Eric. Ron Dudley had served in the Royal Corps of Signals attached to 56th Anti Tank Reg. 5th Indian Division. Ron had written to me having read my books and finding out we were the same age and that our fortunes ran parallel. A Londoner, he now lived at Abergavenny.

I was telling the audience about our button-less uniforms. In their infinite wisdom the power that be had decided that our jungle uniforms should have tin buttons not bone buttons. Burma is a humid country, damp and clammy and during the monsoon season very, very wet. Consequently the tin buttons rusted and rotted the cotton they were sewn on with. The clips that held the five rounds of 303 ammunition were also made of tin and rusted. The Japanese had alloy clips and bone buttons on their uniforms. I knew Ron Dudley had an amusing tale to tell about having vital buttons missing and I asked him to tell it.

The Colonel sent for Ron. He doubled over to his CO and saluted.

'Chico, we are going to Rangoon. Rangoon has fallen. Would you like to come with us?' They called him Chico because he was the youngest in the Company. The monsoon rain was teeming down. Ron was soaked through.

'Well Sir I'm soaking wet and I'd rather go and change. If that's ok Sir!' Ron saluted and went to turn away.

'Chico!' The Colonel pointed to Ron's flies. 'Put that thing away Chico before it frightens the mules!' Ron told his tale with style and vigour and had the audience in stitches.

We all got drenched making our way up from the Museum Shop to the pithead baths and canteen. The canteen staff provided warm towels to dry me off. They wanted to take my photograph next to the locker named after me.

Richard took me to the book signing at Borders, Llantrisant and we met Ceri Thompson of Big Pit there. On the way home we stopped off at Cornelly to see Arthur Smith, the man who on his own kept the short story magazine *Cambrensis* alive for twenty years. Arthur was very ill; he was dying, but was still smoking. The grit, the courage that had kept him going defying the odds to keep *Cambrensis* in print and in the public eye was still there.

I received letters from everywhere and answered them all but two struck a note. One was from a retired head teacher and one time Lieutenant in the Royal Navy, Mr Denys Smith. He was skipper of a ML 200 and went in with the first landings on D-Day. Afterwards he was ordered to Milford Haven to have his launch refitted as a MLGB and in a group, a flotilla and a half, proceed to Burma. They fitted each of the launches with long petrol tanks strapped to the deck to make the long hop to Gib. The Germans used to call the

British army tanks Tommy Cookers. Not to be outdone that must have been the Royal Navy's answer to that. He and his flotilla docked at Rangoon river jetties when there were still dead bodies laying about the place. That's a sight that pulls you up with a jerk, that silent whisper inside your head telling you that the crumpled heaps strewn around the place, like garbage, were standing, breathing, talking, even having a laugh, and woke up the same time as you that very morning. Wellington was supposed to have said while inspecting the battlefield heaped with corpses after Waterloo. 'The next worst thing to losing a battle is winning a battle.'

The Lieutenant and his crew spent their time showing the flag up river and looking for stray Japanese and like us found the Burmese river people helpful and friendly. There was another poignant parallel; his wife who looked, as he put it, 'like your Peggy with dark curly hair', had recently died of cancer. They had both been head teachers.

In the summer 2010 issue of *DEKHO! The Burma Star magazine* there is a letter by a Ken Joyce, Ettalong Beach, NSW Motor Launch Gun Boat 269 and a photograph showing 269 approaching Rangoon, May 1945. Ken Joyce was 19 at the time so I'm guessing that Lieutenant Smith, who wrote me the letter some months before, was Ken Joyce's Commanding Officer. In the same issue of the DEKHO! another letter was published by A Thomas Kean concerning a plane that came down in the Irrawaddy Delta on 31st January 1945. We were sent to Bassein, three launches, to inquire after some French nuns and some missing airmen and to meet up with the Royal Welsh Fusiliers. We met up with the Fusiliers and the nuns but were told by the nuns that the airmen had been executed.

The letter deals with the fate of the airmen. They were made to dig their own graves and then beheaded. They are now buried in Rangoon War Cemetery. The airmen we had been sent to find had after all very likely been brought back to Rangoon by 856 Motor Boats. We had 30 launches and one converted Hull fishing trawler MV14. Its duties were to bring bodies from the battlefields to Rangoon for the War Graves Commission, to be buried with full military honours. I wish I had known that when Richard and I visited the Rangoon War Cemetery; we could have paid our respects at their grave sides. Four Japanese were later executed in 1948 for their part in the atrocity.

Another letter I received that was for me a bit special, was off George E Davies, born in Roman Road, Banwen but living in Senghenydd, Caerphilly; sadly too old and too sick to make the journey to his birthplace. His brother had been great friends with Herbie Regan and was pleased to know that Francis Regan, Herbie's young brother, my old boxing partner's daughter, was now Lady Ann Matthews of Celtic Manor.

The Communities First organisation was bringing out a quarterly news magazine and asked me to write an article for each issue. My contribution was entitled 'Uncle George's'.

Received a surprise telephone call from Jan Thomas. I had known Jan for many years. Jan had suffered a crushing loss that winter. Her son Neil had been drowned trying to rescue his dog that had gone through the ice at the local pond. He was a fine young man, a very hardworking junior civil engineer. She had written some poetry and her two remaining sons had told her 'To show the poetry to George.' I told her to bring her work down. I'm no expert on poetry. I could read the work but I could not read it out loud; it was that moving. These were the words of a mother with a broken heart, her life shattered by the death of her beloved son. I gave Jan some publishers' addresses and begged her to send her work to people better qualified than me to judge her work. Her poems were accepted and published not just in London but New York too.

Naomi came dashing up to the house from her father's car. 'She's courting, Gramps!' she gasped.

'Emily?'

'Yes!'

'What's he like?'

'Alright! He works on the docks with his Dad.' Nick, Nicholas Lemos, is of Greek Welsh stock and worked as a stevedore. He was as wide as a barn door and the hardest-working young man I had met for a very long time. He sent a photo of himself taken on his mobile phone, as black as a collier, in the hold of a large Russian ship unloading Russian coal in Barry Dock to burn in a Welsh power station. In the year 1913 Barry Dock exported eleven million tons of best-quality Welsh coal. David Davies Llandinam, the man many regard as the greatest Welshman that has ever lived, would be turning in his grave: seeing the magnificent docks he had built to bring wealth into Wales now being used to suck Wales dry. D.I. Williams, the one-time head of Geology for British Coal Wales and the West, told me in 1988 there was more coal still under our feet than we'd mined and that the amount of methane gas under our feet was immeasurable.

Britain survived the Second World War because we had sufficient home-produced energy to keep the war effort going.

We are now so vulnerable in terms of energy production, our country is open to blackmail from any ragbag outfit in the world and this appalling situation is the result of one woman's blind hatred of the British Trade Unions: an attitude she very likely inherited from her father, sadly a Welshman, a *Gog*, whose family hailed from Anglesey. Her genuine loathing of the lower order made her a strong supporter of apartheid, a system that kept wages in those countries at starvation level and dividends high.

Emily now teaches and works for the City of Newport. Some time ago Newport council thought it would be a good thing if some of the teachers took the driving tests for a Heavy Goods Vehicle licence. They could then drive the school buses instead of calling in strangers. Emily told me about it. I told her to go for it; one day the only job on offer perhaps would be driving a lorry. She did the course and passed first time. Now she tells me, 'If you are in Newport City Gramps and you see a pink school bus, I'll very likely be the driver.'

I was asked to write the foreword to the Library of Wales reprint of George Ewart Evans's 1947 *The Voices of the Children*. I had known George Ewart Evans very well and he had been instrumental in getting my first short story published in 1978. I felt very honoured to be asked.

I attended the celebrations of the centenary of his birth, held on 1st April 2009 at the newly established George Ewart Evans Centre For Storytelling at the ATRiuM Cardiff, where I had the pleasure of meeting his son and his daughters. Professor Gareth Williams his biographer spoke of his great admiration of George Ewart Evans. Colin Thomas the filmmaker presented his film *Let Dogs Delight* based on a famous George Ewart

Evans story. Richard Davies interviewed me and I told of the pleasure my father had got, not from reading about mining, but from the tales of the farm workers. He had gone into service at fourteen years of age as a servant boy, hired at Brecon fair, £6.00 for six months working from sun up to sun down, and how at fifteen he would cut the throat of a lamb that was born crippled and skin it to use the skin on an orphaned lamb. I went on to say that I thought that George Ewart Evans really understood what made men of my father's generation tick – men who worked in industry but still had one foot stuck in a furrow of a ploughed field. George Ewart's daughters told me afterwards that, walking in the fields with their father in Suffolk, he would show them how to dispatch an injured rabbit with one merciful blow.

They do say like attracts like: Naomi, a granddaughter and great-granddaughter of coalminers, has found herself a sweetheart, Radoslav Krstic-Tomic jnr., grandson of Radoslav Tomic, a coalminer. He is studying engineering at university.

There was a tragic accident on the inter-valley road and the victim was someone I had got to know, Terrance Bishop. He and his wife Jeanine were members of the Historical Society. Terrance was a Royal Marine Bandsman who had taken part in major parades all over the world; in the band accompanying the Queen on the Royal Yacht; having to keep in strict formation at every step and read the music at the same time, in all kinds of weather. Discipline and awareness had been drilled into him since he was a boy soldier. There were no witnesses other than the driver of the car. Terrance's ashes are scattered along the Roman Road, the Sarn Helen near Clwydi Banwen (The Banwen Gates) at the top of the mountain.

I walk to the DOVE most days when the weather is fine to eat at the Café Sarn Helen and on Tuesdays Jeanine comes with me. She is a very talented artist and is that good at copying I think she could earn a living as a forger. Jeanine is a Flemish-speaking Belgian. I asked Owen to take the easel he and Patricia had bought me to Jeanine. I no longer painted and bent over a table painting is hard work.

Jeanine and I were back in Maple House after lunch at the DOVE when Pat Bowden turned up. I had heard that she had been diagnosed with cancer of the eyelid that had been operated on. Her eyelid had been removed and sewn back and there was no trace of a scar. Pat had been as good to Peg and me as any daughter could have been and I was as pleased and as happy with the good result as if she was my daughter. Pat had bought a copy of *Boys of Gold* and *Where The Flying Fishes Play* and wanted me to write something in each of the books as her thank you to the consultant surgeon who had performed the operation.

'This is Eleri Edwards of Mentorn Media. We are making a programme *Rolf and art in Wales* and are hoping you'll be willing to take part?'

The day of Rolf Harris's arrival it was raining. Rolf turned up, bush hat, white beard and red shirt, a grand splash of colour on a damp cloudy day and not looking a day over sixty. Eira had come up meaning as usual to help but there were so many people and so much film gear in the room she gave in, told them to take the telephone off the hook and I think went upstairs out of the way.

Rolf explained to me that the programme would be based on the work of the Polish emigrant Josef Herman and that

285

he, Rolf, was to going to paint in Josef Herman's style. Rolf asked me what style of painter I thought I was? I told him I thought I painted in the style of a cave painter. There are no messages in my painting; they are just pictures of what I can see in front of me. I went on to explain that I really had tried to understand abstract art, surrealism and cubism but was unable to. I put it down to my lack of formal education. Similarly, the cave painter: he painted to show off a bit. He probably knew no one in the cave could draw as well as he could. It never ever occurred to him that some art critic would look at his work 20,000 years from then and read something into it. I said in the BBC Two film, 'It was bitterly cold, raining, pouring, the caveman looked out and said "Bugger this I'm not going out in this!" and drew a deer on the wall and told the kids, "If it's fine tomorrow I'll bring you one of these back for dinner."'

I asked would one of the crew take a video of Rolf and me on my camera so that I would have a record of Rolf Harris being in my house. Rolf readily agreed and sang a song he had written in Welsh at full blast in my back kitchen. I think he enjoyed himself at Maple House. I received a note off Eleri Edwards a few days later in which she wrote: 'You were fantastic'. I wondered how much of the Maple House episode they would use if any. It turned out none.

I received a letter from Melissa Munro of the Department of Modern and Contemporary Art at the National Museum of Wales asking me would I take part in a project for their touch screen computers for their new galleries, talking about Josef Herman's painting *The Three Welsh Miners*. It had to be done on a Monday when the Museum was closed. I had never seen this particular painting before. One miner stood, his fist holding his lapel, in the stance of a squire; another his thumb in his trouser belt. They had the look of confidence about them. Josef Herman came to live in Ystragynlais in 1944. The country had been at war for four years. There was severe rationing, everything was threadbare, yet he saw in these three anthracite miners a self-assurance and poise. In my interview I said that Josef Herman had been born in poverty in a Jewish ghetto in Warsaw. I on the other hand I had been born in the anthracite coalfield of West Wales. We had playing fields, bowling greens, tennis courts, swimming pools, cinemas, ambulance car services, convalescent homes, research into miner's lung disease all funded by the South Wales Miners' Federation. All these amenities available to everyone, the butcher the baker the candlestick maker. If there's one thing I've done in my life that I'm pleased about, it's having that message recorded for posterity. The original Big Society that Mrs Thatcher smashed with the enthusiastic help of the likes of David Cameron.

My efforts in my interview on Josef Herman's painting pleased Naomi if no one else. She went to see the finished product and reckoned I should be up for an Oscar. She told me she had gained a BA (Hons) and had been accepted to read for her Masters at Cardiff. That was the youngest and the last through successfully, and I thought how much that would have meant for Peg. Just like Noel's wedding. He married Lalayn on 1st of July 2011 at Cambridge Cottage, Kew Gardens. I could have spent days admiring the fabulous paintings and drawings hung on the walls. There were etchings, drawings, watercolours, the works of many of the most famous botanists in the world. I had never been to a civil wedding ceremony before. Lalayn came in on her father's arm wearing a gorgeous ivory coloured dress her jet-black hair fastened by bejewelled brooches. Noel and Jamie, tall and straight-backed, looked splendid in their morning dress, Emily and Naomi looked beautiful, especially now Emily was pregnant. Peg would have been bursting with pride if she could have been there. Our first great-grandchild was born on Saturday the 22nd of October 2011. As well as the joy and the pleasure I felt at each of their achievements it brought too a pang of sadness that Peg was not there to enjoy it too. Remembering her tears of joy when seeing two-year old Noel that beautiful summer's day on Haverfordwest railway station.

A young man called Duncan from BBC Manchester telephoned me and asked would I take part in a Melvyn Bragg programme *The Reel History of Britain*. I said I would. They transported me to Big Pit. I was there for ten hours. Thankfully Eira came with me. Big Pit is on two levels; there is the pithead and at altitude the pithead baths and canteen. The second time I climbed the hill I was knackered. Eira had my dinner on the table ready. There was the former manager of Six Bells, an ex-Yorkshire miner in his seventies who had worked in the same mine as Arthur Scargill and had ridden on his motorbike all the way down from Yorkshire, a nursing sister and a lady from the Isle of Wight who had a diary that had belonged to her great uncle who lived in Cresford aged 13 at the time of the great explosion. Each of us were interviewed separately.

I tried to make the point I had made in Cardiff. I told them my father started work as a farm servant at 13 years of age. Then came WWI, an infantryman on a shilling a day.

Demobbed with his brother Jim they started work as miners at Jebs Mountain Colliery Crynant. By 1925 when I was born he lived in a new three-bedroomed company house with hot and cold water and a large garden, plus he'd bought himself an Ariel motorbike, so I said I expect my father had thought he had definitely made the right move.

Then the interviewer, a lovely-looking Irish lady, asked me would I recite a poem because they thought I had a strong South Wales accent. At first I said no but gave in at the end. I practised reading it a few times. Then they filmed me. It must have pleased them; the lovely interviewer came over and kissed me.

I waited to see what, if any, of my contribution would be used in the programme, which was supposed to be about the 1930s. Two of the contributors would not have remembered the thirties. Of my contribution nothing!

I had the honour and the pleasure of meeting Susan Robeson, the granddaughter of one of the greatest men of the twentieth century, Paul Robeson, on her visit to the DOVE. She talked about her grandfather: an athlete, scholar, multi-lingual Shakespearean actor and renowned throughout the world for his beautiful, magnificent singing voice. Gained a law degree at Columbia Law School but gave up practicing law when a vicious white secretary refused to take dictation from him because he was black. In those days segregation was legal in the USA and the law backed the spiteful little madam. If it had not been for that white typist Paul Robeson may well have been the first black President of the United States of America, but times were very different then. The Bund of America was the largest Nazi party in the world.

Supported by very powerful people, the likes of George Bush's grandfather Senator Prescott Bush, whose company's assets were seized in 1942 under the Trading with the Enemy Act. Robeson's passport was revoked in 1950 when McCarthy's 'Reds under the beds' was at its peak. Imagine the loss of international earnings that entailed. Susan Robeson's grandfather's ties with the miners of South Wales go back to the 1920s and they were cemented into the history of the South Wales mining communities by his transatlantic telephone message to the Miners' Eisteddfod at Porthcawl in 1957. Many believe that that broadcast caused such embarrassment to the government of the United States that Paul Robeson's passport was returned to him in 1958.

Jan Thomas and I were invited to the National Eisteddfod at Ebbw Vale. Both of us had contributed to the magazine *GLO*. We went first to the University of Swansea marquee; I wanted Jan to meet Susan Robeson. I gave her the photograph I had taken of her and Siân Williams of the South Wales Library at the Banwen Miners' memorial stone.

After our visit to the Eisteddfod Jan drove us to Six Bells. We wanted to see the Guardian of the Valleys, unveiled by the Archbishop of Canterbury a week or so before. It is a magnificent, colossal sculpture, as high as the Angel of the North but for me with a more real human presence. The valley sides are steep and heavily wooded. The Guardian stands as if in a cupped hand in the warmth and love there was in the mining communities.

We went on to Merthyr Tydfil and had lunch in a restaurant that had once been the mansion of one of the great iron masters. I knew Jan's father had served as an infantryman in Burma with the Lincolnshire and had read that the Lincolns had taken part in the recapture of Rangoon. Jan told me that he had died of malaria when she was thirteen. I asked Jan what his name was.

'George!' She laughed and still smiling she said, 'My mum keeps telling me to find someone. Not to be on my own.'

I looked at the smiling, good-looking, very intelligent woman sitting opposite me and I understood the rage the great Shakespearean actor Sir John Gielgud had exploded with, when asked: 'What's it like to be old Sir John?' Was he remembering the Saunders Lewis line, 'To stop lusting is to die'?

22

I am now in my eighty-fifth year to heaven or wherever.

I covered the first twenty-two years of my life in my second book *Where The Flying Fishes Play*, and, in this book, try to cover the last sixty-four years. In the years since I returned to work underground the valley has changed, totally unrecognizable. Not one colliery chimneystack in sight except for the one left standing at the Mining Museum at Cefn Coed, once the deepest anthracite pit in the world. No winding engines chuffing and puffing twenty-four hours a day. No giant pyramid of slag heaps, no aerial ropeways dominating the skyline. No horse drawn milk floats or coal carts.

Now the streets are lined with privately owned cars. No buses to Aberdare or the Swansea Valley and perhaps worst of all, the railway, The Neath and Brecon, that for one hundred years had puffed its way through one of the most beautiful, picturesque train rides in Britain, that could now be bringing tourists by the thousands to the area, has been dismantled by the man people refer to deservedly as Lord bloody Beeching.

The direct bus service from Neath to Banwen was stopped. We were having to change buses at Seven Sisters going and coming from Neath to Banwen. I had to go to Crynant; it was a bitterly cold day and the only other passenger was Lily Tuck Shop, Mrs Lilian Davies. Her mother had kept the school tuck shop the whole time I was at school hence her nickname. I knew Lil was recovering from a very serious illness but being Lil Tuck Shop she was not going to grumble about the freezing cold we were standing in. I could see Lil's colour changing and thought shortly I'm going to be in trouble with a very sick lady on my hands. Eventually the bus arrived. After witnessing Lil's distress I wrote to the *Western Mail* and to our AM Gwenda Thomas and to our councillor Ali Thomas and our MP Peter Hain. Their joint efforts had the service restored.

People it seems have always been fascinated by other people's sexual behaviour. But unlike today, in 1947 reams of pornography were not available at the flick of a switch. I remember gangs of us fourteen-year-old collier boys walking all the way from High Street Station, Swansea, right the way down High Street on Saturday afternoons just to see a packet of French Letters in Joe Black's window, and bragging about seeing them in work on Monday morning.

When television was in black and white, on Sunday afternoons the only entertainment were talks, The *Brains Trust* and the like. There was one programme where an eminent biologist said something like, 'Maybe our lopsided aggressive sexuality has been put on us as a curse!'

Peg agreed with him. 'He's right. Whoever created us, if we must procreate, they could have given us a more dignified way of making babies, say by just hooking our little fingers together? And not a performance that leaves us both looking, after ten minutes, like we've been dragged through a hedge backwards!'

'You want to stop doing it then?'

'No!' she laughed and punched me on the shoulder.

In 1947 our country was still recovering from the shock of a world war, many of our towns and cities were still little more than a heaps of rubble plus we were stony broke – not two pennies to rub together. The Americans, who, according to David Cameron, were the senior partners in 1940 had had most of our money. We needed silver to process reconnaissance photography. The deal we made with the Americans was daylight robbery. Debt! We were over our heads in debt. Even Winston Churchill was close to broke and the Labour Cabinet, threadbare would be an apt description but Aneurin Bevan was ready to stuff the consultants' mouths with gold to give the people the National Health Service in 1948 and he did but some Tories even then, with the sanatoriums packed to the gunwales with TB patients and droves of war wounded to be looked after were trying to persuade British doctors to leave the country. Clem Attlee, one-time barrister and soldier, who had served in the trenches in WWI, built council houses from Lands End to John o'Groats; he found the money from somewhere.

Now we have a government that has 18 millionaires sitting at the Cabinet table; who, it seems, aim to pay off the country's debt by lowering the standard of living of the poorest people. Sincerely explaining to the people that the painful decision a pensioner will have to make deciding whether to buy a meal of food or turn the heating up will be as difficult a decision for Nick Clegg and his friend David Cameron as it is for the old-age pensioner and people believe them! Are public school boys really taught to fart and put the blame on someone else? The banks they told us had caused the mess we're in and I don't suppose there are very many bankers in the Labour Party.

A team of hard-working, brilliantly clever doctors, scientists and engineers have saved the life of a forty-year-old man by fitting him with a totally artificial heart, another man's life saved when he was fitted with a totally artificial gullet, and between them these outstandingly fabulously clever people are not being paid as much as a thick-as-two-short-planks footballer. Maybe it will not be this generation but the next, or perhaps the next generation again which will decide to wheel the guillotine back out of the cupboard.

Yesterday the 3rd of August 2011, a lovely summer's day, I'd been to the DOVE for lunch. I met a young man originally from Glyn Neath now living in Sweden with his Swedish wife. The young couple wanted directions on how to get on to the Roman Road. They wanted to walk the Sarn Helen from Banwen to Neath. I didn't know it then but I was to make the longest walk that day I had made for a very long time. It was a very warm day and I had fallen asleep watching television. A tap on the window woke me; it was Jeanine. I had promised her that I would walk the Bog (Gors Llwyn) with her and she had arrived to take me at my word.

The Bog is all that remains of an Ice Age lake now officially a site of special scientific interest. I had made a painting of it and it was my father's favourite painting. I had not walked the Bog for twenty or more years. Then you crossed it by way of what in all probability was one of the oldest boardwalks in Britain with golden reeds taller than a man on either side. Sadly now buried under tons of stone chippings.

I wondered who was the thicko who ordered that to be done. We turned off the Bog pathway onto the pathway that follows the track of the Banwen Iron Works Railway and here again the same thicko must have been at work. The path is now covered with flagstones hiding all the stone railway sleepers of the railway that had first linked this part of the world with the port of Swansea and the world in 1845. Historically important because Banwen Iron Works along with Onllwyn Iron Works and Ynysgedwyn Iron Works were unique being fired by anthracite. The method of smelting iron using anthracite was taken to Pennsylvania by David Thomas who became known as the father of the American anthracite iron industry. There was an abundance of wild flowers in the warm sun.

On my eighty-sixth birthday my paintings *Cogging Four Feet*, the painting used for the cover of my book *Boys of Gold* and *The Death of Silver*, a painting that Peg entered in the *Artist* Magazine's International Exhibition in London in 1967 where it gained a place, were officially accepted by The South Wales Miners' Library at Hendrefoelan House, Swansea. To mark the occasion Richard Davies had arranged for me to present to the Library the complete set of Parthian's *Library of Wales* series and later said he'd send me the bill.

Siân Williams the Librarian and Mandy Orford laid on a real treat for my birthday: a buffet and a beautiful cake adorned by the photograph of me at nineteen used on the back cover of Boys of Gold. It was a great honour to have my work hung in the South Wales Miners' Library, a living memorial to the people of industrial South Wales and probably the cradle where the idea of the National Health Service was born.

I have just got back off a four-day holiday in Torquay and on one day of that holiday we were taken on a tour of Plymouth. Our guide was a young woman from Bangor, North Wales, married to a Royal Marine. The bus approached the massive walls of the Royal Citadel, in appearance a frightening place, and I remembered that in 1947, after twenty-three months on active service in Burma and five weeks in the coldest winter on record in Thetford, that resulted in both my feet being frozen, I thought I'd arrived in paradise. Now, looking back, it was the first day of the happiest six months of the eighty-six years I've been alive. My father had put the allowance I had made out of my army pay into a post office account, so I had enough funds to pay my train fare home to be with Peg at weekends and get back before Reveille so I wasn't missed on Monday morning.

I often doze off watching television and wake up with a start half expecting Peg to be there. Strangely, wandering around the cobbled dockside of the Barbican with Ken Cook, where for that six months, from Monday to Friday, I spent my time, Peg's presence was tangible.

EPILOGUE

RETURN TO BURMA

My grandson Noel had gone to Burma on his gap year and hiked from Rangoon to Mandalay: a journey I had made more than fifty years before. Now in 2005 the British Legion were asking if any member would like to visit Burma for the sixtieth anniversary of the end of the war in the Far East and to visit the graves of fallen comrades, the trip partly funded by the National Lottery. I thought I would use the opportunity to visit the graves of two of our lads; one I knew well, Ernie Read of A section, same section as me, and Taff Ellis of C section.

Ernie was one of the battle-experienced men brought into 856 Motor Boats when the company was urgently wanted in the Far East. To the majority of us eighteen- and nineteen-year-olds, Ernie was an old man in his late twenties. Taff Ellis was my age; he was lost, swept over the side into the powerful current of the Irrawaddy. I had got to know Ernie on the troop ship on our way out. The convoy had spent five days in the worst storm many of the crew of the troopship had ever experienced off the west coast of Ireland. We did not know it at the time but it was the biggest troop convoy ever to leave for the Far East and was now somewhere off Cape Vincent. The weather was calming and I had gone on deck for a breath of fresh air. It was pitch dark.

'Taff?'

I recognised Corporal Ernie's voice. 'Corp!'

'How are you? We've had a bit of a going over. You OK?'

'Aye! I'm alright.' I was leaning on the ship's rail alongside him. For a while we stood in silence.

'Where exactly in Wales are you from Taff?'

'A small village near the town of Neath.'

'Neath! I had a mate came from a small village near Neath when I was stationed in Gib. He said it was called I think he said Banwen or something like that?'

I was dumbfounded. 'Banwen! That's where I come from! What was this bloke's name?'

'Butler. Hayden Butler.'

I really could not believe what I was hearing. A bloke from London who had heard of Banwen and my father had told me Hayden Butler had been killed.

'But Hayden Butler's dead?'

'Yes! He was in our lot Taff. His boat was blown up and he was badly burnt.' There was a crew of three on our boats: coxswain, engine man and waterman. Ernie was an engine man; I was a waterman.

Arriving in Bombay was like a dream. I had read so much about India, it was as if I had been there before. The rest of the troops on board were shipped off on trains, taken in lorries or marched off. We were given the day off to go into the city. We went to a whites-only swimming pool where Bob got badly sunburned. A very long train ride and boat ride down the river Ganges followed to cross India to reach Chittagong, to be billeted in a large tented camp. There we were kitted out in our jungle greens, issued with live ammunition (fifty rounds), enough to fill our webbing pouches, and another fifty rounds in a cotton bandolier and asked to sign proxy forms for the coming Parliamentary Elections. Most of us were old enough to vote.

Thirty of us volunteered for our first assignment into Burma, Akyab where I got to know Ernie quite well. For a while we were in the same crew. The most memorable event for me in my short time on Akyab was meeting Leyshon Griffiths of 42 Marine Commando. They were dishing out something to drink; it was blazing hot. He must have heard my accent.

'Where you from?'

'Neath!'

'I'm from Abercraf!'

'I'm from Banwen!

'Bloody hell! Do you know Nancy Josh?' Nancy was one of three very pretty sisters who lived in our street. Leyshon lived in the next village with his grandmother, a well-known local herbalist who the miners went to if a cut turned septic. About a week later he had persuaded Bob and me to accompany him and two of his mates skiving off to an American Air Strip after dark to see a film. We went in a 30 cwt truck that had been abandoned and they had managed to get going. It was in the open air. We had to sit behind the screen; all the seats in the front had been taken. The writing was back to front but that made no difference.

The film was Jennifer Jones in the *Song of Bernadette*. I was smoking Indian cigarettes.

'They smell like horse shit!' moaned Leyshon. 'I'll get you some decent tobacco.' He was on Navy issue, being a Marine.

The following night Bob and I were sat on deck of our D-tug moored under the stern of an ammunition ship, in the moonlight. The moon hung like a silver disc in a dark velvety-blue sky. There was the sudden roar and swish overhead of fighter planes flying very low causing us instinctively to duck. The Japanese were flying straight into a hail of British gunfire. Ploughing up the British lines with a stream of flames and explosives. They wheeled away and back they came roaring and screaming, shooting red glowing streams of tracers and incendiary bullets, making long red lines in the dark velvet-blue sky and causing us to drop to our knees.

The following morning I went ashore on an errand for Captain Belton and to inquire after Leyshon to see if he was ok and hopefully collect the tobacco he had promised me. His mates told me he had bought it.

He hadn't! Two years later I found out he had got back home before me and married Mildred, one of the prettiest girls in the valley.

Our work finished on Akyab. We were brought back to Calcutta to a tidy up. About a week or so wandering around the swanky shops of Chowringhee and the not so swanky brothels. Suffered a morning's collective punishment drill in 120 degrees because someone shouted at the CSM to go and fuck himself.

They asked for forty volunteers. The forty of us were taken to a place that seemed miles from anywhere, under canvas. Spent our time swimming in the river, the medics sticking us with needles and charging Bren Gun weapon magazines, in strict order, two tracers, three ball and an incendiary twenty-eight rounds to each magazine. Over the last week or so, Indian army cooks had been preparing our food. Then as Sergeant George Ashby described them, the worst fucking cooks in the world took over. British army cooks.

It was the last meal of the day. Meat and Veg canned for the First World War. It looked like vomit. I went to tip my mess tin into the waste bucket and a voice behind me said: 'Stuff it down you Taff! Stuff it down you. It looks bloody awful and tastes bloody awful. But get it down you Taff. God knows where we're going. So get it down you!

'There's a good lad!' Ernie Read urged me. They do say, 'It's a good job we don't know what's in front of us or we wouldn't get out of bed in the morning.'

A few weeks from then Ernest Edward Read would be dead, killed on the banks of the Twante Canal. Now I was hoping to go on a Royal British Legion pilgrimage to Rangoon to pay my respects at his grave.

Because of our ages we were all asked to take an escort. Geraint was working overseas, Owen was involved in a project that needed his full attention, but thankfully Richard very kindly offered to accompany me. But that was not without its obstacles. Received a letter from the Burma Embassy in London inquiring into Dr Richard Davies's suitability for a visa because of his writings. I telephoned the Embassy and a very soft-spoken young lady answered. She asked, 'What does Dr Davies write about?'

'He writes novels. His most famous is *Work Sex and Rugby*.'

'Can you get me a copy?' she laughed. Richard's visa was in the post that day.

When we arrived in London there were that many people on the station platform, if Richard had not been there I would have caught the next train straight back home. Our next stop was the Union Jack Club, Richard pushing his way through the crowd, me following in his wake. It was a splendid lodging, the main reception area, its wood panelling embossed in gold lettering with the names of military heroes, everything about the place was elegant and impressive.

Heathrow take off for Bangkok 10th March 2005 arrive Bangkok 6am 11th of March then Bangkok to Rangoon. Leaving Rangoon airport very large notice at the side of road, the size of the side of a house: 'DRUG CARRYING YOU FACE THE DEATH PENALTY'. Next stop the Dusit Inya Lake Hotel.

Sixty years before when we retook Rangoon it was May and the Monsoons had begun, the heavy downpour of rain stripping the flowers from the trees. Now it was March, every tree and bush was in flower, a giant Chelsea Flower Show. I had a fine large room with an en suite, television, easychairs and a balcony looking over the parkland that lend to the lake. At our evening meal we found out the Burmese made top-notch beer. The meal was a carvery type, you walked along a long bar laden with every kind of meat, fish and vegetables imaginable. At our table Jim Jones MM and his wife Doris of Oldbury, Albert Clarkstone and Tony Mee of Nottingham, both former Royal Corps of Signals, Richard and myself.

The following morning we attended a service of remembrance and wreath laying, first the Taukkyan War Cemetery that had been the site of a large and bloody battle and then the Rangoon War Cemetery. Medals and headdress to be worn. Both Richard and I were given a small wreath of poppies. Buses took us first to Taukkyan War Cemetery. It was immaculately kept, not a blade of grass out of place. Each grave marked with a bronze plate bearing the name, rank, age, regimental badge, and date of death: 6,368 bronzed plates lie in orderly ranks as would six and a half British battalions.

Running the full width of the cemetery was the Rangoon Memorial, a massive columned archway, its white stone, brilliant in the morning sun, commemorating 26,380 men with no known grave.

At the far end of the cemetery a memorial to the 1,049 officers and men whose remains were accorded the last rite by their religion of committal to fire.

The service was taken by the Revd Samuel Hitang, an address by the British Legion Vice President. Then a white wreath laid by the British Ambassador Ms Vicky Bowman, followed by others of red poppies. The Burmese army provided the buglers.

A short bus ride and we arrived at the Rangoon War Cemetery. This was the cemetery I had come to visit. There are 1,391 men buried here, among them Ernie Read and others killed in the fighting in and around Rangoon, also the men who died as prisoners of war in Rangoon jail.

First an official wreath laying ceremony then Richard and I set out to find Ernie's grave. I had a plan and a location. Plot 2 line D grave number 17. Read, Ernest Edward, Corporal, Royal Army Service Water Transport. Age: thirty-one.

We found the grave. I had brought with me some pebbles from the stream that runs through my garden to put on

Ernie's grave. I decided to take the pebbles because Ernie, a Londoner, had been a good friend to two soldiers from Banwen and I thought I'd leave a bit of Banwen on his grave. Before I left for Burma the children had bought me a digital video camera. Richard used it to film me putting the pebbles and the poppies on Ernie's grave, with Paul Harris the Standard Bearer standing at my side.

George Hammersley from Hornsea who was accompanied by his son John was overwhelmed with grief at the side of his young brother's grave. The last time George had seen his young brother the lad was just seventeen. George went back off leave; he was serving in the Royal Navy on the convoys to Russia. Some time after his young brother was called up and sent to Burma, and a week before the war ended, his young brother was killed. George I expect was seeing his young brother still a carefree boy, laughing, standing before him. There was a retired army nursing sister from Fife, aged ninety, in another group. She came over and took charge. She and George went off to sit in a quiet corner.

One of the other pilgrims, old in his eighties, his brother had died as a prisoner of war in Rangoon's infamous Insein Prison. He had paid to travel halfway around the world to put soil from the grave of their mother and father onto his brother's grave. His brother had died in the most brutal of places, more than sixty years before. The look of peaceful contentment on his face as he patted the soil into shape onto his long dead brother's grave. To him it was obvious that the expense and long journey had been well worth it.

My first experience of prisoners of war came after the capture of Rangoon. These were not the usual prisoners of war. These men had been serving in the British Indian Army and had been first taken prisoner by the Japanese, perhaps at the appalling surrender of Singapore – where it was said one hundred thousand fully armed men were handed over to fifteen thousand Japanese. It was where a good friend of mine, someone I had worked with, was taken: Gavin Scott. The Japanese had given the Indian soldiers the opportunity to fight on their side with the promise that they would drive the British out of India and India would have home rule or suffer the brutal treatment the Japanese handed out to prisoners of war. These men had sworn allegiance to the British Crown so could face a charge of high treason.

The thirty launches of 856 Motor Boats were the Army's only means of high speed water transport after the capture of Rangoon and the launches needed to be serviced. Large water pumps were loaded on to rafts, the rafts floated to the riverbank, the pumps sending powerful jets of water into the grey mud carving a creek that would fill with water at high tide allowing our launches to reach our workshop. It was a dirty job; the prisoners were covered in mud from head to toe. They were guarded by armed guards but nobody abused them.

In the afternoon we went to a service in Rangoon's Cathedral and then to a reception at the British Embassy. The trees of the beautiful garden were festooned with tiny lanterns and waiters served you with wine and refreshments. I bought a book of an old Burma army veteran telling the story of the brave fight against the Japanese and that the Japanese were as fearful of the jungle as anyone else. One gruesome incident recorded: 'A small Japanese patrol *bivouac* on the outskirts of a village disturbed a swarm of giant hornets. In the morning the villagers found all the Japanese soldiers dead.'

Vicky Bowman didn't look like anything I expected an Ambassador to look like. She was young and very good-looking. 'Hello,' she said and held out her hand. We shook hands and went on to chat. Her father was a master at Oxford and he had told her to go to Cambridge, 'and that whatever subject you take make sure you take a foreign language as well! I went down the list alphabetically and came to B, Burmese, and I've got this job.'

The following morning Richard and I went to the Shwedagon Pagoda: 2,500 years old, 321 feet high, covered from top to bottom in twenty-four carat gold leaf. It is a golden bejewelled cone, its beauty breathtaking and unforgettable. Apparently, 8,688 gold blocks hold the top *stupa*. The umbrella-like design that shades the crown in which are set 5,448 diamonds, 2,317 sapphires, rubies and topaz with an emerald in the centre to catch the rays of the sun. Below there are 1,485 small bells, 420 solid silver and 1,065 pure gold, but then covering the golden edifice like a second skin, bamboo scaffolding, made of bamboo shafts two to three inches in diameter at most. The scaffolding was a work of art in itself. They were cleaning the elegant curving structure.

The temple was crowded when we arrived. We took off our shoes and proceeded up the splendid stairway. Everything was spotlessly clean. A procession was coming our way. Men carrying small boys on their shoulders, the boys dressed in monks' robes and shaded by parasols. Our guide told us the very young boys were trainee monks. Our guide asked me what day I was born on. I told him I did not know. He asked me my date of birth; I told him and in a flash he said you were born on a Wednesday and you are in the house of the elephant. He asked Richard the same question. Richard belonged to the house of the Tiger.

'You pay homage at the shrine of the elephant,' he told me; he told Richard to go to the shrine of the tiger. We each bought a bouquet of flowers; back home such a bouquet would have cost a fortune. I pushed in with the crowd. A fountain of water gently emptied into a carved stone basin, from which you filled a small cup and poured it over the head of a small carved Buddha. We were literally jammed against each other, men and women, but no one seemed to mind. Then, the Burmese bathe often during a day, which may account for the fact that they don't seem to mind you touching them or them touching you. Our guide told me to put my arm around him having our photo taken and said the same to Richard.

From there we went to see the Reclining Buddha. The very sight of it made you take a step back. Thirty feet high and at least seventy yards long: to sculpt a figure of such huge proportions and to arrive at such outstanding beauty demanded great artistic skill. The first-class maintenance was obvious, not even a speck of faded paintwork. Visitors give money in the hope of gaining merit. While we stood there a little girl of about three or four walked up confidently to a large transparent plastic box full of money and pushed the money her mother had given her into the box.

Later we went in search of the houses which 856 Motor Boats had been billeted in, sixty years before in 1945, at the Irrawaddy Flotilla Company Iron Foundry. This was a company that before the war boasted the largest inland waterway fleet in the world: nine hundred steamers trading along Burma's great rivers.

We headed for the river and found the place. What had been an area of six superb very large houses to accommodate the managers of a large industrial complex was now a slum. When we had arrived in May 1945, after spending a night in the engineering department of a railway station, the property had been very well maintained. Except for a few dead bodies about the place, that people said were looters, but others said were the victims of trigger-happy Indian soldiers. Yorkie Brown found a tank of fuel oil in the foundry and soaked some sacking in it. Captain Belton ordered Yorkie with a couple of lads to cremate a swollen maggot-filled corpse, and Bob and me to take a Bren Gun and stop anybody coming down the road. It had been a Japanese billet; their beds were still there, a piano turned on its side and some family photos scattered about the place. The beds three eight-inch-wide planks by six feet long plus a wooden pillow, a block of wood with a hollow carved out, and a piece of canvas nailed over the hollow.

There were two main gateways into the complex. I walked on to what had been the front lawn through the top gate in front of the house that been the billet for C section. I turned to the left and walked past the house that had been the billet of B section and on to the house that had been the billet of A section, the house I had come back to from river details and upriver patrols, the house I had stormed back to, and had had a dressing down off Captain Belton, because I had rushed upstairs not answering when he had called me. It was half an hour after leaving Challagan, a friend and comrade, in the brutal hands of the Red Cap prison warders at Insein Prison. It was too the house where I had had my twentieth birthday.

Now there was barbed wire draped everywhere. The ground floor of the house that had been screened with beautiful teak latticework was now crudely bricked up. The teak walls of the upstairs rooms opened like Venetian blinds controlled by a lever in the corner of each room. The Burmese must be among the best carpenters in the world.

Two young women came to the door and then a young man. I offered my hand. 'Hello!'

The young man smiled and took my hand. I pointed to the house and told I had lived here sixty years before. He laughed and told the two young women what I said in Burmese. They smiled broadly and were holding hands.

He told me he was a lecturer at the university where he taught chemistry. I told him my youngest son had done chemistry. Richard had followed me and was recording the goings-on on the video camera. One of our Burmese drivers had said, it's only the army that get everything like new cars and the like. I wondered, seeing the poverty this teacher was living in, had some of the evil influences of the Khmer Rouge spread here to Burma from Cambodia. I hoped not.

That night at dinner everyone had a story to tell. The story that we found the funniest was Doris Jones cajoling her husband into telling us where he'd got shot when he won his Military Medal. Jim insisted that the lads didn't want to know.

'Go on James tell them!' she laughed.

'No!' James resisted.

'James come on, don't be a spoil sport,' Doris coaxed.

'I got shot up the arse lads! Right!' James burst out. After

311

we had stopped laughing James explained what had happened. They had put a charge under a small road bridge and it didn't go off, so James went back and reset the charge, and climbing out of the ditch a sniper got James in the backside.

The following day Richard and I decided to go on the river. Being on the jetty watching the surge of the river transported me back body and soul sixty years, more completely than any other place in Rangoon. For the best part of two years we had spent all our time on the river, working and sleeping. However long I live, this sight and this sound of this great river will be a part of me.

The day Bob, Smithy and I watched transfixed as a huge oceangoing junk went down. First, its hemp bow spring snapped then its hemp stern spring snapped. She was swept broadside, not a sound from anybody, on to the bows of three moored Tank Landing Ships. She capsized in an instant, her mast snapping on the bows of the TLS. We ran the length of the TLS. There was nothing, just the grey surging current tumbling, rolling and speeding towards the open sea. Then a couple of hundred yards downriver pots and pans started bobbing up, but no people.

There were some Tamil boys on the jetty and like all Tamil lads had more than a bit of savvy. The eldest of the lads cottoned on that we were going to board the steamer and volunteered to come with us. He could speak English, Burmese and Tamil. He'd come if his brother could come with him.

'OK!' said Richard but then his brother wanted to bring his friend.

It wasn't going to cost much, so!

We got ourselves to the top deck. There was a small café selling cold drinks and tea. Richard bought the boys a Coke each. We were under way and as the boat made its way against the current you became very aware of its enormous power. The river was about a mile wide at that point.

We got ashore and asked a bloke with a jeep to drive us to the town of Twante. The metal road soon gave way to a dirt road; a bus passed us doing a fair old whack. We passed two groups of protesters with placards demanding that the road be made up.

The town of Twante was threadbare; apparently nothing stopped at the town any more. Not the steamers that day, anyway. So how to get back? With the help of the eldest Tamil boy, I think, Richard found a woman who owned a motorized *sampan* but she had to find a coxswain. After a while they found one. We clambered down the bamboo poles into the *sampan*, Richard, the three boys, and me. Not a lot of room in the *sampan*, about twelve foot from stem to stern and a four-foot beam, no life jackets and we set off.

It seemed like forever, the long journey back. The sun blazed down, not even the smallest amount of shade. The three lads went to sleep and Richard recorded when he could. The villages on the banks were as they were when we were here sixty years before, huts on stilts, and as they had sixty years before, the villagers still waved a welcome.

At last the golden Shwedagon Pagoda came into sight as we neared the mouth of the Twante canal. Cross the Rangoon River and we'd be home. We could not land at a jetty so the coxswain beached the *sampan*. The police must have been watching us. As soon as I put my foot ashore a voice said 'Come with me please! And you!' to Richard.

313

We followed the policeman up the riverbank along the road into the police station. There were policemen everywhere, loafing around. Richard was busy going through his knapsack looking for the steamer tickets; thankfully he found them.

That afternoon we were supposed to be having high tea with the rest of the party at the Strand Hotel, in its day, so they said, the pride of the British Empire. We walked into the hotel. We must have looked a sight after spending the afternoon in an open boat in the blazing sun.

Back at our hotel, there was a knock on my door. I opened it and there were two lovely-looking Burmese girls. They had brought my laundry back. Smiling they walked into the room: one, the bold one, took hold of my arm. The shy one hung my shirts in the wardrobe; the one who had hold of my arm was stroking me on the chest. I remembered a village girl, all those years ago, wetting the tip of her finger, standing close in front of me, and removing a peeper from the corner of my eye and smiling. We hadn't even spoken. I was nineteen and she'd be about the same age.

'You live in hotel?' I asked the girl hanging my shirts in the wardrobe.

'No,' she shook her head. 'Me home help Mama.'

'Her Papa he bad she help her Mama,' said the bolder one still holding my arm and now her head against her my chest. 'How old?' she asked me then.

'Eighty,' and I drew the figure eighty on my hand with my finger.

'Eighty good! Very good!' she said patting and stroking my chest and laughing, her beautiful dark almond-shaped eyes shone, and the scent of her as fresh and as clean as monsoon rain.

For a split second I thought to myself: write home to the boys, tell them sell up and split the money between you. I'm staying here, love Dad.

Instead I made do with watching Wales play Scotland on television with Richard. They say people get bloody rude with old age. Now I think they get bloody gutless as well.

The next morning Richard and I went to one of the main bazaars to buy presents to take home and we picked up a young trainee monk on the way, at least that what he said he was. His name was Charcoal. I wanted to buy the girls Burmese dresses. I had bought them earrings and Bassein umbrellas. I had been calling them parasols. Sixty years before I had taken two rice paper parasols home, I thought, but their proper name was Bassein umbrellas. The two young Burmese girls working in the hotel gem shop enlightened me. They were from Bassein and their grandmother still lived there.

'How old is your grandmother?'

'Eighty.'

'Has she lived in Bassein all her life?'

'Yes!'

'Well she must have been there sixty-one years ago when I was there!'

Sixty-one years ago three of our boats under the command of Captain Frank Belton, as I said before, left for Bassein to meet up with a detachment of Royal Welsh Fusiliers to try and locate some French nuns who had been running a school in the town since before the war and inquire after some British airmen who were missing. The airmen had been executed. I gave a pretty girl a tin of pilchards; she gave me the hand painted parasols.

It was returning from Bassein to base that Ernie Read was killed. Four years later Peg gave one of the parasols to our flower girls at our wedding, sisters Angela and Ena Lewis.

I bought a red and gold outfit for Naomi, a blue and gold outfit for Emily, blue for Patricia and grey for Jayne. Richard bought an outfit for Gill his wife and daughter Ela and one for himself; an exquisitely carved elephant in sandalwood for me. There were four or five girls working on the stall, all pretty but one was absolutely stunning.

Charcoal said to me, 'Do you think she is beautiful?'

I said, 'Yes.' She smacked Charcoal a whack right across the chops. The other girls laughed, Charcoal just smiled. Charcoal never told us why she had whacked him. Then he asked us could he have a lift back to the monastery.

The flight home was a nightmare. I must have eaten something and poisoned myself. I could not stop vomiting. Geraint picked me up at Heathrow. I sat in the backseat, glad the sickness had gone. The time passed quickly. We were soon pulling up in front of Richard's parent's bungalow at Bryncoch, Neath. Richard would drive home to Cardigan from there.

Geraint and I got home and packed the presents for the girls. I would give the boys money. Sitting on my own, in an empty house, after Geraint had left for home, it took me a while to realize I had travelled all the way to Burma and back in such a short time. The first time, in all it had taken the best part of five weeks to get there and coming home I remember it took nineteen days just from Bombay to Southampton. It was the end of November and about three o'clock in the morning when I got home.

My arrival had my father, mother, my brother David, my sister Ceinwen who was then courting Des Jackson, out of bed. Like all coal miners' houses, the fire had been banked up for the night, so the kitchen was lovely and warm. Ceinwen laid the table and we sat down to a breakfast of cold lamb which cousin John Ty Mawr had butchered, telling the man from the ministry the count was down because one animal had 'fell over the quarry', Aunty Mel's home chutney, thin bread and butter and Yorkshire pudding left over from dinner.

In a few hours, tasting of mountain rain, eighteen-year-old Peggy Jones the Papers would be there. Now, of them all, there was just Ceinwen my sister left.

ACKNOWLEDGEMENTS

My everlasting thanks for the help so readily given to me by the staff of the South Wales Miners' Library, the DOVE, Communities First, Banwen, and Big Pit Wales National Mining Museum.

Doctor Dafydd Aubrey Thomas, Harry Green, Kitty Black, George Ewart Evans, Professor Dai Smith and Alun Richards.

Acknowledgement to John Harvey, Professor of Art, Head of the School of Art, and Director of the Centre for Studies in the Visual Culture of Religion, University of Wales, Aberystwyth – for permission to use the painting *In the Bath*.

REFLECTION

The Ransome Rapier
It walks, it digs and dumps,
And it has the displacement
Of a small warship -
And the feel of a warship:
Steel, concentration, purpose,
The hard beauty of sheer function.

From Harri Webb's 'The Big Job'.